History of the
Argyll & Sutherland Highlanders
7th Battalion

From El Alamein to Germany

Plate 1   Major-General D. N. Wimberley, C.B., D.S.O., M.C., Commander of the 51st Highland Division in Africa and Sicily

History of the Argyll & Sutherland Highlanders 7th Battalion

From El Alamein to Germany

Captain Ian C. Cameron

With a Foreword by
Major-General D. N. Wimberley
C.B. D.S.O. M.C.

The Naval & Military Press Ltd

Published by

The Naval & Military Press Ltd
Unit 10 Ridgewood Industrial Park,
Uckfield, East Sussex,
TN22 5QE England

Tel: +44 (0) 1825 749494
Fax: +44 (0) 1825 765701

www.naval-military-press.com
www.military-genealogy.com
www.militarymaproom.com

In reprinting in facsimile from the original, any imperfections are inevitably reproduced and the quality may fall short of modern type and cartographic standards.

This book is the official record and history of the 7th Battalion The Argyll and Sutherland Highlanders from 1942 to the end of the war in Germany in 1945. It has been written from war diaries and records and also from the personal experience of the author. The gratitude of all ranks are due to him for his accurate and excellent work.

(Sgd.) J. C. CHURCH, Lt.-Col.
Commanding the 7th Battalion
Argyll and Sutherland Highlanders

February 1946

FOREWORD

TRADITIONALLY the Highland clans of Scotland all have slogans of their own, and " Cruachan," after a high hill in Argyll, was the reputed war-cry of Clan Campbell, the most powerful clan in that district, from which most Argyll and Sutherland Battalions take the pipe tune which has become their Regimental March. True to their history and their past, more than one famous Highland regiment has inherited, collected or used some slogan in Britain's wars, but probably not one has been better known in this war than

" Up the Argylls "

which I have heard used many a time in Africa and Sicily, as a sign of pride of regiment, both by officers and men of the famous fighting Battalion whose campaign from Alamein to Germany is described in this book.

I remember particularly coming forward on one occasion and visiting what was left of the 7th Argylls, as they were assembling by the roadside after their gallant fight at Gerbini in Sicily. I arrived, feeling inwardly a little sick at heart, thinking of how, while we at Headquarters had been living in safety, so many of our gallant friends and comrades were now lost to the Division in the fierce fight which had taken place a few hours before ; and then how cheered I became when some of those greathearted " Jocks " of this Battalion, battle-tired and exhausted as they were, exchanged that greeting with me.

Many fighting battalions of British Infantry are supposed to have their own marked characteristics—characteristics imprinted upon them, as on the individuals who compose them, both by their heredity and their environment. The

FOREWORD

7th Battalion Argyll and Sutherland Highlanders, during the two and a half years it was under my command in the 51st Highland Division, ran very true to type. A goodly number of the real 100 per cent. "Jocks" of central Scotland formed its backbone. Many of them were miners—to some who might only have superficially noticed their hands and speech, perhaps rude and even rough, but sterling fighters and men both loyal and true. Further, being Scotsmen, they were to a man right well aware of the great part in British military history which the Argyll and Sutherland Highlanders, and the Highland Division, had always played and the fighting standard they were therefore expected to maintain.

To give them their final training, to lead them in all their early battles, they had as their Battalion Commander a great Highland gentleman also of the Clan Campbell, whose leadership was finally crowned at the battle of the Wadi Akarit with the Victoria Cross. How could such a Battalion fight but superbly well!

Lastly, may I remind the readers of this narrative that the author who tells their epic story was himself wounded on two occasions when serving with this Battalion.

(Sgd.) DOUGLAS WIMBERLEY, Maj.-Gen.
Commander, 51st Highland Division 1941–43

PREFACE

THE history of the Argyll and Sutherland Highlanders is one long tale of glory and honour, and when one thinks of the sturdy troops who fought at El Alamein on the 23rd of October 1942, dashed across the Desert in appalling conditions, took part in the great Desert battles at El Agheila, marched triumphantly into Tripoli, fought at Medenine, Mareth, Wadi Akarit, and finally Enfidaville ; landed on the southern shores of Sicily, marched and fought their way to Gerbini, and, after Sicily was conquered, came home to England to take part in the greatest invasion of all time on the beaches of Normandy, there is no doubt that the 7th Battalion of the Argyll and Sutherland Highlanders have added yet another page to the glorious record of the Regiment which has long been famous as " The Thin Red Line " for its heroic stand at Balaclava.

It was during the month of April 1943 that two officers of the Argylls were awarded the Victoria Cross for gallantry during the fighting in North Africa. The first award went to the Commanding Officer of the 7th Battalion, Lt.-Col. Lorne M. Campbell, for his admirable leadership during the battle of Wadi Akarit. A fortnight later Major Anderson of the 8th Battalion was awarded the Victoria Cross for his part in the battle of " Long Stop Hill " in Tunisia on the 23rd of April. Throughout the war wherever there has been fighting there has been a battalion of Argylls. In 1939/40 the Argylls played a prominent part in the fighting on the Continent of Europe. Later the 2nd Battalion excelled themselves by their heroic defence of Singapore, and the 1st Battalion covered themselves with glory in the Abyssinian and Desert campaigns. It was while with the

PREFACE

4th Indian Division in the Eighth Army that the 1st Argylls fought so gallantly in the first and second Desert campaigns, and the Argylls' graveyard at Sidi Barrani is a silent reminder of these terrible days when our backs were to the wall.

In the summer of 1942 the 7th Argylls, as part of the famous 51st Highland Division, landed in Egypt and shortly afterwards began their series of spectacular advances after having broken through the toughest part of the enemy defences at El Alamein. From the Libyan Desert they chased Rommel's army across Tripolitania and Tunisia and afterwards were amongst the leading troops to land in Sicily. During this period the 8th Battalion fought with distinction as part of the 78th Division of the First Army. When the invasion of North-West Europe took place the 7th Battalion of the Argylls were there with the " Fighting Fifty-First." By this time a new 2nd Battalion had been raised to take the place of the 2nd Battalion which had done so gloriously in Singapore. This new 2nd Battalion was in the 15th Scottish Division during the fighting in North-West Europe. The 1st and 8th Battalions continued to fight through Italy until the end of the war in Europe.

The spirit of the 7th Battalion was Second to None, and I make no apology for quoting the following little verse which the troops sang heartily on many occasions even when conditions were pretty grim :

> Ye may talk aboot yer Gordons and yer gallant Forty-Twa,
> Yer Silver Streakit Seaforths and yer Camerons sae braw,
> But gi'e to me the tartan o' the lads who look sae fine,
> Th' Argyll and Sutherland Highlanders, " The Thin Red Line."

In this history of the 7th Battalion of the Argyll and Sutherland Highlanders, an attempt is made to present an accurate account of the campaigns in which they took part from El Alamein on the 23rd of October 1942 up to the end of the war in Europe. On the author was placed the

PREFACE

responsibility of editing the war diaries of the 7th Argylls throughout the African and Sicilian campaigns, and during part of the campaign in North-West Europe, until transferred to the General Staff of the 154th Infantry Brigade in August 1944, and later to the General Staff of the 1st British Corps. This history, consequently, is compiled from the information contained in these war diaries together with incidents from the author's personal experiences with the Battalion. I am indebted to Lt.-Col. J. C. Church, M.C., for his valuable help in sending me the war diaries and records of the 7th Argylls for the period from August 1944 until the end of the war in Europe, and it is hoped that the reader will find the narrative as interesting as the writer found the actual experiences. I am also much indebted to Capt. C. G. Mackie for the information relating to the campaign of the 7th Argylls in France in 1940 which has been incorporated in the introductory chapter.

The author takes this opportunity of expressing his thanks to the Editor of *Punch* for permission to use the verses by Capt. Hugh Murray Bailey on the battle of Gerbini, and to Mr. and Mrs. Burge for permission to reproduce the sketch by their son, the late Lieut. R. G. Burge, R.E., who was killed in Tunisia in May 1943. In particular, I owe thanks to my friend Dr. C. A. Malcolm, M.A., Ph.D., Librarian of the Signet Library, Edinburgh, who, besides revising and correcting the typescript, made numerous helpful suggestions; to my father, Major W. G. Cameron, T.D., J.P., and to my brother-in-law, Surgeon Lieutenant-Commander G. H. Finlay, R.N.V.R., for their assistance.

The author regrets that he was unable to obtain the photographs of all the Commanding Officers of the 7th Argyll and Sutherland Highlanders for inclusion in the history before publication.

CONTENTS

Foreword v
Preface vii

INTRODUCTORY CHAPTER

Their Darkest Hour 1

PART I

THE NORTH AFRICAN CAMPAIGN

I	The 51st Reborn	27
II	The Turn of the Tide	39
III	Across Libyan Sands	54
IV	The Advance on Tripoli	63
V	Tunisian Battles	76
VI	Enfidaville and the End of the African Campaign	98

PART II

THE SICILIAN CAMPAIGN

VII	The Invasion of Sicily	107
VIII	Victory in Thirty-nine Days . . .	121

CONTENTS

PART III

THE INVASION OF NORTH-WEST EUROPE

IX	The Normandy Landings	131
X	The Caen Break-through	138
XI	Beyond the Dives	156
XII	Across the Seine	165
XIII	Through Belgium and Holland	174
XIV	The Battles of the Canals	187
XV	The Nijmegen Floods	195
XVI	Von Rundstedt's Ardennes Offensive	201
XVII	The Reichswald Forest	211
XVIII	The Rhine Crossing	217
XIX	The Final Advance	227

LIST OF APPENDICES

I	Nominal Roll of Officers, 1940	235
II	Awards during the Campaign of 1940	236
III	Nominal Roll of Officers, October 1942–May 1945	237
IV	Honours and Awards, October 1942–May 1945	241

LIST OF PLATES

1 Major-General D. N. Wimberley, C.B., D.S.O., M.C.   *Frontispiece*

facing page

2 Lt.-Col. E. P. Buchanan, M.C. xiv

3 In the trenches at El Alamein 38

  Sappers at work in the Libyan desert 38

4 Field-Marshal Lord Montgomery of Alamein . . . 46

5 A procession of German prisoners 50

  "Impressions of a night attack," a sketch by Lieut. R. G. Burge, R.E. 50

6 The Massed Pipes and Drums of the Highland Division . . 66

  Victory Parade in Tripoli 66

7 Brigadier Lorne M. Campbell, V.C., D.S.O. and bar, T.D. . 98

8 Troops of the Highland Division in Sicily 114

  Pack mules in southern Italy 114

9 Lt.-Col. R. Mathieson, D.S.O., O.B.E., T.D. 118

10 Lt.-Col. J. C. Meiklejohn, D.S.O. 126

11 Major-General T. G. Rennie, C.B., D.S.O. 146

12 Crossing the Seine at Elbeuf 162

  Greetings from the citizens of Rouen 162

13 Sounding the Last Post at St. Valery 166

14 Lt.-Col. A. MacKinnon, D.S.O., M.C. 174

15 Occupation arrangements being discussed in Bremerhaven . 210

16 Victory March Past at Bremerhaven 226

  Lt.-General Horrocks takes the salute at the handover of Bremerhaven 226

Plate 2 Lieut.-Col. E. P. Buchanan, M.C., Commanding Officer, 7th Argyll and Sutherland Highlanders, France, 1940

INTRODUCTORY CHAPTER

THEIR DARKEST HOUR

ALTHOUGH this history describes chiefly the campaigns of the 7th Argyll and Sutherland Highlanders from El Alamein onwards, it would be incomplete without an account of the short but disastrous fighting which took place in France in 1940. Then, as in 1942, when the 7th Argylls covered themselves with glory at El Alamein, the battalion was in the 51st Highland Division, and distinguished itself as part of this famous division during the disheartening retreat across France prior to the evacuation from the Continent of Europe.

After the First World War military enthusiasm flagged and territorial units were hard pressed to keep up their numbers. The 7th Argylls, which consisted entirely at this time of Territorials from the Stirling district, was no exception to this general rule. In 1937, however, people began to realize that something more than pacifism was needed to prevent Hitler and his Nazi gangsters from attempting to dominate the remainder of Europe by force of arms. Consequently young men of this opinion chose the obvious course, and enlisted in one or other of the many volunteer units, and the numbers in territorial battalions gradually began to increase. It was not, however, until after Chamberlain's visit to Munich in the autumn of 1938 that the decision to double the strength of the Territorial army was reached. A recruiting drive was then started, and the Highland regiments were very soon brought up to strength, until in the spring of 1939 the 7th Argyll and Sutherland Highlanders were able to form two complete infantry battalions. Stirling, the regimental depot, was also the headquarters of the 7th battalion.

In July 1939 the battalion, at double strength, went to camp at Strathpeffer for its annual field training. Shortly after this, however, the official division of the battalion was made, and the two battalions thus formed were called the 7th and the 10th. The division was made by districts, so that each battalion should have a proportion of trained personnel, consideration being paid to the fact that the 7th battalion was to be the first line battalion.

While the Territorial army was thus reorganizing, the political situation was worsening. In the summer of 1939 the inevitability of war was becoming generally accepted, and preparations were made for the immediate mobilization of the Territorial army. It was on the 1st of September, 1939, that the 7th Argyll and Sutherland Highlanders received orders to embody. Then on that fateful Sunday, the 3rd of September, 1939, when the Prime Minister announced to the nation that Britain had reluctantly declared war on Germany, the whole battalion was mustered at Stirling.

In those first days of war much had to be done. Medical inspections had to be carried out, equipment had to be issued, and a hundred and one things had to be done before the battalion could be said to be on a war basis. The battalion embodied thirty-two officers and six hundred and thirty other ranks, but with men released to industry, and soldiers under nineteen years of age being posted to second line units, over two hundred trained men were lost to the battalion by the end of the month.

One month after the declaration of war the battalion said good-bye to Stirling and entrained late one night for Aldershot, which was to be the final concentration area for the 51st Highland Division. Before leaving its home town, however, the battalion was reviewed by the honorary colonel, Brigadier-General Sir Norman Orr Ewing, Bart., D.S.O., on the "King's Knot," and the colours were handed over to Stirling Castle for safe custody. This move to Aldershot meant that the war was starting in earnest for the 7th Argylls. Aldershot is the premier military centre in the United Kingdom, and a move to this area meant only one thing, that the battalion was shortly to be sent overseas. Apart from this knowledge, leaving Scotland was a big event in the lives of many of the soldiers, many of whom had never been very far away from their homes before. As an illustration of the spirit then prevailing, it is worth mentioning that not one soldier deserted the troop trains. On arrival in Aldershot the battalion received drafts of men, battle equipment poured in, inoculations were carried out, and intensive training both night and day began. This busy existence continued until Christmas time, when it was learned that the period of training, short and insufficient as it was, had come to an end. The battalion was now granted embarkation leave, and was warned to have an advance party standing by ready to proceed overseas at short notice.

Fortunately the majority of the men were able to be on leave at home for the New Year, a season all Scotsmen associate with holidays and celebrations. Shortly afterwards the advance party set off for Southampton, where they embarked for France. The remainder of the battalion was not long in following, and subsequent to a visit of the King and Queen, later to be accepted as a normal prelude to departure overseas, orders were received to join the B.E.F. It was on the 2nd of February, 1940, that the battalion embarked on the *Fenella* at Southampton and sailed for Le Havre. Before embarking, however, a sad formality took place when all soldiers handed in their kilts. The traditional uniform of Highland regiments was not considered by the War Office as suitable for modern war. Correct as this opinion may have been, it was regretted by all ranks.

France

After berthing at Le Havre little time was wasted at the port before moving up to the area occupied by the British army in the vicinity of Lille. The 51st Highland Division was certainly the second, if not actually the first, territorial division to join the B.E.F. The division was placed in a reserve area, and Annoeullin, a little town in the centre of the coalmining district about twenty miles south-west of Lille, was allocated to the battalion. All Frenchmen of military age had been called up to their various regiments, but the inhabitants who were left made the battalion most welcome. Traditionally the French have always been kindly disposed to the Scots, but in addition the older people remembered the Highland Division from the 1914–18 war.

During this period a great deal of work had to be done, such as the digging of anti-tank ditches and intensive training. Above all, there was the weather to contend with, for this winter it was particularly severe. For six weeks the time passed happily enough in the contented and friendly atmosphere of that little town. The end of March, however, brought a change, and although it could not be foreseen at the time, started a chain of moves which was to send the battalion along with the rest of the Highland Division on a trek around half of France.

The first move was to an area close to the Belgian frontier in Flanders; the actual village occupied by the battalion was Strazeele. The role of the B.E.F. at this period was to stand in readiness on the Belgian frontier, prepared, at the first sign of the Germans attempting to violate Belgian neutrality, to advance into that country and, in conjunction with the French and Belgian armies, to attack the Germans and prevent any further invasion. This was a difficult task, which was not made any easier by the fact that the Belgians stuck to a rigid neutrality, and would not be a party to any joint plan of action. The battalion only stayed in this area for a week, after which it was pulled back to the neighbourhood of St. Pol, fifty miles further west. Before another week had passed orders were received to proceed to the Saar district.

Saar

The Saar meant active service for the first time. During this static period it had been the policy for formations of the B.E.F. to have a brigade at a time attached to the French army, where they could get experience of actual warfare and contact with the enemy. In the Saar valley the French held a defensive position along the Franco-German frontier about eight miles in front of their famous Maginot Line. It was the one place where any fighting had taken place up to this time, but even this was on a minor scale. For the first time a whole division was to be attached to the French, and not just a brigade. It was a piece of good fortune that the division could get such an opportunity of being gently broken into the serious business of war.

It was a beautiful spring morning in the middle of April when the reconnaissance party, headed by the Commanding Officer, Lt.-Col. E. P. Buchanan, M.C., went forward to examine the positions which were to be taken over by the battalion from the 5th Gloucesters. The 154th Brigade was the first part of the Highland Division to take over a sector of the line. Two days previously the battalion had moved to Metz, where it was billeted in a small village in its environs. It was a welcome change to come down into the pleasant wooded and hilly country of Lorraine after the flat and uninteresting coalmining district of the north. It was a land of orchards, streams, and villages, and although German in character rather than French, this was not to be wondered at on account of the troubled history of the province. It struck one as odd to observe notices posted in German as well as in French. It could not have been a better time of year for visiting Lorraine with the green touch of spring refreshing everything, and the orchards just beginning to blossom. This was not a holiday, however, and one was reminded at every turn of the real purpose in hand by the fortifications of the Maginot Line spreading like some sinister monster over the countryside with tentacles thrown out in the most unexpected places.

The British troops did not occupy the Maginot Line proper, but the defensive screen, " La Couverture," which was put out in front to prevent the enemy from making any close investigation of these formidable and elaborate fortifications. " La Couverture " consisted of three main lines of defence, the " Ligne de Contact," the " Ligne de Soutien," and the " Ligne de Receuil." One brigade occupied the " Ligne de Contact " on a single battalion front, while the other two battalions of the brigade occupied the support lines. The battalion was initially to occupy the second line, and as this was not in contact with the enemy no difficulty was experienced in effecting the relief on the morning of the 20th of April. The normal routine was one week's tour of duty in this line, followed by a week in the front line, and lastly a week in the third line; but before the 154th Brigade had completed this prearranged programme the irresistible flood of invading German armies began.

While the battalion remained in the reserve position a battle patrol was organized, which consisted of twenty men under the command of 2nd Lieut. Alan Orr Ewing, who later earned the M.C. for his work. This patrol, in conjunction with similar patrols from the other two battalions of the brigade, took its turn at deep nightly penetration into the enemy's positions. Every night a patrol, with blackened faces, rubber boots, and every type of infantry weapon from a Tommy-gun to a hunting knife, would sally forward into " No Man's Land." There were frequent encounters with the enemy, and usually the enemy got the worst of it. The usefulness of these patrols was undoubted. The front-line troops were as a result allowed considerably more peace at night and freedom from enemy interference. Nevertheless, it was an eerie experience to set out for the first time knowing that an enemy patrol bent on the same purpose might be encountered at any moment. Once this happened there was little time to think—a flurry of flashes, Tommy-gun shots, exploding grenades, and then all was over.

The week in the support line soon passed, after which the battalion took over the " Ligne de Contact " from the 1st battalion The Black Watch. This relief was carried out without any interference from the enemy, and the battalion settled down to its operational role. About this time people at home were becoming bored with the monotonous nightly B.B.C. news report, " Another quiet day on the Saar with minor patrol activity." To the troops who carried out the patrolling, however, it was a different matter. It might have been a quiet day and the patrol activity might have been negligible, nevertheless the tension was there, and the shells landing beside a section post were very real to that section. After having completed the necessary period in the " Ligne de Contact," the battalion was brought out for a much-needed wash and rest.

On the 9th of May the second tour of the three defence lines began, and once more the unit took over the " Ligne de Soutien," but this position had not been occupied for twenty-four hours when events began to move rapidly. The German armies had now invaded Holland, the Luftwaffe carried out extensive bombing on French and Belgian towns, and the general alert was announced by the French Army

Headquarters. The French plan had never been to hold a position in front of the Maginot Line in the face of determined opposition, and preparations were accordingly made to carry out an orderly withdrawal to the Maginot Line whenever the Germans launched their large-scale offensive.

The Germans, however, did not attack at once. In fact they were, if anything, less aggressive than usual, and this fact tended to increase the tension. This suspense did not continue for long, however, for at 4 o'clock in the morning of the 13th of May the 1st Black Watch in its positions in the forward line was heavily attacked. This attack was preceded by a heavy artillery bombardment, and for two or three hours a fierce engagement with the enemy took place. The Boche made determined efforts to dislodge our troops from the forward positions, but by 10 o'clock that morning they withdrew, decisively worsted in this first major encounter. The casualties on our side were slight, but the Germans suffered severely, and when the battle patrol from our battalion went forward to cover one of the Black Watch companies during the after-battle reorganization no fewer than forty dead Germans were observed lying in front of that company's position. On the 14th of May the battalion relieved the 1st Black Watch in the forward positions, but remained there only for a day, as on the 15th of May orders were received to withdraw to conform with the movements of the French. It was not an easy withdrawal, as the French on the right were falling back, closely followed by the enemy, and the other two brigades of the Highland Division on the left were being heavily attacked. The battalion's battle patrol had the task of covering D company out of its positions in the " Grossenwald "—a very awkward spot to withdraw from. All went well, however, and by dawn the battalion had successfully withdrawn to the " Ligne de Receuil," which was about one mile in front of the Maginot Line proper. As the infantry retired the sappers had blown their charges, leaving a series of demolitions and blocks to hinder the advancing enemy. At this period the fortifications behind the battalion were manned by the French, and a French major in command of one of the forts appeared very anxious that we should withdraw quickly and allow the advancing Germans to come up against his positions. He had commanded a fort in this particular sector of the Maginot Line ever since it had been built ten years previously, and his admirable ambition was to bring his guns into action against the enemy.

For three days the battalion held these positions without enemy interference. On the 18th of May a German patrol was observed in the little village of La Croix, and immediately Alan Orr Ewing and his battle patrol, accompanied by Capt. Jack Ritchie, were sent out to deal with it. They reached the village unobserved and entered the house where the enemy were hiding. Creeping quietly upstairs, the door of the upper room was flung open, then followed a rapid exchange of shots, and shortly afterwards a party of dejected German prisoners, including an officer, were brought in to battalion headquarters. It was a fitting climax to the career of the battle patrol, and a just reward for their energy and initiative.

The time had now come for the battalion to leave the Saar, and that same night the Lothian and Border Yeomanry took over the positions. On looking back, the incidents which spring most readily to mind are often those completely unconnected with actual fighting. During the relief of battalion headquarters that night the adjutant of the Lothians suddenly loomed up out of the darkness at the command post, and was promptly greeted with howls of laughter. In one hand he held a kettle, and in the other a long stick with which he was driving a cow. On being asked what on earth he was doing, he replied that the colonel liked fresh milk with his early morning tea.

After marching back to a rendezvous behind the Maginot Line, the battalion embussed and proceeded westwards for eight or nine miles. It was a welcome change to be completely non-operational for the first time for over a month. New equipment was immediately issued, and general tidying up was carried out, which was just as well, as orders were received to move on the following day, the 20th of May.

The Trek to the Somme

This was the first of a series of moves which, after a roundabout of some 500 miles, was to lead the battalion to the Somme. War news was practically unobtainable within the battalion. Newspapers were not to be had, and one had little chance of listening to the B.B.C. news report, but it was rumoured that the Germans were having phenomenal success, and that the major portion of the B.E.F. were in dire straits. No-one knew what the plan for the Highland Division was, although, as is usual in a crisis, countless rumours got around. A general withdrawal seemed to be indicated, however, as the battalion marched all night every night for five nights—always in a westerly direction. The German air force was very active all the time, and it was considered inadvisable for troops to move by day unless absolutely essential, and so marching by night and hiding in woods by day became the battalion's existence. By the 23rd of May information was received that the Germans had broken through between Sedan and Montmédy, and the plan for the Highland Division was to help to restore the situation. Consequently the battalion was ordered to proceed via Verdun and Varennes-en-Argonne to an area some miles south-west of Montmédy. Within twenty-four hours the plan was again changed, and the Highland Division was ordered to entrain on the night of the 25th of May for what was then to the battalion an unknown destination. The battalion entrained at the little village station of Autry. Early in the morning of the 26th of May the train moved off and for forty-eight hours the battalion travelled by train, uncertain until the very last of their final destination. The train journey followed a huge semi-circle round Paris, passing through Varennes, Troyes, Orleans, the Loire valley, Le Mans, Rouen, and finally ended up at Neufchâtel. The journey lay through some of the loveliest parts of France, and when one looked at the rich and peaceful countryside, it was hard to believe or realize the stark tragic events now engulfing the Low Countries. The battalion arrived at dawn on the 28th of May, and immediately the false tranquillity of these last two days was destroyed as the appalling destruction of a modern bombing attack on a small town was observed from the carriage windows. Quickly the battalion was collected from the train and moved off at breakneck speed in a convoy of French buses to the Haute Forêt d'Eu, a large wood overlooking the River Bresle, which runs parallel with the Somme some twenty-five miles to the west of it.

The 154th Infantry Brigade was the last brigade of the Highland Division to arrive in this new sector, and consequently was placed in reserve. The task assigned to the battalion was to hold, if necessary, two bridges across the Bresle. Uncertainty and ignorance of war news still prevailed within the battalion, but perhaps this was a blessing in disguise as the news was none too cheering. However, that night a French wireless truck parked near battalion headquarters, and Paris was tuned in. The news was even worse than expected. King Leopold of the Belgians had surrendered; the British army along with French troops were retiring on Dunkirk, and the French were establishing a new line of

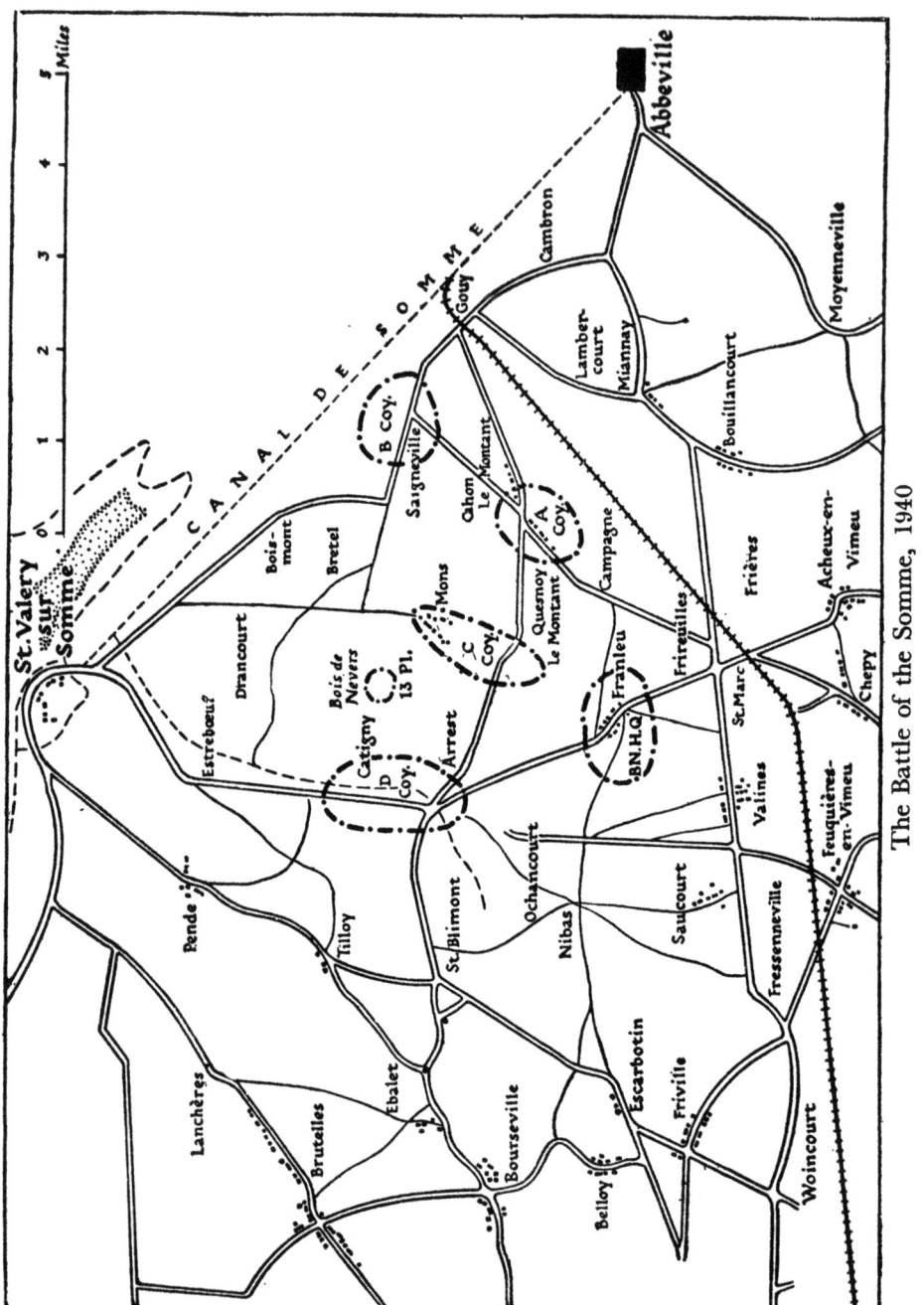

The Battle of the Somme, 1940

defence along the Somme. This new line was what concerned the Highland Division, and as they were now under the command of the French IX Corps, they were ordered to hold the line of the Somme from the sea to Erondelle, a village a few miles south of Abbeville.

The Battle on the Somme

On the 31st of May the battalion took over a sector of the front on the Somme from the 11th Cuirassiere—a French cavalry regiment. The position at the time of this change over was that the Allies had driven back the Germans to the line of the Somme, but had not succeeded in eliminating the two German bridgeheads, one on the coast at St. Valery-sur-Somme, and the other to the south-east of Abbeville. The Highland Division, therefore, in addition to holding a very long front of twenty miles, had also to contain two enemy bridgeheads. The 154th Brigade was on the left of the divisional front, and was responsible for the sector from the coast for a distance of eight miles south-eastwards. The brigade held its position with two battalions forward, the 7th Argylls being on the right. There was no battalion in reserve, as the third battalion of the brigade was placed under the command of the 153rd Brigade. The battalion had, consequently, to hold a front of approximately four miles, no easy task considering the nature of the country, which was mainly arable, with large fields of growing corn, ideal for infiltrating patrols. In addition the countryside was bespattered with straggling agricultural villages; these in accordance with French custom consisted of numerous small farms, each with its own orchard and rambling farm buildings. In the battalion's sector there were some six or seven of these villages, and the battalion's defensive plan was based around them. The drawbacks to this plan were obvious, as the four rifle companies had to form their own individual strongholds, which could not give each other any effective fire support in the event of an enemy attack. There was, therefore, no co-related battalion defensive system, but it was the best that could be done under the circumstances. The dispositions of the companies were: B company held Saigneville, on the right—a dangerous salient between the two enemy bridgeheads; C company held Mons Boubert, in the centre; and D company held Cattigny and Arrest, on the left. A company, after initially holding Guoy and Cahon, was given a reserve area at Quesnoy. Battalion Headquarters and Headquarter Company were based in Franleu.

This was the position on the 1st of June. The battalion had a lot to do now, as the French had not constructed any real defensive positions. The problem of dealing with the civilian population had also to be tackled, and arrangements had to be made for their evacuation along with their livestock. This task was not made any easier by the fact that the French civilian administration had broken down completely. During the next two days—those same days that the remnants of the B.E.F. were being evacuated from the beaches of Dunkirk—a semblance of order was introduced into the area. It was realized that a strenuous battle would have to be fought against overwhelming odds once the German forces around Dunkirk turned their attention to the west, and everything possible was prepared for this day. However, it was not a quiet time of preparation for the coming attack, as daily the battalion suffered casualties. On the 1st of June 2nd Lieut. A. S. Haig of A company took out a patrol and encountered several enemy observation posts, and during the skirmish which followed Private Sutherland was killed. Then again on the same day one of D company's platoons in the Bois de Nevers was very heavily shelled about midday and sustained casualties. In fact, all the time the enemy kept harassing the battalion by constant heavy shelling and patrolling. One day two British anti-aircraft gunners of the 54th Light A.A. Regiment came into the battalion lines. They had escaped from Boulogne and wandered about behind the enemy lines for ten days before they finally managed to reach the Somme and swim across to safety.

On the 4th of June, just before dawn, the Highland Division launched an attack in conjunction with the French on the German bridgehead at Abbeville. The attack failed mainly because it was launched against greater odds, and there was insufficient time for preparation. Many objectives were taken, but they could not be maintained for lack of support. By the evening, despite many a bitter fight, the enemy had regained his positions, from where he was soon to launch his main attack against the " Thin Red Line."

The 5th of June dawned to the accompaniment of a thunderous barrage of shell and mortar fire. It was a memorable day for the battalion—the day on which they made their last gallant stand against the overwhelming flood of the German armies. Actually, the battalion was not in a position to conduct a co-ordinated fight, as its positions were too scattered, and so the battle developed into a series of isolated actions, with each company holding its own stronghold and fighting gallantly to the last. The best description that can be given is extracted from a narrative compiled (in a German prison camp) by the Commanding Officer, Lt.-Col. E. P. Buchanan, M.C., from accounts given to him by the company commanders concerned, who were all taken prisoner with Lt.-Col. Buchanan that day.

Just after daylight at battalion headquarters it was clear from the noise that something had started. The first information to be received came from a despatch rider, who brought back a message from one of C company's platoons in the Bois de Nevers, that they were being heavily attacked by the enemy on all sides. This platoon, as it transpired later, never had a chance. Hemmed in on all sides, the sections soon ran out of ammunition. 2nd Lieut. Moore, the platoon commander, realizing that his men were completely outnumbered, started to withdraw to his company, but there was open ground to the rear of the wood, and when the platoon came into the open 2nd Lieut. Moore was seriously wounded, and the few remaining wounded men of his section were rounded up by the enemy. No sooner had the message from C company been received than D company reported that the forward platoons at Cattigny were in contact with strong forces of the enemy. A section of carriers was at once sent forward under the command of 2nd Lieut. Powell to take up a position south-west of C company at Mons Boubert, with the task of preventing the enemy from cutting off C company from battalion headquarters. On arrival in C company'a area, the carriers went into ground action on the west side of the village, and immediately engaged the enemy at 200 yards' range, and as a result inflicted many casualties. A threat, however, was developing on the right flank of the company, and consequently the carrier section moved over to meet this threat, where again they successfully beat off the German attack. Two further " sorties " were made, but the enemy brought up his anti-tank guns, and after one carrier was knocked out the remainder withdrew to Mons Boubert, where they were used to strengthen the defences of the two remaining platoons of C company, the third platoon having already been " wiped out."

During all this time battalion headquarters was fighting its own private battle, as the enemy had advanced close up to Franleu and were engaging the posts on the forward edge of the village. Soon the enemy infiltrated into the village itself, and came within 50 yards of the command post. It was obvious that the limited personnel of headquarters could not hope to hold the position for long without assistance, and A company was ordered back from Quesnoy to render this much-needed help. The company commander, Capt. Handley, and the reserve platoon under 2nd Lieut. Haig, were first to arrive, but on entering the village Capt. Handley's truck received a direct hit from an enemy mortar bomb and Capt. Handley was mortally wounded. Haig, however, got through successfully, and took up a defensive position in the orchard immediately in front of battalion headquarters. By this time two patrols had been organized by R.S.M. Lockie and C.S.M. Dyer, and the enemy were cleared from the immediate vicinity of the command post. Some little time later the remainder of A company reached the village and took up positions on the east side of the village.

About 6 o'clock in the morning B Company, under the command of Capt. Logan, reported that enemy were advancing on their positions, but that they were being successfully shot up by the Kensingtons, the machine gunners who supported the company. In addition the enemy were observed to be massing in a ravine about 1,000 yards west of Saigneville, and a successful shoot on this target was undertaken by the battery of artillery attached to the battalion. After this, however, the situation became worse. All communications were cut, and all hope of controlling the battle from battalion headquarters was lost. The last message to brigade was passed at about 9 o'clock in the morning, after which the wireless truck was blown up and the battalion was left to fight its own isolated battle against incredibly overwhelming odds.

The Commanding Officer, however, had a hard enough task even to defend Franleu, as all day long the enemy pursued the attack. One attack was repulsed only to be followed by another, and throughout all this a constant shower of mortar bombs kept crashing down on this isolated band of brave men fighting to the end without hope. The battalion's mortars were not inactive, and, moving frequently from one position to another, they retaliated under the enthusiastic direction of their commander, Capt. Hendry, until their ammunition ran out. From the church tower could be seen masses of enemy troops and equipment passing to the west of the village, apparently unconcerned by the presence of British troops on their flanks and rear, but, true enough, not much could be done to hinder their advance. Each company of the battalion was surrounded and besieged by enemy formations who were thus actively engaged, but it did not hinder the main flow of the enemy westwards. The number of casualties within the battalion increased hourly as the battle raged all day long, and little could be done for them with no medical attention available. The padre, Rev. D. MacInnes, did noble work, but the cellar at battalion headquarters, which had been converted into a regimental aid post, presented a sorry spectacle.

In the early afternoon plans were made at brigade for a counter-attack to be delivered by a battalion of the Black Watch, assisted by British and French tanks, the object being to relieve the 7th Argylls. The troops went forward for the attack, but it was decided that it would be impossible for such a small force to expect any success, and the attack was called off. The battalion was now left to its fate, not from any lack of effort on the part of the rest of the division, but through the sheer impossibility of stemming the onrushing tide of enemy infantry and armour.

In Franleu the situation at battalion headquarters became hopeless. A shell which landed at the entrance to the command post wounded the adjutant, headquarter company commander, and the intelligence officer, and by 4 o'clock in the afternoon the only officers remaining unwounded were the Commanding Officer and 2nd Lieut. Haig. By now ammunition was practically exhausted, and all the reserve ammunition was blown up. 2nd Lieut. Haig was instructed to take the remnants of his platoon—now one section—and endeavour to break through to the rear in his platoon truck. In addition, the wounded who could move were told that if they wished they could take their chance at escaping. The padre, who had volunteered to remain with the badly wounded, was told to surrender battalion headquarters as soon as he could get in touch with the enemy. Finally the Commanding Officer, along with the gunner officer and two N.C.O.s, attempted to escape on foot, but they had no sooner left the outskirts of the village than they were pinned down by enemy machine guns at close range, and in the end had to surrender.

The above account is one part of the story of the battle which the battalion fought that day, but it is by no means the complete story, as each company had been undergoing a similar experience in its own particular locality. A company along with the pioneer platoon of the 7th Norfolks, on the east side of Franleu, put up a heroic resistance after they had been cut off from battalion headquarters. Lieut. Fisher, who had assumed command, realizing that battalion headquarters had been evacuated during the late afternoon of the 5th of June, decided to concentrate his men and fight on his own to the end. After beating off one German attack after another, darkness descended and they had a comparatively peaceful night. During the night they captured a German artillery officer who, unaware of their position, had tried to gallop through them. The following day more and more enemy formations kept moving westwards on their flank, and although Fisher's men took heavy toll of these closely packed bodies of enemy, it appeared that two platoons of British infantry seemed too insignificant to warrant much attention. By the afternoon, however, the enemy became rattled, and decided to eliminate this little thorn in their side. Consequently repeated attacks were made, each preceded by a heavy mortar bombardment, but each time the attack was repulsed. At about 4.30 p.m. the final determined assault was made, and this succeeded on the right flank but failed on the left. Three enemy officers and a number of other ranks were shot dead within twenty yards of the company headquarters. Ammunition was now almost exhausted, and when the enemy shouted " Cease fire," and sent forward one of A company's own men, who had been taken prisoner, to order them to surrender, there appeared to be no alternative but to agree. The last act of this gallant company under Lieut. Fisher was to destroy all their weapons. Lieut. Fisher was then conducted to the German commander, who asked him to assemble his now weary company of men and congratulate them on the brave fight which they had put up.

B company's battle had also been a grim affair. They were not engaged as early on the morning of the 5th of June as C and D companies were, but by 6 o'clock in the morning an attack had developed on their platoon positions. The first enemy were seen advancing on Saigneville from Boismont, and these were engaged with artillery and mortar fire. Within an hour, however, further large numbers of the enemy began to approach from the east, and shortly afterwards enemy machine guns began opening up from the rear. By 8 o'clock in the morning the company was completely surrounded and all platoons were in action. To begin with, the enemy concentrated on the forward platoon, and working round to its rear separated it from the remainder of the company, and before long the whole platoon was captured. The remainder of the company continued to fight against superior numbers for the rest of the morning. At midday the company commander, along with his company sergeant-major and a runner, left company headquarters to deal with an enemy section post which had penetrated into the centre of Saigneville. After this was disposed of they found themselves unable to get back to company headquarters, and by 3 o'clock in the afternoon, surrounded on all sides, the company were compelled to surrender.

In C company's battle one platoon was captured in the early morning. This was to be expected, as the platoon was completely isolated from the remainder of the company. The carriers were then sent up to assist the company and to keep communications open between the company and battalion headquarters. Taking advantage of their mobility, the carriers took a heavy toll of the advancing German infantry. Two hours after C company had lost its first platoon the remaining platoons were attacked by enemy infantry advancing from the direction of Bretel. Gradually the platoons were forced back into the village of Mons Boubert. At 10 o'clock in the morning 2nd Lieut. Alan Orr Ewing was badly wounded. The company tried to hold the outskirts of the village, but with the enemy infiltrating through the farm buildings and orchards this was found impossible, and again they had to retire. This went on all day, with each platoon putting up a stubborn fight, but being forced further and further back until at 5 o'clock in the evening the company's position was limited to a small ring around company headquarters, but even this small perimeter could not be held. About an hour later Capt. Hewitt, the company commander, was forced to surrender the remnants of his company.

The fourth rifle company, D company, did not have a static fight that day like the remainder of the battalion. The two forward platoons went into action early in the morning against an infantry attack estimated at battalion strength. The frontal attack was repulsed, but meanwhile other enemy troops had penetrated into the southern portion of the village of Arrest, and thereby not only cut the company's communications with battalion headquarters but captured the reserve ammunition and cookhouse. The reserve platoon was ordered to recapture this position, but it was an inadequate force for the task. By 8.30 in the morning all platoons were running short of ammunition, and with the enemy in front and rear rapidly advancing past both flanks, the company commander, Major Young, decided that his company could no longer make any effective resistance, and at 10.30 in the morning he ordered the two platoons of his company to withdraw to the left rear, and if possible make contact with another battalion of the brigade at St. Blimont. This withdrawal was successfully accomplished and all the wounded were evacuated. Communication was now possible with brigade, and as it appeared that D company was the only remnant of the battalion, it was placed under the command of the 8th Argylls, which was the battalion at St. Blimont. Shortly afterwards the company was ordered to proceed to Nibas, to link up with the force there and act as the situation demanded. The company moved via Escarbotin, for it was impossible to move due south across the open ground, and they reached the village at about 3 o'clock that afternoon. The position was entirely unsuited for defence, as it was situated in a hollow and was surrounded by thick woods. Accordingly Major Young decided that his small force would have to pull back once more to the area of Escarbotin and hold that instead. There they made contact with D company of the 8th Argylls, which was placed under command, and the plan now was for the brigade to hold the line Belloy–Escarbotin–Fressenneville. In theory the scheme was sound, but to the south of Escarbotin there was a three-mile gap, through which the enemy were advancing unopposed. Nevertheless, the position was held until nightfall against repeated enemy attacks.

By 11 o'clock that night the situation demanded a further withdrawal. This time the withdrawal was on Woincourt, but no sooner had this been completed than orders were received that Escarbotin must be held at all costs. The tired and weary troops faced about once more, and moved forward again to their old positions. Daybreak on the 6th of June found them holding these positions, except for one platoon under Capt. Ritchie, which had not received the order to return to Escarbotin. It was a hopeless task for such a small force to hold the village, but these were the orders and they had to be obeyed. All day long on the 6th of June they were subjected to bombardment and attacks, and this continued throughout the following day, the 7th of June, until the evening, when ammunition was exhausted, and with more than 50 per cent. casualties Major Young had no alternative but to surrender.

The last of the fighting strength of the battalion had surrendered after what can only be described as the most tragic but nevertheless glorious record of the whole campaign on the Continent. The words " impossible task " and " overwhelming odds " may have become monotonous with repetition in this account of the actions of the battalion on that disastrous day, the 5th of June, but no other words can adequately describe these events. As a Highland river in spate carries all before it in its tempestuous torrent, so did the German armies surge over the obstacles placed in their path. For a brief moment isolated islands of resistance stood firm against the flood, only to be swamped in the end.

The Retreat from France

Little remains to be told. On the 7th of June the effective strength of the battalion was 5 officers and 130 other ranks, virtually B echelon of the battalion. The whole division was now withdrawing westwards to conform with the French army. Two days later the 154th Brigade was ordered to Fécamp on the coast, to cover the withdrawal of the remainder of the Highland Division to Le Havre. The brigade took up defensive positions to the east of the port, but it was cut off from the division by the break through of German armoured units from Rouen. The main part of the division, separated from its lines of communication, with little hope of evacuating eventually from Le Havre, put up its last gallant stand at St. Valery en Caux. The 154th Brigade held a line in front of Le Havre for a further two days, but on the 12th of June orders were received to destroy all vehicles and such equipment which could not be got across to the United Kingdom. The brigade then embarked on transports in the harbour, but even at this late hour it was not the end. Mr. Churchill, in his last gesture of help, had promised reinforcements for the French, and two British divisions were landed at Cherbourg, which was now to be the destination of the brigade. It was a short-lived venture, for after spending two days at Cherbourg the remnants of the battalion along with the remainder of the brigade embarked on the 15th of June on the S.S. *Duke of Argyll* and sailed for Southampton.

It was indeed a dismal return to Britain five months after the battalion had set off from the same port with such high expectations. The battalion had lost 23 officers and 500 other ranks killed, wounded, or missing. During these five months of fighting the battalion had upheld the glorious traditions of the regiment. It is true that they suffered defeat, but only against what has already been described as insurmountable obstacles and overwhelming odds. The second line battalion, viz. the 10th, were by now training in Scotland, and the remnants of the battalion were posted to the 10th after a well-deserved period of leave at home. Reinforced with the survivors from the 7th Argylls, the 10th took on the joint name of 7th/10th, which was later changed back to the 7th when the reformed 51st Highland Division set sail for the Middle East in June 1942.

PART I

THE NORTH AFRICAN CAMPAIGN

CHAPTER I

THE 51st REBORN

THE valiant rearguard action which the 51st Highland Division fought at St. Valery in 1940, where they held in check the elements of six German divisions for several days in order that the British armies could be evacuated to the United Kingdom, will forever be remembered as one of the finest episodes in the history of the Division. The great majority of the Division were then either killed, wounded, or captured, and the remnants which managed to escape across the channel to the United Kingdom vowed to raise another 51st to avenge their fallen comrades.

For two long years after the capitulation of France and the evacuation of the British armies from the continent of Europe, the new 51st which was, during this period, stationed in the north of Scotland, trained continuously, until in 1942 one might say there was hardly a better trained Division in the British Isles. The Division, which consisted entirely of famous Highland regiments, the men of which were recruited from all parts of Scotland, was in excellent spirit and keen to emulate the deeds of the " Fighting Fifty-first " which had earned undying fame during the War of 1914–18. There were three battalions of Black Watch, viz. the 1st, 5th, and 7th battalions ; two battalions of Seaforth Highlanders, the 2nd and 5th ; two battalions of Gordons, the 1st and 5/7th ; one battalion of Cameron Highlanders, the 5th ; and my own unit, the 7th battalion of the Argyll and Sutherland Highlanders. The men of the 7th Argylls were recruited mostly from the Stirling area. There were many fine fellows among them, and having trained together for so long, a comradeship seldom to be equalled existed between us which was to be of inestimable value to us later when we were to be tested in battle. Our commanding officer, Lieut.-Colonel Lorne M. Campbell, came to us from the 8th Argylls, with whom he served with distinction in France in 1940, where he was awarded the D.S.O. Major R. Mathieson was second in command and hailed from Falkirk. He had been with the 7th Argylls for many years, and was affectionately known as " Wee Roy." Major W. L. N. Whyte, who commanded H.Q. company, also came from the same district, although he had been resident in London for many years. Captain G. Horsburgh commanded A company. A native of Stirling, he also was resident in London, where he played Rugby for the " London Scottish " and for Scotland. Captain J. C. Meiklejohn hailed from St. Andrews and was educated at Fettes College in Edinburgh. He had a wide experience as a soldier with the London Scottish before coming to the 7th Argylls. Captain Donald Young, another London Scot, was one of the most popular members of the battalion, and was indeed a tonic to the officers' mess. Major John Lindsay MacDougall of Lunga, Argyllshire, was a regular soldier, and a very courageous one, which the reader will no doubt appreciate in the following chapters. Major A. F. Henry, M.C., from Denny, gained the M.C. while serving in France in 1940 with the old 7th battalion. Another regular soldier was Captain J. D. Milne, who had seen service previously in Palestine. Our Quartermaster, Lieut. J. Richardson, belonged to Stirling. A regular with thirty years' service, he knew his job inside out. One had to be very diplomatic in the Q.M. stores, as " Ginger," as he was affectionately called, invariably refused any request until one was about to leave. Lieut. Billy Thomson was M.T.O., a native of Edinburgh and an inseparable pal of " Ginger." Captain A. R. Wilson, R.A.M.C., our " Doc," was invaluable.

His impersonations of Dave Willis always caused a laugh in the mess. Lieut. " Sailor " Sills, a native of Stirling, was formerly in the Merchant Navy, Lieut. H. P. Samwell and Lieut. Bob Mathieson both hailed from Stirling, and were old members of the battalion. Lieut. Archie McVicar, a native of Campbeltown, Argyllshire, was formerly a teacher in Dunoon Grammar School. Others from the Stirling area were Lieut. Billy Howatt, Lieut. D. A. Goodall, and Captain John Muirhead. Capt. Sinten, our padre, came from Inverness, where his father was a minister. Several of the officers came from Edinburgh, among them being Lieuts. Bobby Kinghorn, Jimmy Gilmour, Bobby Marshall, Walter Lees, and R. Muir Morton. From the west came Captain J. L. Robertson, Captain David Buchanan, Lieuts. W. A. Brechin and J. H. F. Morton. Captain Charlie Mackie hailed from Montrose, and was with the 7th Argylls in France in 1940, where he was mentioned in despatches. Lieuts. Fraser Buchanan, Dougie Adamson, and Alan Bowden were others who hailed from London, and later distinguished themselves in battle. It will be seen, therefore, that the battalion was officered from many different parts as well as from the Stirling area, but the majority of the men came from Stirling and Falkirk.

By the summer of 1942 it was felt that the Division would soon be given the chance to avenge St. Valery, and it came as no surprise when we were suddenly moved to the south of England, where a period of intensive training with tanks was carried out over country which was ideal for the purpose. Here we put the final polish to our training before setting forth on our long and eventful journey, which was to take us over thousands of miles of land and sea, and over many a grim and bloody battlefield ere we returned. Tropical kit was issued and preparations were soon in full swing for a long sea voyage. One hundred and one things had to be done, stores had to be securely packed in boxes, and each box had to be weighed and painted with the unit's serial number, continual kit inspections had to be carried out in order to ensure that each man had his kit intact, for we knew that once we left the shores of Britain it would not be so easy to make up deficiencies. Records of service books were brought up to date, and particular attention was paid to the lists of next of kin, which had to be compiled. At last we were ready, and although we had no idea what our destination would be, we felt that it would be either the Middle East or India.

Nine Weeks at Sea

After a long and monotonous train journey from the south of England to the Clyde, we embarked on the *Leopoldville*, a Belgian Congo liner of 14,000 tons, on the 15th of June 1942. Stores had to be loaded on to the ship, which took some considerable time, after which the ship had to be re-fuelled. It was therefore not until the 21st of June that we lifted anchor and steamed slowly down the Clyde through a thick fog. Foghorns kept up a monotonous chorus all afternoon, and it was not until we reached the open sea south-west of the Island of Islay that the fog cleared, and the impressive spectacle of a convoy at sea was revealed to us for the first time. The convoy consisted of approximately twenty-five large troopships escorted by a battleship and about ten corvettes and destroyers. For the purpose of reference it might be of interest to mention the names of some of the ships in the convoy, as some of them were famous oceangoing liners in peace-time and others had an historic interest. The battleship, *Malaya*, which fought at the battle of Jutland in the World War of 1914–18, joined the convoy just north of the Azores, and among the troopships were the *Arundel Castle*, the *Stirling Castle*, the *Empress of Australia*, the *Strathmore*, the *Stratheden*, the *Cuba*, the *Politska*, the *Awatea of Melbourne*, the *Narkunda*, the *Empress of Russia*, the *Bergen's Fjord*, the *Duchess of Richmond*, the *Adrastus*, the *Obosso*, the *Palma*, the *Banfora*, the *Empire Pride* (which was a German ship and a sister to the *Altmark*), the *Esperance Bay* (which was a sister ship to the famous *Jarvis Bay*), and the *Leopoldville*.

After reaching the open sea the weather became glorious, and the sight of the ocean-going liners rising and falling gently with the Atlantic swell, and the corvettes and destroyers dashing about on the constant look-out for submarines was one never to be forgotten. At that time troop convoys for the Middle East or India preferred the long voyage round the Cape of Good Hope rather than risk the danger of enemy action in the Mediterranean.

For the first few days we steamed practically due west and then south, passing the Azores on the 28th of June, after which we changed to south-east and passed between Cape Verde and Cape Verde Islands on the 1st of July. On the following day we sighted land, and as we had been told on board that our first port of call would be Freetown, we looked forward with a certain amount of excitement to the capital of Sierra Leone, known as the " White Man's Grave." At first Freetown appeared very attractive from the ship, and one was struck with the extraordinarily luxuriant vegetation. The atmosphere, however, was very heavy, humid, and oppressive, and owing to the presence of a very virulent form of malaria, no-one was allowed ashore. As we lay at anchor awaiting our turn for re-fuelling, we began to perspire to such an extent that we wished we had never seen the place. In the officers' cabins it was bad enough where six officers slept in a cabin meant for two, but the troops' decks were simply unbearable. Hammocks were slung wherever there was a corner, and some of the troops had to sleep on their own mess tables. Not a breath of air stirred the appalling atmosphere, and it was with a joyous feeling of relief that we set off again on the 5th of July. Freetown interested us, however, as being our first contact with Africa. We were highly amused at the natives who shot across to us in the little canoes which they build themselves, and endeavoured to sell melons and sandals. We were warned not to buy any fruit from the natives, and those who could not resist the sight of a juicy melon suffered for it later with pains and sickness.

Anchored off Freetown was a vast array of shipping, including the battleships *Rodney* and *Nelson*, which were lit up at night. Indeed it was a surprise to us to find that there was very little blackout in the port, and the ships in the bay presented a perfect target from the air. Fortunately no enemy raiders came our way, and we were able to gaze in peace on bright lights which we had not seen since the 3rd of September 1939. This was not the last time we were to see bright lights, for in Cape Town when we arrived there was no blackout at all.

Two days after leaving Freetown we crossed the Equator. It was 6 p.m. on the 7th of July, and we at once began preparing to celebrate in the usual manner. Lieut. "Sailor" Sills acted as King Neptune and as his Queen he chose 2nd Lieut. W. A. Brechin, and 2nd Lieut. J. Gilmour as Clerk of Court. The ceremony was preceded by the pipe-major playing round the ship from one company to another. About one day's journey from Cape Town we encountered the first rough weather since leaving the United Kingdom. Until now the weather had been glorious, and the sunsets a vast variety of beautiful colour. At night the Southern Cross and the Constellation of Orion were ever present in the sky. The beautiful starlight night, together with the phosphorescent lights in the sea alongside the ship, caused by the passage of the ship through the water, was indeed a peaceful scene amongst a convoy going to war. The ships at night appeared to resemble a number of large greyhounds bounding over a limitless expanse of ocean. Day after day we steamed on in glorious weather. Near the Cape the weather became cooler, which was a relief after the oppressive heat of the tropics. We all found plenty to interest us during the voyage, and we carried out some very useful training. Various denizens of the deep such as whales, sharks, dolphins, porpoises, and flying fish were often sighted.

On the 18th of July we arrived at Cape Town. It was a glorious morning, and as we looked at Cape Town for the first time, we wondered if anything could be more beautiful than the sight of the town nestling below Table Mountain with its white cloth of cloud in the early morning sun. We docked at 4 o'clock in the afternoon, and when we were allowed ashore that evening we found to our intense pleasure that there was no blackout. In addition, all the ships in the harbour were lit up.

The people of Cape Town were exceedingly kind, and as we marched through the town on the morning of the 19th of July all the troops were cheered and fruits of all kinds were showered on us. Our stay in Cape Town was disappointingly short as our convoy moved off again on the 21st. We knew that Cape Town would be the last town of the British Empire which we would see before going into action, and consequently we were very sorry to leave. As we rounded the Cape we had a good view of the Hottentot Holland mountains and the peaks called the " Twelve Apostles." The weather was very pleasant, and the Indian Ocean was as smooth as a mill-pond. At 9 o'clock on the morning of the 26th of July the convoy dropped anchor off Durban and remained there until late evening, when the remainder of the convoy, which had overstayed us in Cape Town, rejoined. No-one was allowed ashore at Durban, but we had a very good view of the town with the Drakensburg mountains in the distance rising to a height of 11,000 feet.

On the following day we re-entered the tropics and crossed the Equator again on the 3rd of August. We now knew we were bound for Egypt, and as we neared Aden the heat became more intense. About midday on the 6th of August we sighted the coast of Saudi Arabia and three hours later we arrived at Aden. As we approached, the pipes and drums of the battalion played the " Barren Rocks of Aden," and how appropriate the name is. No vegetation of any description could we see, and nothing but towering barren rocks confronted us. The heat here was very oppressive, the temperature being sometimes as high as 140° in the shade. On arrival in Aden, our convoy split up, some of the ships going to India and Basra and some to Suez. Our part of the convoy left Aden on the evening of the 8th of August, and on the following day we sighted French Somaliland on the port side and later in the day Eritrea. One could also just make out the Island of Perim and the Yemen province of Arabia on the starboard side.

For the next few days the ship slowed down and steamed around an island in the Red Sea at this reduced speed. The reason for this was that at Suez there was no room for us to berth until the ships in front of us had cleared off. The heat was the most severe we had yet encountered. Not the least suspicion of a breeze did we feel, and our main daily job was to try to find a part of the ship which would keep down our rising temperatures. At night the heat on the troop decks was appalling, but the Jocks stood it with as good a humour as one could expect under such trying circumstances.

At last we began to move faster and to steer a straight course for Suez, which we reached on the 15th of August and disembarked at Port Tewfik after having been at sea for close on nine weeks. The voyage had been full of interest, but we were not sorry when we said good-bye to our troopship, as we felt very much in need of some strenuous exercise to get our land legs back.

Training in the Desert

After our disembarkation was completed we departed by train for El Quassasin, where we camped for a week. Here we acclimatized ourselves to our new surroundings and carried out compulsory sun bathing. During our stay at El Quassasin, Mr. Churchill and the Chief of the Imperial General Staff visited the Division and addressed the officers of each battalion. On the 23rd of August we left our camp for Khatatba. The journey was full of interest as we had our first real glimpse of Egypt, passing through such well-known places as Tel El Kebir, Zagazig, Benha, and Cairo. The reason for this move was to place ourselves in readiness for any urgent move which might take place, as it was expected that Rommel would attack with the intention of capturing the rich Nile delta. One day only we spent at Khatatba, after which we moved in transport along the Alexandria desert road via Giza, where we had a good view of the Pyramids. Rumours went around that Rommel had attacked and our new role was to defend the Nile delta. Mosquitoes in this area caused us a great deal of annoyance and discomfort, and it was with a feeling of relief that we marched out three days later, bound for a little village called Mansuriya. I think that one can safely say that a more filthy village could not be found anywhere. During the course of digging trenches at Mansuriya a certain number of minor arguments arose with the local Arabs who objected to us digging up their pea-nuts. The digging went on, however, as it was definitely established that Rommel had attacked farther to the west. On the 1st of September we received orders to move on the following day to Alam Shaltut, forty miles south-west of Alexandria, in order to defend the aerodromes there. Here the climate suited us much better as it was very much cooler in the evening, free from mosquitoes, and certainly much healthier than it was in the Nile delta. During this period we were able to get hot and cold showers fairly regularly. Later we dreamed about these showers during our advance across the desert, where a thimbleful of water was worth ten times its weight in gold.

On the 7th of September the battalion moved to an area called F Box at Alam El Khadim, about fifteen miles from El Alamein. This locality was a mined area, for the defence of which the battalion, as part of the 154th Infantry Brigade, was responsible. Having now spent approximately three weeks in Egypt becoming acclimatized to the country, and also having moved about from one locality to another, we felt ourselves ready for anything. A great deal of intensive training was then carried out, during which time we took part in no fewer than five full-scale night attack exercises over desert which was practically similar to the desert over which we later attacked at El Alamein on the 23rd of October. In each case we advanced behind an artillery barrage, and in addition had the 1/7th Middlesex Regiment's machine guns in support. The object of these exercises was (*a*) to accustom the infantry to the terrific din of artillery barrage, (*b*) to practise the penetration through enemy minefields for a distance of some five or six miles, (*c*) to practise advancing closely behind artillery barrages, and (*d*) to consolidate by digging-in on the capture of the objective, and thus be ready for any enemy counter-attack at first light. All exercises were slightly different, but in many respects they were the same operation.

Although we had no idea when the Eighth Army intended

to take the offensive or where this offensive would be, it was obvious that something of the kind was brewing. The Eighth Army had been considerably reinforced during the previous six months and consisted of the 10th, 13th, and 30th Corps. Altogether we had the following divisions: the 9th Australian Division, the 1st South African Division, the 2nd New Zealand Division, the 4th Indian Division, the 44th Division, the 50th Division, the 51st Highland Division, the 1st Armoured Division, the 7th Armoured Division, and the 10th Armoured Division. Against this it was estimated that the enemy had about twelve divisions, consisting of the Brescia Division, the Trieste Division, the Trento Division, the Bologna Division, the Folgore Division, the Pavia Division, the Littorio Division, the Ariete Division, all of which were Italian, and the 90th Light Division, the 164th Infantry Division, and the 15th and 21st Panzer Divisions, which were German. Although the enemy had more divisions than we had, the Italian divisions were very much under strength, and were little stronger than our brigades, that is, the estimated strength of an Italian division was about 5,000 men. It was therefore with a feeling of complete confidence that we awaited the inevitable offensive of the Eighth Army.

During the month of October the battalion relieved the 5/7th Gordons in a reserve front line position west of El Alamein station, on the left flank of the Australians. The Australians were veterans of desert fighting, and in order to gain experience a number of officers from the battalion were attached for a period of four days to the 17th Infantry battalion of the 9th Australian Division. The Australians were very friendly and humorous. They were firm believers in " A nod is as good as a wink," as is evidenced by the dry humour of their advice to desert travellers on the signposts which they had erected in " No Man's Land." These signposts, which were erected at intervals of 200 yards in "No Man's Land" in the Alamein area, put the onus of further advance on the traveller himself. One signpost bore the one word "Hey," the second one had painted on it the words "Where are you going?" and the third one bore the inscription, "If you go much farther take one of these." Beside the last signpost lay a row of little crosses.

Rommel's attack had been a complete failure, and as his armour had been caught in a trap his losses in tanks were very heavy. He had received a very nasty knock and would think twice before he attacked the Eighth Army again. It was now our turn, and the battle which followed shortly afterwards at El Alamein was to be the turning-point of the war in our favour. Rommel had come within an ace of capturing the rich Nile delta, and was only a matter of approximately 70 miles from Cairo and Alexandria. The British army, after having retreated across the desert for hundreds of miles from Agheila, stood firm on a narrow front in the coastal region at El Alamein, where to the south lay the Qattara depression, which in itself was a complete obstacle to Rommel's advancing armies.

Plate 3 (*Above*) In the trenches at El Alamein. (*Below*) Sappers at work lifting Teller mines in the Libyan desert

CHAPTER II

THE TURN OF THE TIDE

About the middle of October we dug and camouflaged trenches south of Tel El Elisa station, one mile behind the front-line positions. At the time we had no idea for whom the trenches were intended, and came to the conclusion that they were intended for some unit who were too lazy to dig for themselves and had got the Argylls to do the job for them. Nevertheless, although the Jocks grumbled about their task, the job was finished in record time. Actually these were the trenches the battalion occupied as an assembly area just prior to the battle of El Alamein on the 23rd of October 1942. Having completed the trenches, the battalion was relieved by the 5th battalion of the Cameron Highlanders, and our next location was an area called E box, another mined locality, not far from our previous area at F box. Here the battalion remained for a few days, until on the 22nd of October the plan for the Eighth Army offensive was at last divulged, and the battalion moved forward again to the assembly area. The battalion by this time was very well trained, and the troops were in splendid spirits and eager to get to grips with the Afrika Korps commanded by Rommel.

The Eighth Army plan was to attack on all fronts simultaneously with the main break-through of the armour at El Alamein. The 51st Highland Division, along with the 9th Australian Division on the right and the 2nd New Zealand Division on the left, were to penetrate the enemy minefields and thereby open up a road through which the armour and transport could pass after the mines had been cleared away by the sappers. Zero hour was 10 o'clock at night on the 23rd of October. In addition to our infantry, masses of guns, tanks, scorpions, and vehicles of all kinds had been well dug in and camouflaged. A clever deception plan had been carried out in which the vast number of tanks in the area of where the break-through was to take place were camouflaged as three-ton trucks. Farther to the south all vehicles were camouflaged as tanks and the enemy reconnaissance planes were consequently hoodwinked, and Rommel thought that the main armour break-through would be attempted in the south instead of at El Alamein. Rommel, therefore, moved most of his tank strength to the south to meet this threat, only to find out his mistake when it was too late. In addition, the enemy did not expect us to attack at El Alamein as it was the toughest part of the enemy defence line.

All day on the 23rd of October everyone lay hidden in his trench with his own food and water, orders having been previously issued that no movement of any kind was to take place during daylight. It is a credit to the discipline of all concerned, and to the excellence of the camouflage, that although several planes passed over during the day, no bombs were dropped. At 7 o'clock in the evening, when darkness came, everyone sprang to life and got out of his trench. Water-bottles were filled and a substantial hot meal was served. Each man was fully armed and carried at least one hand grenade. At 8.30 in the evening the march to the start-line, which had previously been laid by the 5th Seaforths, began. There were four objectives to be captured by 30th Corps, which was the corps to which the 51st Highland Division belonged. These objectives were termed the Green line, the Red line, the Black line, and the Blue line.

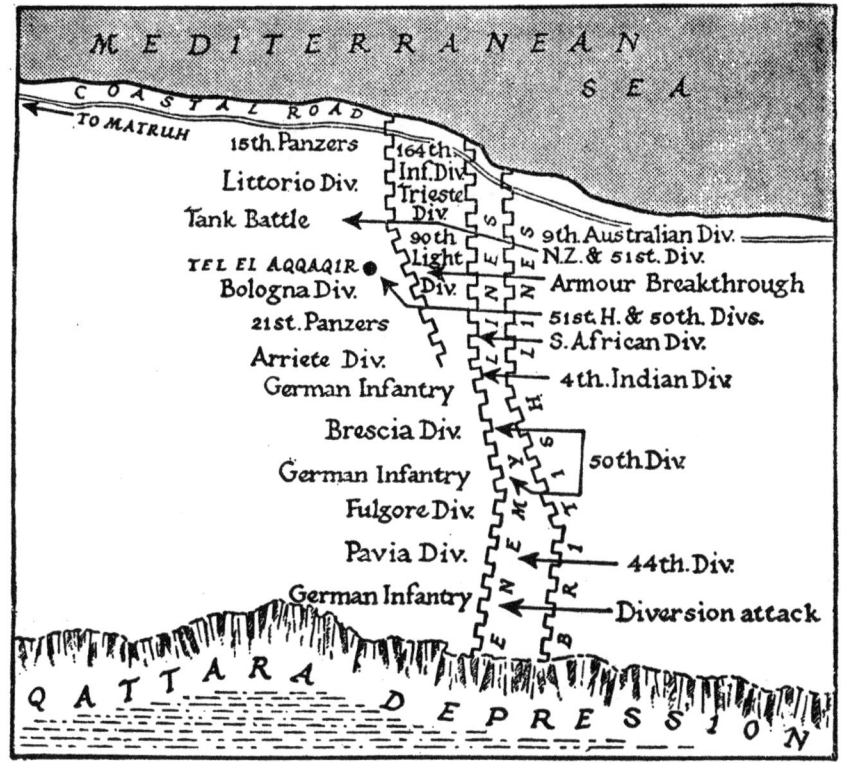

Disposition of forces at the Battle of El Alamein

The Battle of El Alamein

The attack was supported by a previously co-ordinated and timed artillery programme, and the job of the infantry was to keep close up behind the artillery barrage in order that the enemy would have no time to raise their heads before our infantry reached their objectives. The division attacked with parts of all three brigades forward. Of the 154th Brigade, the 1st battalion of the Black Watch were on the right, next came the Argylls with the Reconnaissance Corps on our left and the 7th Black Watch beyond. Certain localities were to be captured, and it is interesting to note that these localities were named, with one exception, after Scottish towns within the battalion recruiting area. These localities were called Renfrew, Falkirk, Mons Meg, Greenock, and Stirling. Just as the battle was about to begin the Divisional Commander, Major-General Wimberley, sent out a message to all units of the Division. The message contained the stirring words, " Scotland forever and second to none." How could such a message fail to rouse us !

We attacked with C company on the right under Major John Lindsay Macdougall, and D company on the left under Capt. David Buchanan. B company under Capt. J. C. Meiklejohn was right rear company, Battalion Headquarters bringing up the left rear, followed by a platoon of A company acting as moppers-up. The remainder of A company under Capt. G. B. Horsburgh was detached, and moved with a squadron of the 50th Royal Tank Regiment. At 9.40 p.m. the deathly silence of the desert was broken by one gun which fired a single round. A second later our artillery opened up for twenty minutes, firing on the enemy's battery positions. The noise was one thunderous roar which, when compared to the death-like silence of a second before, appeared as if hell had been let loose. The distant horizon appeared to be on fire. The desert was flooded by brilliant moonlight, which made it somewhat easier for our troops to make their way through the extensive enemy minefields. Five minutes after the guns had opened up we crossed the start-line, and at 10 o'clock the artillery began their timed programme of firing on the enemy's forward positions. Behind this barrage the battalion advanced at a speed of 100 yards in three minutes. The noise created by our 25-pounder guns was terrific, and was increased when the enemy's artillery and mortars opened up. Smoke, sand, the crumping sound of bursting shells, the shattering roar of air-bursting shells, and the smell of cordite, together with the vicious spattering rat-tat-tat of machine guns appeared to be everywhere, while minefields, trip-wire, and anti-personnel mines all added to the confusion. Sometimes above all this din one could hear the moans of the dying, and the familiar cry of the wounded calling for stretcher bearers. The stretcher bearers performed their grim duties with a courage and determination beyond all praise, and throughout all this hell the men were magnificent.

C company's objectives were Paisley and Mons Meg, after which they were to advance to the Red line, and capture and consolidate on Greenock, while A and B companies went through to capture Stirling. D company on the left had as their first and second objectives, Renfrew and Falkirk, and finally Greenock. The first objectives were captured at about ten minutes to 11 o'clock, C company quickly mopping up on Paisley to the strains of " Monymusk " on the pipes. Behind the first objective a great number of anti-personnel mines and booby traps were encountered, causing many casualties. The second objectives, Mons Meg and Falkirk, were reached at about 11 o'clock, and after these positions were mopped up, the advance to the Red line at 11.30 p.m. was resumed. At about this time Capt. David Buchanan of D company was wounded by enemy mortar fire, which caused a reshuffle of command within the company. The Red line was, however, reached at a little before midnight, and the battalion, which was well up to time in their advance, continued to push on against stiffening opposition. Shortly after midnight, a platoon of B company under Lieut. Kinghorn suffered heavy casualties from enemy shelling, leaving only himself and three men untouched. At the same time Lieut. W. T. Thomson was wounded in the mouth, and Lieut. R. Mathieson had to be evacuated after having been wounded in the hand. The battalion was now about 500 yards from Greenock, and about this time several rounds from our own artillery were found to be dropping short, and, in fact, falling among the forward companies causing several casualties.

The battalion, therefore, as ordered, observed one hour's pause and dug in. The advance was resumed at 1 o'clock in the morning, and as we advanced the enemy shelling and mortaring and machine-gun fire increased. Many casualties were sustained during the final attack on Greenock, which was taken at the point of the bayonet. A favourite trick played by the Italians was to hold their hands up in surrender and as our troops lowered their rifles, over would come a hand grenade. In this way we sustained quite a few casualties, until we got wise to the tricks of the "Ities." The position on Greenock consisted of an anti-tank gun and two machine-gun posts, one mobile field gun, and the usual cluster of mines, all of which was supported by two platoons of infantry. All the enemy in this position were killed or wounded, and our troops were in occupation of the position by 2 o'clock in the morning. By this time C and D companies were considerably weakened, having only about 30 men left in each. The commanding officer, Lt.-Col. Lorne M. Campbell, D.S.O., T.D., then decided not to attack the objective called Stirling, as A company and the tanks had not yet appeared. A company's platoon, which was mopping up in the rear of the battalion, arrived at about 4 o'clock on the Saturday morning and were sent to strengthen D company. The battalion then consolidated just forward of Greenock, the dispositions of the companies being C company on the right, D company on the left, and B company in depth in the rear.

An enemy counter-attack with tanks was expected, and the position at dawn was not a pleasant one. However, no counter-attack took place. We had no communication with brigade as the wireless had broken down. All day on Saturday, 24th October, our positions were subjected to heavy enemy shelling. At about 4 o'clock in the afternoon, a gallant but unsuccessful attack by the 2nd Seaforths was launched on Stirling. At about this time, our pipe-major, Maclachlan, was killed by enemy snipers. Early on the morning of Sunday, the 25th of October, our transport arrived, after having been held up by mines, due to some of the scorpions having broken down. Our task was not yet done, for later in the day orders were received to attack the objective " Nairn," a long low ridge about 1,800 yards in front of Greenock. Zero hour was 11 o'clock at night, and this time there was to be no artillery barrage. About 3 o'clock in the afternoon, Major John Lindsay Macdougall, Lieuts. Archie McVicar and Bobby Kinghorn were evacuated, all of them having sustained wounds during the capture of the objective Greenock. Capt. G. B. Horsburgh, with the remainder of A company, rejoined the battalion at 7 o'clock in the evening. They had been held up forward of the Mons Meg objective by heavy enemy mortars and machine-gun fire, and the minefields prevented the tanks on which they were travelling from getting through. Here 2nd Lieut. Gilmour of A company was killed by enemy shell-fire. A company was quickly reorganized, and along with B and D companies was ordered to attack the Nairn objective, while the depleted C company held on to Greenock, along with battalion headquarters. Three different objectives were to be taken, all of which formed part of the main objective called Nairn. All three companies had the same start-line but their advance was on divergent lines. The order of the attack from right to left was A, D, and B companies. The first objective was a machine-gun nest and an enemy mortar position, along with three machine-gun posts.

All three companies formed up on the start-line, and before they actually started their advance were heavily shelled and machine-gunned. The men were dead tired and exhausted through lack of sleep and constant fighting, and although they had gone through hell since the 23rd of October, they all stood silent and motionless on the start-line, ready once more to do battle at whatever cost, knowing well enough that some of them would never remain alive to tell the tale, and what a tale of heroism there is to tell of this Sunday night battle! Enemy machine guns kept chattering viciously during the attack, and very soon casualties began to mount up. Capt. Horsburgh and Lieut. Bobby Marshall were both wounded, leaving the company without any officers in command. This did not deter the company, which carried on gallantly under the N.C.O.s. The battlefield was bathed in brilliant moonlight which enabled our troops to observe sections of the enemy moving about. The enemy eventually began to retreat, and when this occurred our troops chased after them. There was no stopping them, and it caused some considerable difficulty in control. The way the men went in at the point of the bayonet was magnificent. After the position was captured the companies dug-in on the reverse slope of a shallow depression on the Nairn objective. A and D companies, having no officers left, were reorganized by Capt. Meiklejohn into one company, which, including his own company, gave him a force of approximately 100 men. During this attack Sergeant Gauld of D company was blown up by an enemy discharger cup, but this did not deter him from charging the enemy with his bayonet after he regained consciousness and wiping out a machine-gun post. Throughout this attack the courage and the determination of the men were splendid. All companies were weak and short of ammunition and water. Although Capt. Meiklejohn could not definitely establish his position, he got in touch by wireless with Major Hugh Foster of the 126th Highland Field Regiment, Royal Artillery, and

Plate 4 Field-Marshal Lord Montgomery of Alamein

arranged for defensive fire to be brought down all round his position, thus saving his force from being overrun. An 88-millimetre anti-tank gun on the left was giving considerable trouble, and it was observed that shells were landing near it. Where the shells were coming from it was difficult to say, but eventually it was found that our own tanks were firing at it. Owing to Capt. Meiklejohn's accurate directions our own artillery opened up on it and eventually knocked it out. Capt. Meiklejohn then asked battalion headquarters to fire a Verey light in order to assist him to find his position. As ammunition and water were short in Capt. Meiklejohn's force, battalion headquarters made three attempts to reach the force by sending out carrier patrols with supplies, but all patrols were unsuccessful. On one occasion when Lieut. A. J. A. Stewart was sent out with a section of carriers and a wireless set, he went too far to the right and was directed by Capt. Meiklejohn, who could hear his carriers moving, to bear left. Eventually he was told to halt and that Lieut. Sills would be sent out to find him. Capt. Meiklejohn then sent out Lieut. Sills, who was the only officer left. The last heard of Lieut. Sills was when, quite near to Lieut. Stewart's position, he was heard to shout " Up the Argylls," and then an explosion occurred. Later Lieut. Sills was reported killed. Lieut. Stewart's carrier patrol could not reach Lieut. Sills because of minefields. Later a patrol of five carriers was sent out. Three of the carriers were towing anti-tank guns. The patrol, which went out on a different bearing this time, ran on to another minefield, two carriers getting through, two got blown up, and the remaining carrier returned to battalion headquarters with the crews of the blown-up carriers.

At about midday on the 26th of October armoured units arrived and opened fire over the heads of the forward companies. This, of course, brought down enemy fire on top of

Capt. Meiklejohn's force, but fortunately few casualties were sustained. At 7 p.m. lorried infantry arrived on the right and pushed out slightly westwards. Still no ammunition nor water arrived for the force, which was by now twenty-four hours without supplies. At 10.20 a.m. on Tuesday, 27th October, L/Corporal Wallace of B company was sent to Battalion Headquarters to act as a guide for the long awaited supplies, and this time the carrier got through.

During all this period the battalion was subjected to heavy and constant shelling and dive bombing, and indeed until the attack on Tel El Aqqaqir on the 4th of November, the battalion were almost continuously under shell-fire. On the 27th of October C company under Capt. Donald Young was sent forward to Nairn to occupy the position on the left of B company, D company then being withdrawn into reserve. Patrol activity in the form of both fighting and reconnaissance patrols produced some valuable information, and during one of these patrols on the night of 29th October Lieut. Alan Bowden of C company was wounded. The patrol returned minus Private Shields, who it was thought must have been a fatal casualty. Later, however, Private Shields turned up carrying the body of a wounded comrade whom he had found lying out in " No Man's Land." Private Shields had the presence of mind to strip and bury his Bren gun in order that it might not fall into enemy hands, as he found it impossible to carry both his Bren gun and his wounded comrade also.

On the night of the 30th of October the battalion was relieved by the Royal Botha Regiment of the 1st South African Division and so we left this grim blood-stained battlefield, leaving behind us our brave fallen comrades but never forgetting them for one second. We marched back through the battlefields which all around bore evidence of the terrible struggle that had taken place, and in fact which was still going on. Enemy guns and vehicles lay scattered, the twisted pieces of metal smoking and burning furiously. The night was as usual brilliantly lit by moonlight, and as we marched on, most of us unshaven for days, we could smell the stench of the dead. The sand underneath was beaten into a very fine dust lying nine inches thick on the ground which, as we moved on, rose in choking clouds all about us. The guns kept on firing, but as we neared the end of our ten-mile march we knew we were out of the range of German guns with the exception of their heavy guns. It was rumoured that the battalion had another role, but what that role was no-one could guess. The rest which we expected only lasted for one night, that is, the night we marched out of the line, and we had no sooner arrived than we were ordered back into another part of the line. Our next location found us in the centre of a minefield. In addition a great number of mines were scattered over the area and were unmarked. It was while in this area that a few of us while travelling in a truck were blown up on a Teller mine without injury to any. The experience is difficult to describe. The accident occurred so quickly that we were only stunned for a second or two by the quickness of the explosion. One of the wheels was blown completely off the truck and generally the truck was a total wreck. On yet another occasion while on a recce in a Bren carrier at 5.30 in the morning, a heavy enemy artillery concentration was brought down on us. Everything went all black and the carrier was struck by several pieces of flying metal. We, therefore, decided to stop temporarily and make for the nearest trench, which incidentally was only one foot deep. We only got there just in time, as two trucks only a few yards away received direct hits.

 On the 2nd of November we took over a front-line position from the 2nd New Zealand Division, the location of which was in the El Wishka area to the north of our old front-line sector on Nairn. This relief was carried out at night, fortunately without much enemy interference except for spasmodic shelling.

The Attack on Tel El Aqqaqir

On the 3rd of November orders were received to attack and capture a feature called Point 44, Tel El Aqqaqir in the El Higeif area. This attack, which was of vital importance in order to allow our armour a complete and final breakthrough, was supported by seven regiments of artillery firing on a front of six hundred yards. The objective was to be captured by our battalion alone, and a quick recce from the area of a depression was made before dark by Brigadier Houldsworth, D.S.O., M.C., along with our Commanding Officer and Company commanders. Through a haze a line of telegraph poles could be seen running diagonally across the front about 1,400 yards distant. The objective was a little rise in the desert about 800 yards beyond this line of poles. Darkness then came on, and we had great difficulty in finding our way back to the battalion. Eventually we arrived back about midnight, to find the battalion all ready to move.

The plan was that our gunners would bring artillery concentrations down on the line of telegraph poles from 5.15 a.m. until 6.15 a.m., after which the gunners would move their barrage forward to form a protective screen 500 yards beyond the objective, but with the centre point on the objective, Point 44. The battalion left its location at 1.30 a.m. on the 4th of November and marched across country for approximately five miles. We were rather doubtful as to whether or not we would arrive in time, and in fact we were none too happy about our ability to find the assembly area at all. During our advance we again met the Brigadier, and after a short discussion it was decided that we

Plate 5 (*Above*) A forlorn procession of German prisoners captured by the Highland Division in the desert. (*Below*) "Impressions of a night attack," a sketch by Lieut. R. G. Burge, R.E.

could not be far from our assembly area, and as time was absolutely vital we formed up the battalion for the attack at once. Actually we found ourselves in the area occupied by the 5th battalion Cameron Highlanders and were therefore too far to the right. The gunners had already opened up on the line of telegraph poles, and without any ceremony we started our advance almost immediately. The original bearing was 293° for the advance, but as the assembly area was slightly wrong we changed the bearing to 280°. The sound of our own bursting shells helped us considerably in finding direction. C company under Capt. Donald Young were on the right, and A company under Capt. Seymour on the left during the advance. B and D companies and battalion headquarters brought up the rear. After we had advanced about 1,000 yards C company disappeared in the smoke which the gunners had by this time laid for us in order to cover our advance. The line of poles was crossed at 6.15 a.m. according to schedule, and we now had only 800 yards to go to reach the objective. As navigator I had some difficulty in keeping the two forward companies in line, as by this time the smoke was very thick, and A company on the left had lost touch with one of its platoons. C company on the right had also lost one of its sections. Unfortunately some of our guns were firing short, and in consequence caused a number of casualties within the battalion. On reaching the objective at about 6.45 a.m. we found that the enemy had made a quick getaway, and the position was unoccupied except for a couple of snipers who were soon rounded up. One of the snipers took a pot-shot at the commanding officer as he was in the act of lighting his pipe. Although there was no opposition it is unfortunate that we sustained casualties amounting to 8 killed and 23 wounded, as a result of some of our own guns firing short. In the hurry and confusion of the advance, and also owing to the fact that we moved off from a different start-line to the one we had previously so very hurriedly recced, battalion headquarters, and B and D companies, led by the commanding officer, arrived on the objective from a different angle to A and C companies, led by myself.

Our objective was a former Divisional Headquarters, and after we consolidated we made a reconnaissance of the area and found masses of signal equipment of great value, a complete Orderly Room, Intelligence Office, and Regimental Aid Post, and a store full of valuable equipment. Documents which we captured were considered of such great importance as to merit sending them off by special plane to General Headquarters at Cairo. In addition to this, bottles of chianti champagne, etc., were found in large quantities. A headline which appeared in one of our home newspapers referring to the attack on Tel El Aqqaqir read, " The Boche got the wind up and the Argylls got the wine." A number of Iron Crosses and Afrika Korps badges were also among the newly discovered treasures which we found in a store. In the afternoon we held a mock investiture at which we invested our commanding officer with the Iron Cross, and eventually a number of " Jocks " were seen wandering about with Iron Crosses pinned on their chests.

By this time the battalion had lost a number of its original members, but drafts were arriving, thereby bringing the battalion up to strength again. The total number of casualties since the beginning of the battle of El Alamein up to and including Aqqaqir were 2 officers killed and 11 wounded, and 70 other ranks killed and 192 wounded. This was the end of the battle of El Alamein, which, starting with that bright moonlight on the 23rd of October when the 51st Highland Division bore the brunt of the attack and added yet another page of glory to the history of the fighting 51st, or as they were known to the Germans, " The Ladies from

Hell." St. Valery was avenged in no uncertain manner by twelve days and nights of the most bitter fighting, finishing up with the 7th Argylls doing the last attack of that mighty struggle at Aqqaqir on the 4th of November, and thus enabling our tanks to break through and begin the historic chase across the desert.

We remained in this area for three days, during which time we had visions of canteens and rest camps after having carried out three different attacks in such bloody fighting. Prisoners came streaming in, and on the 5th of November one batch alone numbered two thousand two hundred.

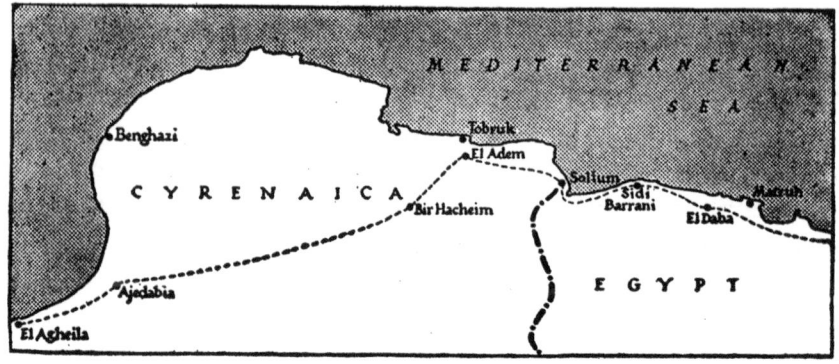

The Pursuit of Rommel's Forces from El Alamein to El Agheila
The dotted line shows the route taken by the Highland Division

CHAPTER III

ACROSS LIBYAN SANDS

ON the 7th of November we began our famous dash across the desert continually moving westwards trying to catch up with Rommel's Afrika Korps. Our first move was to an area south-west of El Daba in the locality of Ras El Kanaysis East. We were now well out of the battle, the enemy having retreated so speedily that only what were termed " Flying Columns " could keep in contact with him. The amount of destroyed enemy equipment and burnt-out vehicles which lay scattered around the countryside spoke volumes for the good work done by the Western Desert Air Force.

While in the El Daba area, a party of thirty-three German Luftwaffe drove into our camp one morning in an Italian three-ton vehicle. They were unarmed, and said they had been wandering about lost for days. A corporal of the particular Nazi type—a student of languages—was among the prisoners, and seemed very much to resent his captivity. At this time we had just heard that the British First Army and several American divisions had landed in North Africa, and when we told the prisoners this, to see what effect it would have on them, the corporal's reply was, " The longer you keep us prisoners in Egypt, the sooner we shall be free. We have the whole of Europe. Heil Hitler." We then told him that Rommel was travelling in the wrong direction for freeing prisoners in Egypt.

The battalion did extremely well in salvaging enemy equipment and transport in the area. One captured gun which excited great interest in the camp was a French six-inch naval gun on wheels in perfectly good condition. Each company had picked up a number of German and Italian vehicles, and it was an amusing sight to see troops driving about in vehicles of the most weird design. On the 16th of November we were again on the move, but this time we marched instead of using transport a distance of forty miles, which was done in three stages, arriving at our final destination on the 18th of November. We had by this time become accustomed to the heat of the desert, but although this was so, we found these marches most exhausting in the glaring heat of the midday sun. When we halted for a short rest it was not possible to find a shaded spot anywhere, and the sun's rays burned unmercifully into our skins until we felt we would soon be the colour of the Arabs. Now we were on much shorter water rations, and one water bottle full per day for all purposes—that is, for washing and shaving, making tea, and drinking—was all we were allowed.

On the 23rd of November we were ordered to move to the area of El Adem, which was about twelve miles south of Tobruk. The role of the division was now to assume control of Western Cyrenaica and to be responsible for operations west of Benghazi. We all looked forward to this fresh move, which meant the probability of passing through many places well known to us by name, such as Mersa Matruh, Sidi Barrani, Sollum, Fort Capuzzo, Bardia, and Tobruk itself.

Actually Bardia was by-passed, and few of us had the time or opportunity of visiting Tobruk. Sollum, however, was seen to advantage, and we had a fine panoramic view from the top of the escarpment overlooking the bay. Hellfire Pass was most impressive, winding up on to the high Libyan plateau, which presented a beautiful view of the little white-washed buildings of Sollum nestling down below at the head of the bay with the greenish-blue waters of the Mediterranean lapping across golden sands which stretched away to the east as far as the eye could see. We were now across the Libyan frontier and in enemy territory. Our next move was to take us a stage farther and much nearer to where we expected the enemy to make a stand, so on the 2nd of December we raced across the desert via Bir Hacheim, where the French had made such a gallant stand in the previous campaign. Near Antelat we encountered a vast minefield which compelled us to halt and form our vehicles into a single column from the desert formation which we had been employing up till now. After passing through the minefield, however, we reverted to our desert formation once more. The sight of a convoy of vehicles moving across the desert in desert formation is a very impressive one, and the formation is very similar to a convoy of ships at sea. First of all there is a vanguard of one platoon in vehicles, each vehicle being two hundred yards from the one on either side of it and one hundred yards from the one behind it. Next comes the remainder of the battalion some distance behind, all the vehicles of which are spaced similarly. The leading truck of each column, being the company commander's truck, flies the company flag. The convoy is led by the battalion navigator, who is usually the intelligence officer, and who uses a sun compass as a guide. The reason for this formation is to keep to a minimum casualties through enemy air action, as the vehicles are so well dispersed. Another reason is that should the battalion be required to fight a battle at a moment's notice, they are already deployed for it.

Unfortunately, by following the route across the desert, we by-passed Bomba, Derna, and Benghazi, all of which we were rather anxious to see. This journey, a distance of some two hundred and fifty miles, took us from the 2nd to the 5th of December. We camped in an area just west of Ajedabia, but not for long, as the following day we were ordered once again to take over front-line positions from the 2nd Seaforth Highlanders in the area of Mersa Brega, approximately twenty miles east of Agheila. An amusing story worth mentioning here refers to the forward elements of the Eighth Army when they entered Benghazi for the third and last time. It was early morning, and an Arab chieftain who saw them coming went to greet them with the words, " Good-morning, gentlemen. You are earlier than usual this year."

Mersa Brega and its Mines

The village of Mersa Brega appeared to be a very strongly defended position, and this time we were to hold the line while the 152nd Brigade of the Division attacked. During the next few days active patrolling was carried out. Shelling of our positions by the enemy was intermittent, and by the morning of the 11th of December we began to suspect from information received that the enemy were thinning out, leaving only a rearguard with some mobile guns to defend their positions. On the night of the 12th December, a raid by a company of the 1st Battalion of the Black Watch on our right was preceded by an artillery barrage of seventy-two rounds per gun. The enemy obviously thought that this was a full-scale attack, and on the morning of the 13th of December a platoon of our C company entered the village only to find that the enemy had already flown. The village was found to be full of booby traps and anti-personnel mines of various types, booby traps also being attached to Teller mines in the minefield in front of the village. Sometimes booby traps were discovered on the under-side of dead bodies, which caused casualties among the troops detailed to bury the dead. Mersa Brega was the worst place we had yet encountered for mines, for wherever we went we found mines, even outside the enemy wire. These mines caused a number of casualties. It was while going to the rescue of a sapper officer that Capt. W. A. Brechin received wounds from mines from which he later died. 6 other ranks were killed, and Capt. Seymour and 13 other ranks were wounded as a result of mines, most of which were of the German S type commonly known as " Jumping Jack."

We spent Christmas Day here, and while the commanding officer and I were visiting one of the companies, our car ran over a cluster of anti-personnel mines, but fortunately the only damage done was to the petrol tank of the car, which was perforated. The commanding officer in his usually calm manner proceeded to mark the spot with two barrels which we found at the side of the road, in order that the sappers would know where to look for and clear the mines.

In addition to the discomfort of mines we experienced a violent sandstorm. Anyone who has not been in a sandstorm cannot visualize how annoying and uncomfortable it can be. On this occasion, far away in the distance could be seen a wall of sandy dust about a hundred feet high coming towards us. It struck us with terrific force and the fine sand got into everything, including the hair, eyes, ears, and throat. It turned day into night while it lasted, and afterwards came torrential rain—a truly unpleasant experience. On top of all this the water which we had to drink came from a nearby well which, on account of the district being composed mostly of salt lakes, was extremely salty and unpleasant to drink. The more we drank of it the more thirsty we became.

By now the 153rd Brigade of the Division were moving up beyond Mersa Brega from a position to the south of us, and one had hopes of the New Zealanders, who were doing an outflanking movement from the south aimed at Marble Arch, fifty miles away to the west, being able to cut off at least some of the enemy forces. The day after Christmas we left Mersa Brega and its mines and moved forward in transport to Ras El Aali. The role of the battalion here was the unloading of ships at the pier, and road-making. We anticipated a stay of at least five or six days, but on the morning of the 27th of December a warning order was received to move on the 28th of December to the Wadi Matratin to take up an operational role. No sooner had we arrived in the Wadi Matratin than we were told that our next move would be to an area beyond Sirte on the 30th of December, and this time we were to act as advance guard to the 154th Brigade Group. This move was postponed until the 5th of January, and we had the doubtful pleasure of spending the New Year at the Wadi Matratin.

Making Contact at Buerat

On the 5th of January, 1943, we moved in transport again in three stages, doing approximately sixty miles per day for the first two days and thirty miles on the last day. The move was carried out without incident and, indeed, was very monotonous. On arrival we took over positions on the Wadi El Chebir, about fifteen miles east of Buerat. Our role was to form a firm base with the Brigade Group, and to send forward Observation Posts protected by a keep consisting of one infantry platoon, one section of Bren carriers, and two six-pounder anti-tank guns. The object of this was to gain information of the enemy's strength, dispositions, and intentions. There were two reasons why the brigade at this time did not move closer to the enemy. One reason was that the strength of the enemy was unknown to us, and as we had very little in the way of support behind us, the brigade might easily be wiped out by numerically superior enemy forces. The second reason was that we did not, on the other hand, want to show too many troops in the area in case the enemy withdrew without our being able to catch any of them. This, of course, we did not want him to do, and the plan was therefore to form this firm base until the remainder of our Division should arrive. The dispositions of the enemy forces at this time in the order from north to south were the Trieste Division, the Pistoia Division, the Ramcke Division, the Spezia Division, the Young Fascists, the 164th Infantry Division, 88th Force, and the 90th Light Division. This last-named division was reckoned to be one of the best divisions in the German army, and were our opponents on many memorable occasions. During our move up to the Wadi El Chebir, several Stuka raids took place, which kept us constantly on the alert. On the night of the 13th of January the battalion again moved forward in transport to the Wadi Uesca, about twelve miles west of Wadi Chebir, the object being to make contact with the enemy positions south west of Buerat. D company under Capt. Horsburgh was detached for a special job to an area west of Buerat. Their job was to prevent the enemy moving east along the roads in the Buerat area, and subsequently to protect Corps Royal Engineers working parties who were clearing mines in the area. Along with D company were a battery of anti-tank guns and a section of carriers. One platoon was already in close contact with the enemy on the coast five miles northwest of Buerat. It was not until the battalion arrived at Zliten on the 17th of January that D company rejoined us.

On the night of the 14th of January the battalion, less D company, again moved, this time to Wadi Chfef, thus coming into closer contact with the enemy. The enemy were known to be holding positions in the Wadi Chfef area, which positions had to be attacked before the advance on Tripoli began. It was estimated that the enemy's foremost defended localities were only a matter of two thousand to three thousand yards distant. The move took place at night, and in spite of the amount of transport and the open nature of the ground, which was devoid of any cover whatever, no enemy shelling took place. Finding a place in the desert at night is an exceedingly ticklish business, and on this particular occasion it was a nightmare to the navigator. In the desert one has to travel on a previously selected bearing for a certain distance which is measured from a map. On arriving at the end of the preselected distance, one finds just another piece of desert no different from the rest of the desert for hundreds of miles. C company under Major John Lindsay Macdougall, M.C., acted as advance guard, and established itself on the right flank of the brigade position. Several casualties occurred in C company during the night from what was thought to be accurate enemy mortar fire, but which turned out to be German S mines. Owing to the noise of our transport the enemy evidently thought that there would be a dawn attack, as the battalion was very heavily shelled just before daybreak.

On the afternoon of the 15th of January two companies of the 1st Battalion of the Black Watch moved forward into the next wadi. Throughout the afternoon our carriers made four reconnaissance sorties on the right flank, the object being to draw enemy fire. One sortie under Sergeant Proffitt was severely shelled, the carrier receiving several hits and Sergeant Proffitt and one of the crew being wounded. The last carrier patrol was commanded by Capt. Douglas E. Adamson, who was able to penetrate a distance of five miles along the Wadi Chfef in a northerly direction. When the patrol returned they reported that they had been followed by accurate shelling, and that the enemy were still in occupation but that a certain amount of transport was observed moving in a north-westerly direction, which seemed to indicate that the enemy were thinning out.

On the night of the 15th of January the 153rd Brigade carried out their attack. The attack was preceded by a machine-gun concentration and an artillery barrage. Prior to the attack, General Montgomery, the G.O.C. in C. of the Eighth Army sent the following message to all troops.

"The leading units of the Eighth Army are now only two hundred miles from Tripoli. The enemy is between us and that port, hoping to hold us off. The Eighth Army is going to Tripoli. Tripoli is the only town in the Italian Empire overseas still remaining in their possession. Therefore we will take it from them; they will then have no overseas Empire. The enemy will try to stop us. But if each one of us, whether front-line soldier or officer, or man whose duty is performed in some other sphere, puts his whole heart and soul into this next contest, then nothing can stop us. Nothing has stopped us since the battle of Egypt began on the 23rd of October, 1942. Nothing will stop us now. Some must stay behind to begin with, but we will all be in the hunt eventually. On to Tripoli. Our families and friends will be thrilled when they hear that we have captured that place."

The attack by the 153rd Brigade was successful. Little enemy resistance was encountered, and on the afternoon of the 16th of January we prepared to move forward towards Misurata preceded by the 152nd Brigade. This move was postponed until the morning of the 17th of January. The casualties during the battle of Buerat were 1 officer and 12 other ranks wounded and 6 other ranks killed.

CHAPTER IV

THE ADVANCE ON TRIPOLI

AT long last we had rounded the monotonous gulf of Sirte, which stretched for hundreds of miles from Benghazi to Buerat. In the previous desert campaigns the Eighth Army's advances did not get beyond the area of Agheila, but this is quite understandable, as they had many fewer troops to do the advance with, and generally the position so far as supplies were concerned was not quite so healthy as with us. Nevertheless, there is no doubt that our present advance was one of the most spectacular in history. We knew that as soon as the Buerat position was captured, a long advance was in front of us, and we anticipated that the enemy would make his last stand in Tripolitania around the area of Homs, where the country was suitable for defence.

It was on the morning of the 17th of January that we set off in our trucks in a northerly direction. The thrill of moving northwards for the first time after having travelled about one thousand miles in a westerly direction, can well be imagined. The country was now beginning to look much more civilized. Little farmhouses soon came into view, and growing crops, although sparse, were indeed a change from the everlasting sands of Egypt, Libya, and Cyrenaica.

The advance on Tripoli was divided into two columns. Briefly the plan for the advance was that the 51st Highland Division would advance along the coast road via Misurata, Zliten, and Homs, and this column was to be known as the " Coastal column." The 2nd New Zealand division along with the 7th Armoured Division were to advance through Beni Ulid and Tarhuna, and were to be known as the " Inland column." It can well be imagined that an advance of this nature over such a long distance is difficult to control without jeopardizing our position by giving away information on the wireless, but an excellent system of codes got over this difficulty. Between these two columns another force consisting of the 22nd Armoured Brigade were to operate.

We were all very tired before we started, but in good spirits, and if anyone had given the troops the choice of staying behind for a night's rest rather than push on immediately for the glittering prize of the capital of Mussolini's tottering Empire, there is no doubt that "On to Tripoli" would have been the cry.

The Divisional plan was that, following the capture of the Buerat objective by the 153rd Brigade, the 152nd Brigade were to pass through and commence the pursuit of the enemy. There was a certain time-lag between the break-through of the 153rd Brigade and the follow-up by the 152nd Brigade, which was due partly to the bottleneck caused by the narrow-

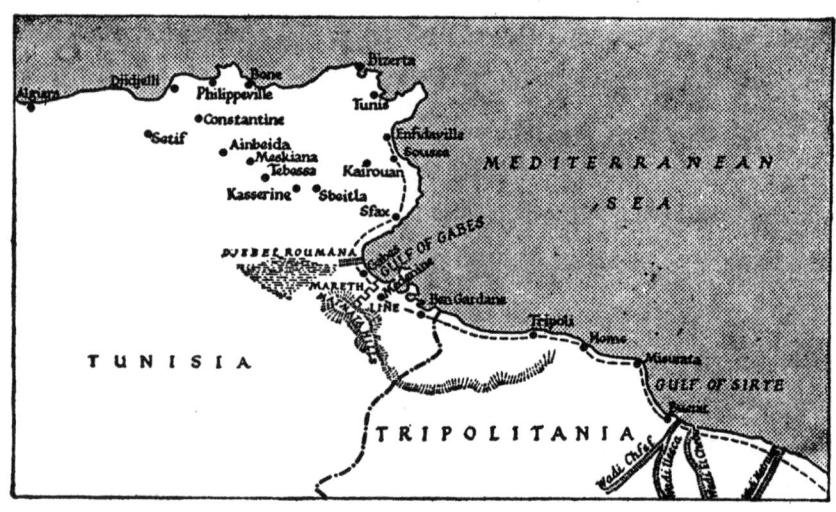

From El Agheila to Tripoli and Tunis
The dotted line shows the axis of advance by the Highland Division

ness of the minefield gap (which was being feverishly widened by the Royal Engineers), and partly because of the time required for the collection of our guns, which were still in action. Petrol shortage at this stage also became temporarily acute, and the 126th Field Regiment R.A. found it impossible to move, as the tanks of their vehicles were dry.' This petrol shortage was to handicap the Division from time to time during our long advance. Following the 152nd Brigade came the 154th Brigade, who were to advance northwards towards Misurata, which was one of the objectives of the 152nd Brigade. The 154th Brigade were ordered to by-pass Misurata and make for Zliten.

Our battalion moved across country on the west side of the Misurata road via Garibaldi, and harboured for the night of the 18th of January in an area a few miles south-west of Zliten. No enemy resistance was encountered by us. What a sight for sore eyes it was to gaze on the cultivated belt along the coast from Misurata after having experienced nothing but wilderness for three months. I shall never forget the thrill we all experienced when, after crossing the coastal ridge above Misurata, the Mediterranean lay before us once again. Stretching along the coast for miles were attractive little white-washed farmhouses, all of which appeared to be deserted. The great chase for Tripoli was now well under way. Our morale was exceptionally high, but our supply of petrol was low. Indeed our supply of petrol was non-existent, as we had to syphon petrol from some of our 15-cwt. trucks to enable our three-ton vehicles to carry on.

On the 19th of January we again moved on in transport to a position at Leptis Magna about two miles east of the village of Homs. This advance was temporarily delayed by a small minefield and crater a few miles west of Zliten. The advance was across country on the ridge to the south of the coastal road, and the track, which was extremely bad, slowed up progress considerably. Eventually we found the track so difficult that we had to use the road. The road was very badly cratered in many places, and the battalion had therefore the job of repairing these in order to let the transport through. This work was, however, speeded up by the help of local Senussi labour. Eventually, after an arduous advance of 23 miles, we reached Leptis Magna. A certain amount of intermittent shell-fire was encountered here, but this did not worry us unduly. To the west of Homs the enemy were holding what was considered to be a very strong position. The country round about here was very hilly and not like the desert at all.

The Attack at Corradini

We did not stay long in our position at Leptis Magna as brigade reserve, for at about 9 o'clock in the morning of the following day, the 20th of January, we advanced behind a recce screen of one company of the 7th Black Watch. The village of Homs as we passed through it was being heavily shelled by what was found later to be enemy mobile guns, and so instead of advancing along the roads our route was along the coast north-west of Homs. Our intention was to cut off the enemy's rearguard by moving westwards along the coast, then swinging south-west through Beni Hassan towards the main road. It was then discovered that the enemy were stronger than we anticipated, and a brigade attack was ordered.

The plan was for the 1st and 7th Black Watch Battalions to attack the left flank and take up positions astride the main road at Corradini, to cut off the enemy's retreat. Our battalion, along with B Squadron, 40th Royal Tank Regiment, were to act as forward body to the brigade. At this time the commanding officer was recalled by the general to be informed of these orders, and command of the battalion

Plate 6 (*Above*) The Massed Pipes and Drums of the Highland Division at the Victory Parade in Tripoli. (*Below*) Victory Parade in Tripoli

temporarily devolved on the second in command, Major R. Mathieson, T.D. It was found impossible to move the transport along the coast as the going was much too soft and sandy. The gunners' wireless truck got stuck in the sand, and no communication between the battalion and brigade was possible. The commanding officer then endeavoured to catch up with the battalion by travelling along the coast in a tank. On the way he picked up the remainder of the tanks at Zambra, but the going was so bad that by nightfall he had still failed to catch up, and the tanks were recalled to join the rest of the brigade in the attack. Meanwhile we had marched a distance of about sixteen miles across what was at first loose sand dunes and later rough bumpy ground. When we arrived within sight of the road we found about twenty enemy vehicles including guns lined up along the road at a distance of about 3,000 yards to 4,000 yards from us. Unfortunately no artillery or mortars had been able to move with the battalion. An advance over the open appeared impracticable, and small-arms fire alone was of little value against the vehicles at such long range. It was, therefore, decided to attack as soon as darkness fell. It was most annoying to sit there awaiting darkness and do nothing, as the enemy were quite unaware that they were being observed. We attacked when darkness fell, but we arrived to find the enemy already gone and a clash with the advancing troops of the 1st Battalion of the Black Watch was narrowly avoided. The 1st Black Watch had a particularly nasty time in their attack and sustained quite a number of casualties on the feature known as " Edinburgh Castle." This feature was a high rock which bore an extraordinary resemblance to Edinburgh Castle.

During the night the Divisional advance guard ran into the enemy again, and there were rumours that we would be required for an attack that night, but the 5th

Seaforths came up and attacked in our place. We were then warned for an attack at 1 o'clock on the 21st of January, and this was prepared. About one hour before the attack was due to take place, when we had just returned from a reconnaissance, the Divisional Commander arrived and told us that the enemy had withdrawn, and our attack would not now be required. It is perhaps just as well, as we were by this time all dead tired, having had little or no sleep since our advance on Tripoli had begun four days before. In addition, the position appeared to be a very awkward one to attack, as the enemy were concealed on the slopes of the surrounding hills overlooking us.

Tripoli is Ours

It now seemed that everyone was making a race of it for Tripoli. The roads were jammed full of transport, and in our role of advance guard to the 152nd Brigade we found great difficulty in getting to the head of the column. When we did, and the column eventually moved off, it was found that the roads were badly cratered and all bridges were blown. We were about sixty miles from Tripoli, and although tired, we were eager to push on as quickly as possible. Sometimes we did not even have time for a meal, and on many occasions when we came to a halt and " brewed up " as from habit, along would come the general with words of encouragement that we would get plenty rest and food in Tripoli, but in order to get to Tripoli we would have to leave our meal for the present as he required our help to fill in craters. Sometimes we had to march long distances between one crater and another throughout the night, and although there was a certain amount of the usual grumbling, the troops were in splendid spirits. In the late evening of the 21st of January we emerged from the hilly country of the Homs area and gazed for the first time across the plain of Tripoli. In the far distance we thought we could just make out Tripoli, but it is doubtful whether it was that town, as we were still some fifty miles from the capital of Mussolini's Tripolitanian Empire. While filling in the last crater before we emerged on to the plain, we were subjected to a certain amount of enemy shelling by mobile guns. Our own howitzers very soon got into action and silenced them. On we went after this, commandeering any empty vehicle that passed us on the road. It was a case of Gordons, Seaforths, Camerons, Black Watch, and Argylls scrambling forward by any means until halted by the next crater, when once again we would set to and fill it in.

On the morning of the 22nd of January more craters had to be filled in, and it was while we were working on a diversion where the Germans had blown a bridge that General Montgomery, along with the 22nd Armoured Brigade, passed through us. What a cheer went up for " Monty " as he drove past us on his way with the leading troops to Tripoli ! Altogether there were eight large craters on the road between Corradini and Tripoli. During our advance across Tripoli plain we came across quite a number of artesian wells, and it was obvious that we were nearing a large town from the number of white-washed dwellings in the area, most of which were still occupied. Some of us visited a local farmhouse to trade tea for eggs as was the custom, and enjoyed the luxury of sitting in a farmhouse kitchen for the first time since landing in Egypt in August 1942.

At long last the craters were filled in and the companies of the battalion, which were by this time miles apart, pushed on as quickly as possible for Tripoli. C company under Major John Lindsay Macdougall was the first of the battalion to enter the town, which they did at six o'clock in the morning of the 23rd of January, strangely enough exactly three months after our attack at the Battle of El Alamein. The remainder of the battalion were hot on the heels of C company, and for the first time in history the British flag was flown over the castle in the main square in the city which has known a dozen conquerors in the two thousand years of its chequered history. The inevitable paint-brush then came into action and large H.D.s were painted all over the town, for, if the Division got the nickname of "The Highway Decorators," we saw no good reason why we should not live up to our nickname.

Our role now was to garrison the city, guards being provided for the various gates which were considered to be vulnerable points. The city was surrounded by a wall, and the following were the gates for which guards had to be provided : Benito Gate, Azizia Gate, Taguira Gate, Gurgi Gate, El Amrus Gate, Tarhuna Gate, Fornaci Gate, Bir Accara Gate, Gargaresh Gate. In addition, certain factories and works of importance had to be guarded against looting. Some of these factories were the Fiat and Lancia Works, the Refrigerating Plant, the Flour Mills, the Water Pumping Station, the Wireless Station, the Railway Station, certain hospital stores, and the cavalry barracks in Sciara el Seidi. In addition to all this the battalion had to provide working parties to unload ships in Tripoli harbour. Battalion Headquarters established itself near Bir Accara Gate, all the companies having their location in an orchard just outside the city wall. Shortly after our arrival in Tripoli the following message was sent to all troops of the Eighth Army by General Montgomery :

"To-day, 23rd January, exactly three months after we began the Battle of Egypt, the Eighth Army has captured Tripoli and has driven the enemy away to the west towards Tunisia. By skilful withdrawal tactics the enemy has eluded us, though we have taken heavy toll of his army and air forces.

THE ADVANCE ON TRIPOLI

The defeat of the enemy in the Battle of El Alamein, the pursuit of his beaten army and the final capture of Tripoli, a distance of some fourteen hundred miles from Alamein, has all been accomplished in three months. This achievement is probably without parallel in history. It could not have been done unless every soldier in the army had pulled his weight all the time. I congratulate the whole army and send my personal thanks to each one of you for the wonderful support you have given me. On your behalf I have sent a special message to the Allied Air Forces that have co-operated with us. I do not suppose that any army has ever been supported by such a magnificent air striking force. I have always maintained that the Eighth Army and the R.A.F. Western Desert together constitute one fighting machine, and therein lies our great strength. In the hour of success we must not forget the splendid work that has been done by those soldiers working day and night in back areas and on the lines of communication. There are many soldiers quietly doing their duty in rear areas who are unable to take part in the triumphal entry into captured cities, but they are a vital part of our fighting machine, and we should gain no successes if they failed to pull their full weight. I refer especially to stevedores at our bases, to fitters in the workshops, to clerks in rear offices, and so on. I would like to make a special mention of our R.A.S.C. drivers. These men drive long distances by day and night for long periods and they always deliver the goods. The R.A.S.C. has risen to great heights during the operations we have undertaken, and as a Corps it deserves the grateful thanks of every soldier in the army.

"There is much work still in front of us, but I know that you are all ready for any task that you may be called on to carry out.

"Once again I thank you all from the bottom of my heart."

Shortly after our entry into Tripoli the massed pipes and drums of the Division played Retreat in front of the castle in the main square of the town. It was very impressive to see the Union Jack flying over the castle, which was draped only a few days before with the Italian flag and the German swastika.

The town itself has a very fine harbour. Many of the larger buildings are to be found along the sea front overlooking the harbour. Such buildings as the Banca D'Italia and the Governor's palace are worthy of special mention as being very fine pieces of architecture. The main square is called the Piazza Italia, and many fine streets radiate from it, such as Via Lombardia, Passegiata Marescialla, and Corso Sicilia.

The history of Tripoli has been a long tale of sack and pillage. Its commanding position in the central Mediterranean, which it shares with Tunis, has made it one of the most coveted and most bloodily fought for cities in the Mare Nostrum.

In pre-christian times, it was an emporium for the Phoenician traders until conquered by the Romans, who held it until the fourth century A.D. Since then it has been conquered and reconquered in turn by practically every nation in the Mediterranean basin, by the Vandals in the fifth century, the Byzantine Emperor, General Belisarius in the sixth century, by the Arabs in the seventh century, by the King of Sicily in the twelfth century, by the Genoese in the fourteenth century, by Spain in the sixteenth century. During the fifteenth and sixteenth centuries it was the chief lair of the Corsair Pirates, and it was finally conquered by the Turks in 1835. Not until 1911 did Italy occupy the place during its war against the disintegrating Turkish Empire. 1943 is the first time in history that British troops have set foot in Tripoli.

THE ADVANCE ON TRIPOLI

Mr. Churchill's Visit and the Victory Parade

On the 4th of February Prime Minister Churchill visited Tripoli and inspected units of the Eighth Army. The saluting base was in the main square below the castle. The streets were lined with tanks, guns, Bren carriers, and the personnel of the armoured and infantry forces. The massed pipes and drums of the Division gave a most spectacular and colourful display as they played the various Highland regiments of the Division past the saluting base to the strains of the regimental marches of each battalion in turn. The troops looked exceedingly smart, and one would have thought that they had been practising for this parade for months if it was not for the dark tan on their faces, instead of having arrived in Tripoli only three days before as war-begrimed warriors. Mr. Churchill was accompanied on the saluting base by Generals Alexander and Montgomery and our own Divisional Commander, Major General Wimberley.

Mr. Churchill in the course of an address to us said :

" You have altered the face of the war in a most remarkable way. The fame of the Desert Army has spread throughout the world. When a man is asked after the war what he did, it will be sufficient to say, *I marched and fought with the Desert Army.*"

During our stay in Tripoli, in addition to the various guards which we provided, we had a very busy time unloading ships in Tripoli harbour, and even after we moved to Tagiura, about seven miles east of Tripoli, working parties had to be provided.

On the 18th of February we were again on the move, and camped in an area six miles west of Tripoli in readiness for a move across the Tunisian border. Before we left, the Army Commander spoke to most of the officers of 30th Corps in the Miramare Theatre in Tripoli. During his address he passed some very complimentary remarks about the 2nd New Zealand Division, or "Kiwis," as they were affectionately known, the 7th Armoured Division, or "Desert Rats," and the Highland Division. He brought back to our memories that bright moonlight night at El Alamein, when the German line was broken. He said that the Highland Division, being a new and untried division, was placed between two experienced divisions, the 9th Australians and the 2nd New Zealanders. During the battle of El Alamein the 51st Highland Division attacked where Rommel's defences were strongest and completely smashed through. After the battle, some of the Division had to be left behind during the ensuing chase for a day or two, but when transport became available they soon caught up. General Montgomery then said that he would never leave the Highland Division behind again, and true to his word he never did. Not even after the Sicilian campaign was over and the invasion of Italy was going well, when General Montgomery got command of the 21st Army Group for the invasion of north-west Europe, did he leave us behind. Instead, he took us home to England to train for the European invasion as a member of the 21st Army Group.

This ends a chapter which refers entirely to desert fighting, starting at El Alamein and finishing up with Tripoli as our prize, and which we all look back upon with pride and a certain amount of sorrow for the loss to the battalion of many brave lives. The lack of water was now beginning to be a discomfort of the past, as we knew that in Tunisia we could always fall back on the artesian wells which were dotted about the countryside. In fact, the appalling conditions of the desert, although not entirely over for us, would certainly not cause us so much annoyance in future. Desert sores had been a source of great discomfort, and such illnesses as jaundice, sandfly fever, and dysentery were quite common.

Malaria had not as yet touched us, as mosquitoes could not live in the desert without water. But if mosquitoes could not live, the flies undoubtedly could, and thousands of them at that. It was considered that flies were the root of all the trouble. For instance, if a fly settled for a second on the smallest scratch on one's hand, within a very short time a desert septic sore had formed. Food was very often contaminated by flies, causing dysentery, and we felt that indeed the fly was our worst enemy.

Tripoli served us as an excellent port where supplies were unloaded to feed us as we pushed on into Tunisia. No longer did we have to rely on our long desert lines of communication, where petrol, ammunition, and supplies of all kinds necessary to feed an army had to be brought hundreds of miles across the desert. Benghazi harbour had been wrecked by a storm in January, and since then supplies through Benghazi were comparatively small.

CHAPTER V

TUNISIAN BATTLES

On the 22nd of February we moved in transport across the Tunisian border to an area east of Ben Gardane. The country in Tunisia was much more like our own country than Tripolitania. The soil appeared to be a rich brown, and much more of it was under cultivation than any we had yet seen. The terrific heat of the desert and the constant glare of a blazing sun with not a bit of shadow anywhere to take shelter was now a thing of the past. The day after we arrived at Ben Gardane we moved again to an area six miles east of Medenine. A party of us then left the battalion for a period of three days and became attached to the 5/7th Battalion of the Gordon Highlanders, who were occupying a position in the northern sector. The object was to get to know the ground, so that when our battalion eventually arrived in that sector information about the enemy positions would be readily available. Lieut. A. M. Leslie with a patrolling party from A company came with us, but unfortunately he was wounded on the night of his first patrol.

The battalion had by this time moved to an area south of Medenine, where their task was to guard the roads running south and south-west. On the 25th of February, however, the battalion took over front-line positions from the 2nd Battalion of the Seaforth Highlanders, and our party was ordered to return to our battalion immediately. Obviously there was a change of plan. On the 26th of February we again had a change, this time taking over positions from the 6th Queen's Regiment of the 131st Brigade in the Wadi Moussa. This was a particularly unhealthy spot, and the route up to the position came into view of German observation posts. While looking for an alternative route to the wadi which would not be under observation, some of us got completely lost for a short time. However, we took over the position under cover of darkness without any enemy interference except for spasmodic shelling of the wadi as we entered it. Sidi Guelaa and Glieb et Tine were prominent features in the foremost defended localities of the Mareth Line, and as they were used as observation posts by the enemy we had to exercise great care when moving about during the daytime.

Rommel attacks at Medenine

On the morning of the 1st of March the Divisional Commander told us that a German attack was expected in about three days' time. That morning the general along with the duty officer climbed a vantage point near Battalion Headquarters to view the company positions. As they were peering over the top, half a dozen shells landed in the vicinity, which brought the following wrathful remarks from some Jocks who were down below : " Get off that skyline, you idiots ! " The general laughed and complied with the Jocks' request, remarking, " I do not think the Jocks like us being up here."

After reviewing our positions it was decided that they were untenable and so on the night of the 2nd of March the battalion moved to positions in the Wadi Segdel, about one mile farther back. This wadi was a feature which presented an obstacle to tanks. Numerous smaller wadis ran into the main wadi from the east, and in these smaller wadis the companies took up their positions in the order from right to left : D company, C company, H.Q. company, Battalion H.Q., A company, and B company. Then began a race against time. Mines and wire were arriving in small quantities, and Hawkins mines were laid along the ridge in front of the positions, trip wire also being erected. The battalion had very little sleep for the next few nights as, in addition to mining and wiring, active patrolling in the form of both fighting and recce patrols were carried out. An outpost position called a " keep " for want of a better name was established well forward, the object being to delay the initial advance of the enemy and to give warning of enemy troops or transport movement. This keep consisted of one officer, ten privates, two Intelligence privates, and one signaller. Communication was by wireless at first, and latterly by line. The keep was to withdraw at its own discretion when the enemy attack was launched. Patrols brought in reports of enemy transport movement on the road north of Bir Bsir, and on the morning of the 4th of March a dawn attack was expected. The following message was at this time received from the Army Commander, which was read out to all troops:

" The enemy is now advancing to attack us. This is because he is caught like a rat in a trap, and he is hitting out in every direction, trying to gain time to stave off the day of final defeat in North Africa. This is the very opportunity we want. Not only are we well equipped with everything we need, but in addition the soldiers of the Eighth Army have a fighting spirit and morale which is right on the top line. We will stand and fight the enemy in our positions. There must be no withdrawal anywhere, and of course no surrender. The enemy has never yet succeeded in any attack against a co-ordinated defensive layout, and he will not do so now. We have plenty of tanks, and provided the defended localities stand firm, then we shall smash the enemy attack and cause him such casualties that it will cripple him. We will, in fact, give him a very ' bloody ' nose. It will then be our turn to attack him, and having been crippled himself, he will be unable to stand up to our attack, and we will smash right through him. This attack of the enemy really helps us, and is one more step forward towards the end of the war in North Africa. I did not expect for one moment that the enemy would attack us; it seemed absurd. But he has done it, and we must show our gratitude in no uncertain way. Let us show him what the famous Eighth Army can do. Good luck to each one of you, and good hunting."

The attack on the 4th of March did not materialize, and it was again expected on the 5th of March. It was not, however, until first light on the morning of the 6th of March that the battle began. Lieut. Archie McVicar of C company was the officer in charge of the keep at the time, and Lieut. Bowden of C company was out on deep fighting patrols. At about half-past six on the morning of the 6th of March an enemy barrage came down in front of our positions. Obviously the enemy thought that we were still in the Wadi Moussa, as the shelling in that area was fairly heavy. Capt. Bate had gone out the previous night to relieve Lieut. McVicar at the keep, and orders were sent through for both Capt. Bate and Lieut. McVicar to return immediately. Fortunately they all got back safely. Lieut. Bowden's patrol got split up while he had gone forward to make a recce. Bowden returned at about 8 a.m. without his patrol, and reported that they had moved from the area in which he had left them. This caused some worry, but the patrol returned later via the 126th Field Regiment R.A. without any trouble.

Good observation soon discovered the enemy advancing in open formation. In one area a body of approximately two hundred infantry were observed advancing badly bunched up. Our gunners immediately opened up on the advancing enemy causing a considerable number of casualties among them. A platoon of the 1/7th Middlesex machine gunners had a wonderful shoot, and the enemy were seen to be dropping like ninepins. The remainder of the enemy went to ground and wormed their way into the Wadi Hachchana, about 1,600 yards distant. No enemy tanks had as yet appeared, but in any case we were well prepared, with two troops of the 241 Anti-Tank battery well sited in addition to the anti-tank platoon of the battalion. The enemy still continued to advance, and wormed their way forward into the Wadi Moussa and opened up on us with spandau machine guns. B company under Capt. J. C. Meiklejohn were more exposed to this machine-gun fire than the other companies as the enemy had a machine-gun post on the left, forward of the Wadi Moussa, where the previous headquarters of the 7th battalion of the Black Watch was located prior to the move back of the brigade group to the Wadi Segdel. Several smoke shells were fired by the enemy, all of which landed in the Woggery in front of B company, and for a while the smoke in addition to the mist made visibility very poor. At about 8.30 a.m. B company reported that they were engaging the enemy with small arms and mortar fire at 800 yards range. In the afternoon the spandau fire was much closer, and at 4 o'clock in the afternoon a much more forceful attack was launched against us. The enemy were able to take advantage of the dead ground and advanced to within 300 yards of our positions. B company's observation post could not remain for long, and for quite a while the enemy lay up on the ridge just forward of our positions and kept blazing away at us with their machine guns. The artillery forward observation officer in his observation post had the very unpleasant experience of suddenly seeing six Germans grinning at him and just about to throw a few grenades. As the F.O.O. was only about thirty yards away from them, he decided that the observation post was no place for him any longer. The enemy's advance was held up by our platoons on the ridge. C company kept blazing away, but at that time it was difficult to say what was happening. The shelling was not heavy at this time, but the battalion area was dive-bombed several times with the loss to us of only 1 killed and 1 wounded. The commanding officer then sent for the tanks of B squadron, 40th Royal Tank Regiment, who were in support of us. A counter-attack was organized, and the plan was for the tanks to travel along the ridge in front of our positions and as they passed each company area, one platoon was to be picked up and the counter-attack was to begin.

The tanks were slow in carrying out the orders, and A, C, and D companies' platoons advanced without them. The enemy brought down his defensive fire as we began the advance. It appeared that C company's platoon under Capt. Peter Samwell were suffering heavy casualties during the advance, as the mortaring and machine-gun fire was heaviest against them. By some miracle, however, they got through with only the loss of 3 wounded. As they approached the Wadi Moussa they charged down the slope with fixed bayonets and firing their Tommy and Bren guns from the hip. The enemy troops in the wadi soon scampered up the far side under cover of their own machine guns and beat a hasty retreat. Later B company's platoon on the left arrived riding on the tanks. Our counter-attack was a complete success, and not one inch of ground was lost to the enemy during his attack on us. The battle was fast and furious while it lasted, but as General Montgomery had forecast, the Germans received a very " bloody " nose. Our opponents were as usual the famous German 90th Light Division. The following day carrier patrols under Capt. Adamson and Lieut. McGill captured two 7·5 cm. infantry guns, one three-ton vehicle, and one truck in the Wadi Hachchana. In addition one spandau machine gun complete with tripod and sights and one Breda gun were captured by B company.

The morale of the troops throughout was exceptionally high, and everyone fought and worked with the will to win. For the next few days following the attack, the defences were improved and reinforced. More wire and mines were laid and active patrolling was carried out. Local patrols were sent out to guard the flanks against infiltration. On the night of the 8th of March a message was received that the keep, which had again been re-established under Capt. Samwell, was being sniped at by an enemy patrol of twelve men just before dusk. Capt. Samwell gave orders for the patrol to be stalked, but when darkness came the Germans had gone, obviously not wishing to have an encounter with the Argylls in the dark. It was obvious, therefore, that the keep would have to be moved to a new location from Pt. 98 as the enemy had discovered it. Capt. Samwell then received orders to withdraw from the keep at 4 o'clock in the morning of the 9th of March after the fighting patrol which had gone out under Lieut. Rolland of B company had returned. On the way home, while crossing our own minefield, one member of the keep party stood on a mine which exploded, causing 10 wounded casualties. Capt. Samwell was among the slightly wounded. The casualties during the battle of Medenine were 4 other ranks killed and 26 other ranks wounded and 1 officer wounded.

The Army Commander congratulated both the infantry and the artillery on the splendid resistance which they put up. The infantry, unprotected by wire or minefields, saw off the attack of three Panzer Divisions by means of their own weapons. Rommel absolutely bolted, and would think twice before he dared to attack the Eighth Army again. Over fifty-two enemy tanks were destroyed in this battle on the southern sector with the loss of one to ourselves.

On the night of the 12th of March the battalion was relieved by the Grenadier Guards, who took over our positions in the Wadi Segdel. The battalion, less A company, moved to a rest area near Sidi Makrelouf, where they remained for two days. A company, under Capt. J. L. Robertson, was ordered to establish three keeps in the area of the Wadi Melah, their task being to delay any enemy attack and give information immediately to the battalion of enemy movements and intentions. On the night of the 15th of March the battalion moved forward and set up Battalion Headquarters in the Wadi Melah with D company in reserve. A company was again sent forward, this time to the area of the Wadi Zeuse, where they established two keeps. At the same time C company took up position near Pt. 73, a feature approximately 500 yards west of Battalion Headquarters, and B company on Pt. 70, another feature about 1,600 yards to the north-west. The following night B and C companies took over the positions in the Wadi Zeuse occupied by A company. D company, up till now in reserve, took over from B company on Pt. 70, and A company came back into reserve. Positions were well dug in and mined, and no movement was allowed during daylight, as the positions were under enemy observation. Active patrolling was then carried out, and one patrol led by Lieut. J. Robertson of C company had a skirmish with an enemy patrol near the enemy lines. The enemy were identified as Italians, and Robertson's patrol accounted for at least three of them. On the night of the 17th of March the 50th Northumbrian Division and the 153rd Brigade of the Highland Division improved their positions to the north of us by moving forward to make closer contact with the enemy in the Mareth Line. On our left the Grenadier and Coldstream Guards attacked certain enemy localities and also made an advance.

The Attack on the Mareth Line

It was now obvious to us that the Eighth Army would soon attack, and the plan of attack was made known to us on the morning of the 20th of March. The 50th Division and the 4th Indian Division were to attack in the north and create a gap for a pursuit force to pass through. The 7th Armoured Division were to attack through the Brigade of Guards and advance along the main road. The New Zealand Corps, consisting of 27,000 troops and 5,000 vehicles, were to outflank the Mareth Line on the left. The pursuit force, consisting of the 22nd Armoured Brigade and the 7th battalion of the Black Watch and two batteries of the 126th Field Regiment R.A., followed by the 1st Black Watch and ourselves and the remainder of the 126th Field Regiment R.A., were to advance through the gap created by the 50th Division and the 4th Indian Division. Should the enemy decide to hold the Mareth Line, the New Zealand Corps were to cut in behind the line and attack it from the rear. Should the enemy, on the other hand, decide to withdraw from the line, then the New Zealanders were to make a wider sweep in order to encircle them. The Ghurkas were sent into the Matmata Hills to destroy enemy guns, particularly the heavy guns which were shelling Medenine aerodrome.

The Army Commander sent the following message to be read out to all troops before the battle:

" On the 5th of March Rommel addressed his troops in the mountains overlooking our positions, and said that if they did not take Medenine by the 6th of March and force the Eighth Army to withdraw, the days of the Axis forces in North Africa were numbered. The next day he attacked the Eighth Army. He should have known that the Eighth Army never withdraws, therefore his attack could only end in failure, which it did. We will now show Rommel that he was correct in his statement which he made to his troops. The days of the Axis forces in North Africa are numbered. The Eighth Army and the Western Desert Air Force, together constituting one fighting machine, are ready to advance. We all know what that means and so does the enemy. In the battle that is now to start the Eighth Army

(*a*) will destroy the enemy now facing us in the Mareth position ;

(*b*) will burst through the Gabes Gap ;

(*c*) will then drive northwards on Sfax, Sousse, and finally Tunis. We will not stop or let up till Tunis has been captured, and the enemy has either given up the struggle or been pushed into the sea. The operations now about to begin will mark the close of the campaign in North Africa. Once the battle has started the eyes of the whole world will be on the Eighth Army, and millions of people will listen to the wireless every day, hoping anxiously for good news. We must not let them be anxious. Let us see that they get good news and plenty of it, every day. If each one of us does his duty, and pulls his full weight, then nothing can stop the Eighth Army, and nothing will stop it.

" With faith in God and in the justice of our cause, let us go forward to victory.

" Forward to Tunis. Drive the enemy into the sea."

The Eighth Army offensive began at 9.30 p.m. on the night of the 20th of March. All went well and the first objectives were taken. On the 21st of March the 50th Division widened the gap by capturing two more strong-points. On the 22nd of March things did not go so well, and by the morning of the 23rd of March all objectives were lost with one exception. Our battalion then received a warning order to move up north to take over part of the line from the East Yorkshire Regiment of the 50th Division, who had suffered many casualties. We established our headquarters in the Wadi Tarad, about 2,000 yards from the Wadi Zigzaou, which was in enemy hands. Shelling in this area was heavy, and we suffered a number of casualties. Shortly after we took over the positions a strong fighting patrol, consisting of one platoon at full strength, six light machine guns, and four three-inch mortars, was sent out under command of Capt. Corcoran of D company. The task of this patrol was to shoot up enemy in the Wadi Zigzaou, and to mortar the fort in the Mareth Line known as Ksiba Ouest. A certain amount of artillery was in support. The patrol, which went out on the night of the 25th of March, was very successful, and only one wounded casualty was sustained.

While in this position, paths were made through the extensive German minefields by parties of sappers protected by patrols from A and C companies. Unfortunately the battalion suffered as a result of these mine-sweeping operations, 6 other ranks being killed and 8 other ranks wounded. Sergeant Lake of C company, who gained the Military Medal for his part in the Battle of El Alamein, was among the killed.

On the morning of the 28th of March it was suspected that the enemy had once again withdrawn from his positions, and patrols were sent forward by A company under Lieut. Bobby Marshall to investigate. Lieut. Marshall reached the Mareth Line and found it deserted, and immediately wirelessed back to battalion headquarters. B company were then sent forward to occupy Ksiba Ouest. At about 2 o'clock the battalion moved forward by march route across the Wadi Zigzaou. The crossing on the Zigzaou was named " Argyll " crossing. The battalion occupied positions in the Mareth Line, the intention being to wait there until the transport got through. On inspection of the Mareth Line we found plenty evidence of the gallantry of our friends of the 50th Division, who had borne the brunt of the attack on the position.

Many corpses lay about, most of them in a state of decomposition and several of our tanks were still burning, but the Germans suffered even heavier losses. It was a most unpleasant night we spent in the Mareth Line with the stench of dead all around us. The wadi was impassable for wheeled vehicles, and even tracked vehicles could only get across at one place, so it was not until the morning of the 29th of March that the transport was able to cross the wadi and reach us. We then moved forward on foot to a camping-place just east of Gabes, a distance of some sixteen miles. On the way two Bren carriers were blown up on Teller mines and the crews were fatal casualties.

The Battle of Wadi Akarit

On the 31st of March the complete carrier platoon under Capt. Adamson, the Intelligence Section under myself, and three patrolling parties of one N.C.O. and seven privates from B, C, and D companies commanded by Lieuts. Faid and Bowden and Capt. Joe Corcoran respectively, moved up to the New Zealanders' area where a keep was formed in front of the Wadi Akarit position. The task was to gain information of enemy intentions and dispositions, and to get to know the ground. Patrols were sent out each night, and observation posts were established well forward of the keep. Patrol reports and Intelligence information indicated that the positions held by the enemy along the line of the Wadi Akarit and the anti-tank ditch were strongly fortified. Enemy transport movement was observed going on all the time, and it was deduced that the enemy were reinforcing. The position itself formed a natural barrier against attack, as from the sea for some distance inland the wadi was impassable for vehicles. Where the wadi became shallow and passable for vehicles, a very effective anti-tank ditch was constructed which linked up with the hills farther south known as the Djebel Roumana.

On the 2nd of April, after three days' rest, the battalion moved to a brigade concentration area near the Oasis de Usseps about three miles east of Oudref. The harbour party, which left the old location before the main part of the battalion, under the command of Lieut. Walter Lees, failed to turn off the main road at the correct place, and ran on into the enemy lines. An attempt was made to turn the trucks, but the enemy mortar and machine-gun fire was so intense that the order was given, " Every man for himself." Three other ranks including my batman, Private Lang, were the only troops who escaped back to our own lines, and the remainder of the party, consisting of two officers and twenty other ranks, were taken prisoner.

The plan of attack for the battle was somewhat complicated. The 51st Highland Division were on the right of the Eighth Army attack but south of the coast road, the 50th Division in the centre, and the 4th Indian Division on the left. The New Zealanders were to be ready to push through the gap which the attacking infantry made. On the extreme right, north of the coast road, the Guards Brigade were to create a diversion by pushing forward under an artillery barrage and maintain positions close up to the enemy's foremost defended localities.

Of the 51st Highland Division, the 154th Infantry Brigade were on the right, and the 152nd Infantry Brigade on the left. The 154th Brigade ordered the 7th Argylls to attack and capture the positions on the Wadi Akarit, and the anti-tank ditch to the north of Djebel Roumana. The 7th Black Watch were then to pass through us and mop up by swinging left along the anti-tank ditch with a view to linking up with the 2nd battalion of the Seaforth Highlanders of the 152nd Brigade, who were to mop up by swinging right along the

Djebel Roumana. Our commanding officer named the Argyll objectives after the Regimental Battle Honours, such as Somme, Balaclava, Corunna, Beaumont Hamel, and Alamein. The place chosen for the attack was immediately west of the junction of the Wadi Akarit and Oglat es Smala, and the battalion were to break through the enemy positions on a front of one thousand yards and form a bridgehead. Air photographs showed the principal defended localities to be a long low sand-hill running parallel to the Wadi Akarit about three hundred yards behind it. On the right of the front there was another position three hundred yards beyond the sand-hill, and two strong positions were behind the anti-tank ditch which ran north-west from the wadi. Up till a few days before the attack no minefields were discovered by our patrols. On the night of the 4th of April, however, a patrol discovered a minefield one hundred yards deep which covered the length of the wadi and the anti-tank ditch. The mines were mostly the wooden box type, newly laid, widely spaced, and easily seen.

On the evening of the 5th of April I went forward with Capt. Lord Guernsey of the 1st Black Watch to lay and light the start-line, which was on a slope facing Akarit about 1,800 yards due south. At 7 o'clock in the evening the battalion left its location by march route and marched a distance of seven miles to the start-line. On arrival at the start-line all troops began to dig themselves in, and at 1.30 a.m. breakfast was served. After breakfast everyone lay in his trench taking the advantage of about two hours' sleep before the attack began.

At 4 o'clock in the morning the artillery barrage opened up on our left, which was an indication that the 50th Division had started their attack on Pt. 85, an enemy outpost in front of the anti-tank ditch on the left of the Djebel Roumana. At 4.15 a.m. an artillery barrage opened up in our sector, chiefly to disguise the noise created by the scorpions, which had moved forward to gap the minefield, supported by mortar detachments of the battalion under the command of Lieut. David Goodall and eight Valentine tanks of the 40th Royal Tank Regiment towing 6-pounder anti-tank guns of the 241 Anti-Tank Battery who were in support of us. The Valentine tanks were later to support us with machine-gun fire. They and the Royal Engineers' working parties for bridging the anti-tank ditch were seriously hampered by enemy shelling and machine-gun fire throughout the morning. Later, however, in spite of intense shelling, both the gap and the bridging were completed, and by midday the tanks were able to cross the anti-tank ditch.

At 5.15 in the morning we advanced across the start-line supported by a terrific artillery concentration. B company was on the right under Capt. J. C. Meiklejohn, D.S.O., A company on the left under Capt. J. L. Robertson, the navigating party under myself moving in between the two forward companies. C and D companies, with Advance Battalion Headquarters in between, followed 700 yards behind, and Major R. Mathieson, T.D., brought up Rear Battalion Headquarters 700 yards behind the rear companies.

B company was to capture the long sand hill on the right, and A company was to seize the anti-tank ditch and capture the nearer of the two posts beyond it, pause for fifteen minutes, and then push on and capture the second post, after which they were to reorganize 600 yards beyond the ditch. During the fifteen-minutes pause C company was to pass through B company and capture the final objective beyond. D company was in reserve, and moved behind A company to give depth. At the last minute fresh air photographs revealed that the enemy positions were very nearly doubled. A strong position was discovered in front of the sand-hill on top of the wadi whose banks were about twenty-four feet high, and several machine-gun posts appeared on our side of the Akarit. Things went well with us to begin with, and very little shelling or machine-gun fire came down on our start-line. After we had advanced across the open for about six hundred yards, however, the enemy guns opened up and shelling became very heavy. Enemy machine-gun fire came at us from both flanks. This fire steadily increased and caused a considerable number of casualties.

The advance of the battalion continued in good order, and on reaching the minefield it was found to be no worse than had been expected, and although only A company were able to use the gaps made by the scorpions, the rest of the battalion walked through the minefields without sustaining many casualties, as the mines were easily seen. The anti-tank ditch was the next obstacle to be surmounted. This ditch was about ten feet deep with steep smooth sides, and could not be climbed without assistance. It was rather amusing to find several Italian prisoners assisting C company over the ditch with the aid of rope ladders. About this time the shelling was the heaviest the battalion had yet endured in any battle, and this heavy shelling continued all day long. Both A and B companies captured their objectives on time, and prisoners, mostly Italian, began to flow through. When it was observed that B company's attack was going successfully, C company pushed through them to their objective, which they secured. D company, who were in reserve, had little fighting to do up till now, and reached their position without difficulty. On the other hand A, B, and C companies had sustained a considerable number of casualties, and were consequently very weak. A counter-attack was to be expected, and a threat by the Germans who tried to attack B company in the rear was beaten off by B company and one platoon of D company, supported by our artillery and the machine guns of the 1/7th Middlesex Regiment. Meanwhile both the left-hand companies and Battalion Headquarters were subjected to intense shelling by enemy guns of various calibres, and machine guns from the Roumana hills kept up a continuous chattering. At 8 o'clock in the morning the 7th Black Watch attacked and passed through our position.

No fewer than three German counter-attacks were launched during the morning against A company, all of which were broken up by accurate artillery fire. About 1 o'clock in the afternoon the familiar eighteen bombers of the R.A.F., known to the Germans as the " Eighteen Indomitables," passed over. This was a very welcome sight until they accidentally dropped their bombs on A company, who as a result suffered a number of unnecessary casualties. Throughout all this time the enemy shelling continued to be intense, and Battalion Headquarters as well as the companies came under this unpleasant shelling. Shelling and mortaring of the minefield gap caused many casualties, and in some instances ambulances which were evacuating the wounded through the gap received direct hits from armour-piercing shells. At 4 o'clock in the afternoon eight enemy tanks appeared on A company's front about 2,000 yards away. Bodies of infantry were then seen advancing, but our artillery again broke up their counter-attack. At 6 o'clock that evening the most formidable counter-attack of all developed from a force estimated at two battalions with tanks in support. Some of the 7th Black Watch were seen to withdraw, and our A company, which had gone rather farther than was intended, were ordered to draw back three hundred yards at dark. This was done successfully, and A company took up new positions in line with the forward platoon of D company. Our companies opened up with all they had and halted the German counter-attack. One body of infantry, however, penetrated to within fifty yards of C company's headquarters, but Major John Lindsay Macdougall, M.C., was undismayed. Although already wounded, he ordered the only five men he had, consisting of his sergeant-major, his batman, his clerk, his runner, and his wireless operator, to charge with him, shouting at the same time, " No surrender, C company." Ever after this Major Macdougall was called " No surrender John." Twelve of the enemy were taken prisoners, several were killed, and the remainder fled when they saw the bayonets of C company coming at them. This was the last German counter-attack, and as dusk came the battle died gradually away, but what a battle while it lasted! It was the most vicious and furious battle that the battalion had yet to endure. The shelling had been intense all day long, and the positions were even stronger than the air photographs showed, and were bristling with guns and weapons of all kinds. At night vigorous patrolling was carried out. German patrols were also active, and one instance of the trickery of the enemy is shown by the following story. A patrol of twelve Germans approached C company, and in the darkness spoke to some of the Jocks in Oxford English. One suspicious Jock asked his platoon commander, Lieut. Archie MacVicar, " Are there ony English aboot here ? " Lieut. McVicar replied that there should not be, and the Jock then said, " Well, there is something funny afoot." The enemy patrol was then soon discovered and held up at the point of the bayonet. Two Boches were wounded and all but one were taken prisoners.

So ended the battle which will always be remembered by Argylls as the toughest one-day battle they had yet experienced. We took seven hundred prisoners and captured an enormous amount of booty, including seventeen anti-tank guns, two light anti-aircraft guns, two infantry guns, eight anti-tank rifles, sixteen medium machine guns, seventeen light machine guns, three heavy mortars, seven light mortars, and a great amount of other equipment. We suffered very heavy casualties during the battle, and among the killed were Capt. Dougie Adamson, the carrier officer, who received a direct hit from a mortar bomb. Lieut. Pat Stewart Bam and Lieut. Tommy McGill were killed during a heavy spell of shelling on Battalion Headquarters. Thirty-eight other ranks were killed and over a hundred other ranks were wounded. Among the officers wounded were the commanding officer, Lieut.-Col. Lorne M. Campbell, D.S.O., T.D., Major John S. Lindsay Macdougall, M.C., Captain M. J. G. Bate, the padre, Captain T. C. J. Sinten, Lieuts. Marshall, Bowden, and Kinghorn, and myself. The commanding officer made light of his wound, and when asked if he had been wounded in the neck, he replied that he had merely cut himself shaving. Actually it was a mortar bomb which had wounded him. It was for this battle that our commanding officer was awarded the Victoria Cross for gallantry. In France in 1940 he was awarded the D.S.O. for gallant leadership during the ordeal of the 51st Highland Division at St. Valery. At Alamein he received a bar to the D.S.O. for his outstanding part in the capture of important objectives.

Announcing the award of the V.C. the citation says:

" On the 6th of April 1943, in the attack upon the Wadi Akarit position (before the Gabes Gap), the task of breaking through the enemy minefield and anti-tank ditch to the east of the Roumana feature and of forming the initial bridgehead for a brigade of the 51st Highland Division was allotted to the Battalion of the Argyll and Sutherland Highlanders commanded by Lieut.-Colonel Campbell:

" *Took Personal Charge*

" The attack had to form up in complete darkness and had to traverse the main offshoot of the Wadi Akarit at an angle to the line of advance.

" In spite of heavy machine-gun fire in the early stages of

the attack, Lieut.-Colonel Campbell successfully accomplished this difficult operation, captured at least six hundred prisoners, and led his battalion to its objective, having to cross an unswept portion of the enemy minefield in doing so.

" Later, upon reaching his objective, he found that a gap which had been blown by the Royal Engineers in the anti-tank ditch did not correspond with the vehicle lane which had been cleared in the minefield. Realizing the vital necessity of quickly establishing a gap for the passage of anti-tank guns, he took personal charge of this operation.

" It was now broad daylight, and under very heavy machine-gun fire and shell-fire, he succeeded in making a personal reconnaissance, and in conducting operations which led to the establishing of a vehicle gap.

" Throughout the day Lieut.-Colonel Campbell held his position with his battalion in the face of extremely heavy and constant shell-fire, which the enemy was able to bring to bear by direct observation.

"*Went on alone*

"About 16.30 hours determined enemy counter-attacks began to develop, accompanied by tanks. In this phase of the fighting Lieut.-Col. Campbell's personality dominated the battlefield by a display of valour and utter disregard for personal safety, which could not have been excelled.

" Realizing that it was imperative for the future success of the army plan to hold the bridgehead his battalion had captured, he inspired his men by his presence in the forefront of the battle, cheering them on and rallying them as he moved to these points where the fighting was heaviest.

" When his left forward company was forced to give ground he went forward alone into a hail of fire, and personally reorganized their position, remaining with the company until the attack at this point was held.

"*Refused to Leave*

"As reinforcements arrived upon the scene he was seen standing in the open directing the fight under close-range fire of enemy infantry, and he continued to do so although already painfully wounded in the neck by shell-fire. It was not until the battle died down that he allowed his wound to be dressed.

"Even then, although in great pain, he refused to be evacuated, remaining with his battalion and continuing to inspire them by his presence on the field.

"Darkness fell with the Argylls still holding their positions, though many of its officers and men had become casualties.

"There is no doubt that but for Lieut.-Colonel Campbell's determination, splendid example of courage, and disregard of pain, the bridgehead would have been lost.

"This officer's gallantry and magnificent leadership when his now tired men were charging the enemy with the bayonet and were fighting them at hand grenade range are worthy of the highest honour, and can seldom have been surpassed in the long history of the Highland Brigade."

No wonder we are proud of our commanding officer, whose courage was an inspiration to all of us. The Jocks would follow him anywhere.

An amusing incident during the battle which took place between a Padre and a Jock shows the dry humour of the Jocks. The Padre had been burying some Jocks when a little Jock passed him with a batch of Italian prisoners. The Padre shouted some remark to him, and the Jock on swinging round quickly accidentally drew his bayonet across the face of one of the prisoners. His remarks to the Italian then were: "Ah, Tony, Tony, am awfu' sorry, but tak' it a' the same."

On the 8th of April the battalion moved to a rest area seven miles south of Sfax, where the French people received them with open arms. The troops had a much-needed rest and had the joy of bathing in the sea. Once more the pipes and drums of the battalion were brought out and played in the town, to the delight of the natives.

After having been wounded by enemy machine-gun fire in the early stages of the attack at Wadi Akarit, I was conveyed in a scorpion from the battlefield to the advanced dressing station. The speed of the scorpion was not above 5 miles per hour, and on account of my wound temporarily paralysing my left leg, I was laid across the top of the scorpion. Dust rose in thick clouds in my face and the jolting I received on that scorpion is beyond talking about. However, at long last I arrived at the dressing station, was given a cup of tea, a cigarette, and an injection to deaden the pain. Next I was conveyed in an ambulance along with some other casualties, and as we motored along at reduced speed the bumping on the rough desert tracks got worse. Several times the driver had to halt in order to let us settle down for the next bit of the tortuous journey. On we went in stifling heat until we reached Zuara that night, a distance of over a hundred miles. Here we had one night's rest and moved on the following day to Tripoli, fully another 100 miles. When we arrived in Tripoli we were feeling far worse than when we had started out, but what a relief it was to get into bed between white sheets once more.

As time went on other officers from the battalion began to arrive, some with nasty leg wounds, some with abdominal wounds, and one with his left arm off above the elbow. The latest news of the battalion was the chief topic among us. Our hospital was a very modern Italian hospital, staffed, of course, with British doctors and nurses. After spending about four weeks in hospital, some of us were sent to a convalescent depot, where we remained until we were fit to return to our respective units.

CHAPTER VI

ENFIDAVILLE AND THE END OF THE AFRICAN CAMPAIGN

On the 22nd of April an order came for the battalion to take over part of the Enfidaville line known as " Djebel Garcia " from the 2nd battalion of the Ghurka regiment. This sector of the front was about 3,000 yards in width along the line of the road running parallel to the Wadi Boull and about one mile to the north. The southern part of the Djebel Garcia on our left flank was held by our own troops, while the hill village of Takrouna on the right had previously been taken over by the New Zealanders. The country between the battalion and Takrouna was held by the 7th Black Watch. The layout of the battalion for the first night was all companies forward, with B company on the right holding the hillside, C company in the centre astride the road, and on the left D company on the foothills of the Djebel Garcia. On the night of the 24th of April D company was withdrawn to the rear of C company to give depth to the position. Even so, the line was very thinly held, and the battalion was mainly providing protection to the anti-tank guns, of which there were forty-six. In addition the battalion had a company of the 1/7th Middlesex machine guns in support. This part of the line was fairly quiet, and shelling was slight in spite of what our predecessors had evidently experienced. Patrols at first were reconnaissance patrols, but after the third night fighting patrols were sent out with the object of harassing the enemy, making him stand to, and bringing down his defensive fire. On the morning of the 26th of April four Germans surrendered to our anti-tank platoon. They were

Plate 7 Brigadier Lorne M. Campbell, v.c., d.s.o. and bar, t.d.

in a state of exhaustion and hunger, their story being that they had lost their unit fifteen days before, somewhere between Sousse and Sfax, and had since been making their way north in an attempt to rejoin their unit.

On the night of the 26th of April, the battalion went into divisional reserve, and part of the 19th Fighting French Corps took over the line. B company were relieved by the 7th Black Watch, and C company remained in the line under command of the 7th Black Watch. On the night of the 30th of April D company relieved C company, which then returned to the battalion. While in this area the battalion had a counter-attack role known as " Snout " and " Hillock." At this time the awards for the battalion were made known. Capt. Peter Samwell was awarded the M.C. for his part at the battle of Medenine. Other awards were : C.S.M. Archibald and C.S.M. Gauld were each awarded the D.C.M., and the M.M. was awarded to L/Sergeant Wallace, Corporal McColl, Private Monaghan, and Corporal McRae.

The battalion was shortly afterwards relieved in the line, and this finished our fighting in North Africa. We had, however, a lot of fighting still in front of us. Where this fighting would take place we had not the least idea, but we knew it would have to be an invasion by seaborne landings, and we were ordered to move to Djidjelli on the Algerian coast to train in combined operations.

The North African campaign ended in an incredible victory for the Allies. Only seven months separated the final destruction of the German armies in North Africa and that never to be forgotten night at El Alamein, now nearly 2,000 miles away. Approximately two hundred thousand Axis prisoners had been captured, along with thousands of guns and vehicles. Curiously enough, the last Axis troops to fire a shot in North Africa were the Italians. Mussolini's

African Empire had been, as the Prime Minister had forecast, torn to shreds and tatters.

General Montgomery in a personal message to troops of the Eighth Army said :

" Now that the campaign in Africa is finished I want to tell you all, my soldiers, how intensely proud I am of what you have done. Before we began the Battle of Egypt last October I said that together, you and I, would hit Rommel and his army for six right out of North Africa. And it has now been done. All those well-known enemy divisions that we have fought and driven before us over hundreds of miles of African soil from Alamein to Tunis have now surrendered. There was no Dunkirk on the beaches of Tunis, the Royal Navy and the R.A.F. saw to it that the enemy should not get away, and so they were all forced to surrender. The campaign has ended in a major disaster for the enemy. Your contribution to the complete and final removal of the enemy from Africa has been beyond all praise. As our Prime Minister said at Tripoli last February, ' It will be a great honour to be able to say in years to come, I marched and fought with the Desert Army.'

" And what of the future ? Many of us are asking when we will be able to see our families at home, but I would say to you that we can have to-day only one thought, and that is to see this thing through to the end, and then we will be able to return to our families honourable men. Therefore, let us think of the future in this way, and whatever it may bring to us, I wish each one of you the very best of luck and good hunting in the battles that are yet to come and which we will fight together.

" *Together, you and I, we will see this thing through to the end.*"

ENFIDAVILLE AND THE END OF THE AFRICAN CAMPAIGN

Training in Algeria

The difficulty of wounded personnel catching up with the battalion after having been discharged from hospital may be appreciated from the following personal experiences.

On the 9th of May a Hudson plane from Cairo called at Castel Benito aerodrome near Tripoli and conveyed us to El Djem, thirty miles north of Sfax, a distance of three hundred and fifty miles. The trip was most interesting, as we flew directly over the coast. The Mareth Line, our old battlefield, could not be distinguished by us, but the Djebel Roumana at Wadi Akarit stood out quite clearly, and we also had a good view of Gabes and Sfax. At El Djem, which could easily be distinguished from the air by its prominent Roman Coliseum, an air force truck met us and conveyed us to Hergla landing-ground three miles south of the village of Enfidaville, passing through much-bombed Sousse on the way. The following day we arrived at the Rear Headquarters of the 51st Division, and indeed we were very glad to be among " Oor Ain Folk " once more. On arrival we found that part of the Division, including the Argylls, had left the day before for Algeria. However, our commanding officer, Lieut.-Col. Lorne M. Campbell, V.C., D.S.O. and Bar, T.D., who was given temporary command of the 153rd Brigade of the Division, was in the vicinity, and the latest news of the battalion was given to me by him. Shortly afterwards he was given command of the 13th Brigade of the 5th Division.

The following day we set off on our journey to Djidjelli on the Algerian coast. The route was via Kairouan (the Holy City), Sbeitla, Kasserine, Dernaia, Bou Chebka on the Tunisian-Algerian border, Tebessa, Meskiana, Ain Beida, Ain Fakroun, Oued Athmenia, Setif, and finally Djedjelli. The scenery was simply glorious. One was struck by the fertility of the Algerian soil. Rich crops were abundant, and the mountain peaks were mostly covered in forest. From Dernaia to Bou Chebka, over the Djebel Chambi and Djebel Tamesmida, the mountains of Tebessa rise to a height of 5,000 feet, and the view from the highest point on the way through the mountains is magnificent. The Tebessan plain can be seen stretching away for many miles both east and west, and the quiet beauty of the valleys was such a contrast to the hard stony and sandy desert wastes of Egypt and Libya with which we were so familiar during our desert advance. A little farther on a series of cone-shaped hills could be seen in the distance, one of which was the Djebel Roumana. At a distance the hills appeared to be purplish blue, then nearer to us they appeared brown, and nearer still the green fields and fields covered with scarlet poppies and other wild flowers of various colours all blended together to present to the eye a picture of beauty beyond words. In fact the entire journey was through country of indescribable beauty, but it was not until near the end of the journey that we had the greatest sight of all.

It came as a surprise to us when we suddenly entered one of the most impressive gorges we had ever seen. It was the Chabat El Akra gorge, which cuts through the Atlas mountains to the sea. Rugged mountain peaks towered straight above us in the gorge, and in some places waterfalls cascaded down the mountain-sides. As we journeyed along the very narrow winding road through the gorge we observed numerous tunnels through the mountain-sides. Emerging from the gorge, the sea once more lay in front of us, still the beautiful Mediterranean. The scenery along the coast road was what we had always imagined the Mediterreanan coast to be. Narrow winding roads with overhanging cliffs and towering mountains presented to us a truly beautiful scene all along the coast to Djidjelli.

On our arrival at Djidjelli we immediately began training

for our next operation. Of course, we all knew that to get to grips with the enemy again we would have to invade his homeland, and that such an operation would have to be an amphibious one. Which part of enemy territory we would eventually invade was quite unknown to us, although within our own minds we speculated and thought of such places as Sardinia, Corsica, Sicily, and even the Italian mainland.

Landing craft and assault craft of various sizes and designs were at our disposal for this training, which was usually carried out at night. Generally we would march down to the docks at Djidjelli in the evening at about 6 o'clock and embark on landing craft, which would then put to sea and land us in the dark on some part of the coast. Very often the landing was a wet one, and although sometimes we were made to wade ashore chest deep in water, the sea was warm and by keeping on the move no ill effects were suffered. During the day we attended many lectures on combined operations, and also practised according to a certain drill embarking and disembarking with landing craft. Towards the end of June it was considered that we were sufficiently well trained for our new venture, and the battalion were then ordered to move to a concentration area at Sousse. The transport came by road, and the main body of troops by sea. As a member of the advance party which left on the 22nd of June, two days before the battalion, the route was left to our own discretion, and so we chose the coast route through El Milia, Phillipville, Bone, Mateur, and Tunis. We spent a day in Tunis, and during our sight-seeing we paid a visit to the amphitheatre at Carthage. On the following day we set off again through Hammam Lif, Grombalia, Hammamet, Enfidaville, and Sousse. The camp at Sousse was very dusty, but nevertheless we were fairly comfortable and we had some excellent sea bathing. During our stay in Sousse we occupied most of our time checking over equipment and weapons and the hundred and one little items which have to be attended to before a unit goes into action, until on the morning of the 8th of July we embarked at the docks at Sousse for what to us at that time was an unknown destination. Shortly after we had put to sea, however, we were told that we were on our way to invade Sicily. At last we were going to strike at the enemy in his homeland, and a thrill of pride ran through us when the captain of the ship spoke to all personnel on board through the loudspeaker, during which he said that he had the honour to convey in his ship the incomparable 51st Highland Division.

PART II

THE SICILIAN CAMPAIGN

CHAPTER VII

THE INVASION OF SICILY

THE Brigade plan for the invasion of Sicily was to assault with two battalions forward, the 7th Black Watch on the right and the 7th Argylls on the left. The landing was to be made on the extreme south-eastern tip of the island, the nearest town of any size being Pachino, which was about five miles inland.

The weather was fine to begin with, and it was a wonderful sight to watch the thousands of craft of all sizes racing across the Mediterranean. What a memorable day that was! Everyone was keyed up and our morale was very high. We did not know what to expect at the other end but we certainly did not expect the landing to be unopposed, and we had visions of wire obstacles, mines, machine-gun posts, mortar bombs, and shells. Our commanding officer, Lieut.-Col. R. Mathieson, who took over command of the battalion from Brigadier Lorne Campbell at the end of the African campaign, was in excellent spirits, and was keen to emulate the deeds of his predecessor. Lieut.-Col. Mathieson was very much at home in the battalion, as he hailed from Falkirk and was well liked by both officers and men.

When our forward companies touched down at 2.45 a.m. on the morning of the 10th of July 1943 virtually no resistance was met. B company under Capt. Joe Corcoran was the right forward company, and Capt. Donald Young had command of D company on the left. The only casualties during the initial landings were fifteen men of D company, who were all wounded by a " Red Devil " grenade which was thrown into their craft as they were disembarking. To

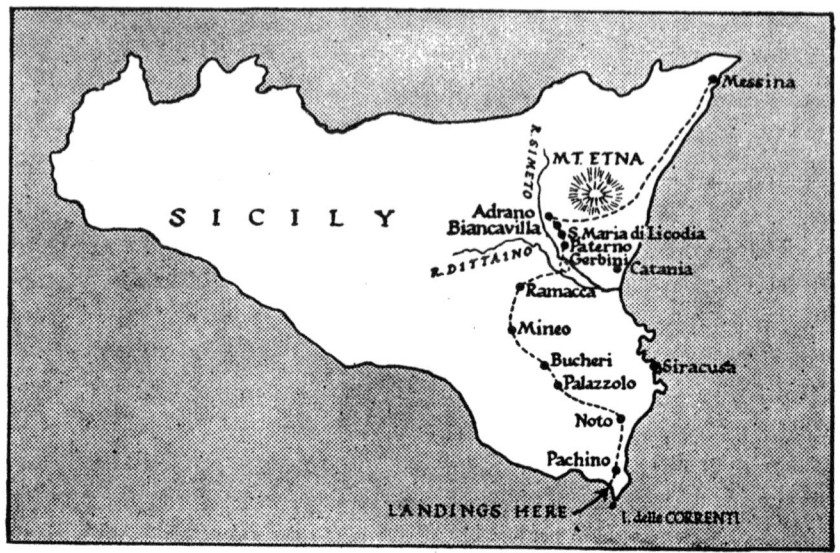

The invasion of Sicily by the Highland Division and the subsequent axis of advance shown by dotted lines

our surprise, and needless to say to our relief, no mines were encountered on the beaches. The value of the air photographs which we had studied before the invasion became evident as we readily recognized the landing beach. Just before we landed the weather became quite rough and our craft ran on to the rocks, as a result of which we had to wade ashore up to our chests. In the half-light we could easily distinguish the I. delle Correnti and the lighthouse, which was captured without any opposition by a party of the 2nd S.A.S., and the promontory on our landing beach with the military hut was quickly recognized.

As the landing was in progress a support ship fired on to the beach defences on the left 790 rockets, each rocket being equivalent to a twenty-pound bomb. This had a tremendously demoralizing effect on the Italians who were manning the coast defence batteries farther along the coast, and when our C company under Major Pat Tweedie arrived on their final objective, known as Pt. 25, they found about 50 very frightened Italians running away from their positions, and who surrendered without any resistance whatever. A company on landing moved forward to positions one mile inland known as Pt. 12, and C company of the 7th Black Watch came under the command of our battalion. B company had the task of mopping up along the beaches, which they carried out successfully without incident. The Brigade bridgehead was now established, and in order to be ready for a counter-attack we dug in during the course of the morning. Mobile guns, tanks, ammunition, and supplies kept pouring in without a halt all morning, and there was no doubt in our minds then about the success of our landing. Having met little opposition on the beaches we knew that farther inland the hard core of the enemy defences would have to be overcome.

At about 2 o'clock in the morning of the 11th of July we marched forward through Pachino and halted to hold a ridge five miles north-west of the town that night. This was the beginning of a series of long and exhausting marches which took us so swiftly through southern Sicily. At 10 o'clock in the morning of the following day we were on the move again, our objective being Noto, which we reached at 7 o'clock in the evening. At Noto we halted for a rest until 11 o'clock that night, when we again moved off, but this time we were on a new axis of advance away from the coast road, which up till now we had been following. We marched a distance of twelve miles up into the hills towards Palazzolo, where we finally halted at 5.30 on the morning of the 13th of July. Until now none of our battalion transport had landed, and every move had to be on foot. These long marches were very tiresome, and since landing on the morning of the 10th of July we had practically no sleep. The bulk of our transport was landed on the 13th of July, however, and joined us. As long as we carried no stores it was found possible to lift the battalion in one load, and we were consequently relieved of some of the heavy marching. During the day we moved to a position about two miles north-west of Palazzolo.

We were all wondering when our battle with the enemy would take place, as so far no resistance at all had been encountered. In Palazzolo two Germans and four Italians were rounded up which, apart from the few enemy we had encountered on landing, were the only enemy we had seen. There was nothing to do but move forward with the utmost speed until we encountered opposition, and on the 14th of July we again moved forward to within two miles of Bucheri, where we rested until the evening. The 231st Brigade, which had edged its way across in front of the Highland Division, was lying in front of Bucheri. Two hills to the right of the village which were held by the Germans were unsuccessfully attacked by the 231st Brigade, and our brigade were ordered to take Bucheri that evening.

The Attack on the Bucheri Hills

The battalion was ferried in transport to an assembly area about eight miles west of the enemy positions near Bucheri. The start-line was along the line of a valley, and the objectives, only 2,000 yards distant, were two hills which we named for reference because of their appearance, Burnt Hill and Scraggy Hill. The 1st battalion of the Black Watch were attacking features on our left. We attacked with B company on the right and C company on the left, with A and D companies in reserve, zero hour being 10 o'clock that night. During the advance an amusing incident occurred when a Maltese interpreter who was attached to us was captured by the 1st Black Watch, but after identification was produced he was released. Both objectives were captured without meeting any opposition as the enemy withdrew a few hours before our attack went in. At about a quarter past three in the morning heavy shelling came down on the 1st Black Watch uncomfortably close to us. It was found to be Canadian artillery, and was quickly stopped by means of the wireless. Although our attack on the Bucheri hills met no resistance, it was a very strenuous advance over exceedingly rough ground, where numerous dykes of lava rock had been built, and which had to be surmounted, thus making our advance rather exhausting.

During the 15th of July we rested until 7 o'clock in the evening when we again set off in transport to within eight miles of Mineo, where we took up positions on the high ground overlooking the town and established road blocks with anti-tank guns in position against a counter-attack by the enemy. Twenty-five Italian prisoners were captured in this area, but as they had been lost for days we got little information from them.

This was quite a pleasant part of Sicily, and the view was magnificent; fortunately we rested here for the whole of the 16th of July, which was the first real rest we had since we landed. The rest was soon broken, however, as we moved off again at 3 o'clock in the morning of the 17th of July to Palagonia, where we debussed from our transport at dawn and marched to Ramacca. During our march we skirted round the foothills to the west of the Catanian Plain. The bridge over the River Caltagirone was blown, and our transport was held up for some time until a good road with an excellent bridge was found a few miles to the west, which was uncharted on the map.

Meanwhile the 1st Black Watch, who were advancing parallel to us on our right, were meeting considerable opposition on the Catanian Plain. Obviously the enemy had expected us to come via the plain, so the Brigadier pulled the 1st Black Watch out and sent them up in our rear behind a ridge which screened the Ramacca road from the plain. On reaching Ramacca our A and C companies were ordered to attack a ridge four miles north of the village. Opposition was very stiff, and both companies sustained a number of casualties through heavy enemy shelling, until they were relieved at 4 o'clock in the afternoon by B and D companies. The ridge was successfully captured and held, however, and served as a good jumping-off place for our attack across the Catanian Plain that night. Several prisoners were captured and were identified as from the Hermann Goering Division. Major John Lindsay Macdougall, who hails from Lunga, Argyll, was rather amused when on looking at the map he found that the river over which we had established a small bridgehead was called the Gornalunga. His remarks were that although we were having a sticky time he felt more at home now. Capt. Ian Campbell had under his command a section of carriers, a troop of Sherman tanks, two troops of anti-tank guns, three detachments of mortars, and an artillery forward observation officer. The section of carriers, which was leading, on coming within sight of the bridge over the river, suddenly came under heavy machine-gun fire from the front and from both flanks. Our Shermans then soon came into action and our mortars and artillery opened up on suspected enemy positions. Enemy tanks could be seen in the plain below beyond the river, but after our Shermans had knocked out two in rapid succession, they made no move across the bridge, which indeed was fortunate for us, as the ground offered few good positions for our anti-tank guns.

On the same night the 152nd and 153rd brigades of the Division each advanced about 13,000 yards, leap-frogging their battalions through each other on to three successive objectives. The speed with which this night advance and attack was launched appeared to have surprised the Germans, and by first light on the morning of the 18th of July both brigades had established bridgeheads across the River Dittaino at Lion and Sferro.

The following day there was very heavy shelling on both sides, and the forward companies had a tiring day and suffered several casualties through shelling. The cornfields in front of our positions were set alight by the shelling, and when darkness fell the countryside was illuminated by a vast circle of burning crops. That night we advanced with the 1st Black Watch leading. The task of the brigade was to establish a bridgehead across the River Simeto, and the 1st Black Watch were given the first phase, which was to take them up to the crossroads where the Gerbini road branches off from the main Catania road. The 7th Black Watch had the intermediary task of capturing the next road fork to Gerbini and a small railway station, and our task was to establish the bridgehead. Zero hour was 10 o'clock at night. Considerable opposition was encountered, and the 7th Black Watch had a hard fight to gain their objective. The leading company of the 1st Black Watch was held up in its advance to Gerbini in the area of the anti-tank ditch, and after a stiff fight consolidated there. By now it was too late to push the Argylls through on to the bridgehead before dawn and the Brigadier decided to bring them up into an area between the 1st Black Watch and the 7th Black Watch where they could be used in a counter-attack role for either of the two battalions and where also they were suitably disposed for any further attack which they might be called upon to do. By about 4 o'clock in the morning of the 19th of July we were in position, and began to carry out some very successful counter-patrol work in conjunction with the 7th Black Watch. In one of these patrols an enemy patrol of about twenty strong were practically wiped out by the mortar and machine-gun fire from one of our own patrols.

It appeared from the amount of enemy shelling, patrolling, and general movement during the day that the enemy was holding Gerbini in strength, thus offering a threat to our brigade's left flank, and so it was suddenly decided that rather than continue with the original intention of establishing a bridgehead, the Argylls were to capture Gerbini, and by doing so strengthen the brigade's position.

The Battle of Gerbini

The plan was to attack Gerbini along the line of the railway rather than up the road, which had been attempted previously by the 1st Black Watch, then to push a patrol down the road, clearing it for transport.

For the purpose of the attack Gerbini was divided into six objectives, A, B, C, D, E, and F, and an artillery plan was arranged with two field regiments and two batteries of mediums, all of which were firing from well up on the left flank on the other side of the Lion bridgehead. Two squadrons of the 46th Royal Tank Regiment were under our command. The start-line was the line of a deep ditch which ran at right angles to the railway. This ditch was about 20 feet deep, and on the enemy side thick wire obstacles confronted us. When we reached the start-line we found a large number of dead Germans, presumably killed by our shelling. C company were right forward company with D company on their left, who were making for the left-hand edge of the wood and the crossroads. In the rear B company were to link up with the tanks at a railway box, and then swing left up a road in rear of D company. A company were in reserve, and were not to be committed until called for. Zero hour was 10 o'clock on the night of the 20th of July.

Plate 8 (*Above*) Troops of the Highland Division foot-slogging along the dusty roads of Sicily. (*Below*) Pack mules in use as transport in southern Italy

Immediately on crossing the start-line we came up against the double apron wire fence, which impeded our advance. Signallers with their wireless sets had great difficulty in getting through. Our wire cutters, however, soon got us through the wire, and the advance continued. Fortunately the enemy defensive fire, which was by this time coming down, was well away from us and did not trouble us much. The enemy machine-gun fire became very troublesome, and several casualties, including myself, occurred in the first thousand yards of the advance. On the right C company, which had one platoon on the other side of the railway, soon became heavily engaged with enemy on the railway line. Soon all officers in the company became casualties, but the N.C.O.s carried on nobly, and this engagement lasted for some considerable time. It was then decided to leave C company in that area, and to bring A company from reserve up the line of the railway. A company went forward under Captain G. B. Horsburgh, but by the time they got on to their first objective their ammuntion was running low. This did not deter them from pushing on, and they made contact with the enemy, who were reported by a patrol to be forming up for a counter-attack. At about this time the wireless was knocked out, and consequently there was no communication with Battalion Headquarters. A company beat off the first counter-attack and consolidated in the area of a railway crossing. Using a deep ditch, they started to dig in near a signal box on the railway. A German self-propelled gun was moving up and down along the line of the railway and seriously threatened their position. Our tanks were then sent over to support A company, arriving just in time to break up a second counter-attack, and for some time they carried out a battle with the self-propelled gun. Shortly afterwards, since A company's position seemed fairly stable, the tanks were diverted to the left to assist B company, who were having a tough fight. A final counter-attack was launched at about 9 o'clock in the morning of the 21st of July by a battalion of Germans supported by a number of tanks. This force surrounded A company, and the tanks kept firing down into the ditch where A company were. After having sustained a number of casualties and realizing that the position was hopeless, as they had very little ammunition left, A company were forced to surrender.

In the meantime, on the left, the other two companies had fared better. D company had met considerable opposition on the aerodrome, which resulted in some stiff hand-to-hand fighting. After overcoming this opposition they continued their advance to the wood, being followed at a distance of two hundred yards by Battalion H.Q. who in turn were followed by B company. B company, after having waited at the rendezvous for the tanks for about a quarter of an hour, decided to follow on without the tanks. D company were well into the woods and beyond the crossroads when B company observed some movement on the left flank. Two sections were immediately sent into the woods to clear up what was thought to be a machine-gun post. Thereupon bedlam was let loose; an armoured car opened up on them, and what later transpired to be a company of infantry holding a pill-box and well dug-in positions, opened up with all their weapons on the two unfortunate sections. This post, although attacked frequently from both sides, was a thorn in the battalion's side for some time before it was finally reduced.

The battle had been fast and furious until now, but at first light the tempo slackened and our tank squadrons leaguered in the woods engaging enemy tanks as they were observed. Later in the morning the battle flared up again, and two companies of Black Watch were sent up to reinforce the position. Successive enemy counter-attacks steadily reduced the strength of the battalion, and at last with only four officers left and the battalion almost surrounded and attacked by enemy tanks after our own tanks had been withdrawn, the battalion was ordered back to hold the line of the anti-tank ditch. The fighting had been particularly fierce, and in spite of our heavy losses the Germans had been dealt a severe blow. The fact that they did not press home their initial advantage, and never again occupied Gerbini, indicates that they were exhausted, and that this battle was the means of breaking the back of the German defence system, which shortly afterwards finished with the withdrawal of all enemy forces from Sicily.

The victory added another page of glory to the gallant record of the Argylls. No fewer than 18 officers and 160 other ranks were killed, wounded, or missing. Considering that the battalion was under strength before the battle started, the position at first looked dismal indeed, but within twenty-four hours officers began to arrive as reinforcements from brigade and division in order to make up the numbers. The following were the officer casualties at Gerbini ; Lt.-Col. R. Mathieson, T.D., while reading a map in the squadron commander's tank, was killed when an 88-mm. shell hit the tank, Major John Lindsay Macdougall, M.C., was severely wounded and taken prisoner. For many months he was reported missing, but later it was confirmed that he had died of wounds in enemy hands. Capt. Donald Young was shot through the head when leading his company, Lieut. Archie McVicar died of wounds, Lieut. Reid Bruce Jones was shot through the head while attacking a pill-box, Lieut. Mathers was killed along with Capt. Donald Young. Capt. G. B. Horsburgh, along with Lieuts. McNaught, Gibb, and Cormack, were all taken prisoners with A company. Among the wounded casualties were Major Pat Tweedie, who lost an arm, Lieut. R. F. Kinghorn, Lieut. W. D. Williamson,

Lieut. Harry Crone, Lieut. R. Muir Morton, Capt. Joe Corcoran, and myself.

Many of these officers had been with the battalion before we came abroad, and their loss was a great blow to us. Although the artillery at Gerbini was not to be compared with the ferocity of the enemy shelling at Wadi Akarit, the enemy machine gunning was very accurate and took heavy toll of us. In addition to machine guns the enemy were using 20-mm. exploding shells, which left the person hit with very little hope of recovery. A favourite trick played by the Germans during the attack was to call out in perfect English, " Is that A company or B company ? " The unsuspecting Jock replied accordingly, and immediately down would come a devastating hail of bullets. Among the enemy dug-outs also were a number of oil drums, and as we fired at the enemy positions the oil drums which had been hit flared up, transforming night into day, thus leaving our troops in full view in the open. This was the last major action that the Argylls fought in Sicily, and although it was a sad ending for many of us, it was a glorious victory for the regiment. In honour of the Argylls the following poem by Capt. Hugh Murray Bailey, appeared in *Punch*, along with a sketch of the battlefield showing the shell-torn trees, the smashed pill-boxes, the burnt-out tanks, and the rows of neat little white-washed crosses where the gallant Argylls were buried where they fell.

> Profane not with profundities these casual graves,
> Words are but platitude to the dead.
> Raise no echoes among those blackened trees ;
>   Their tale is best untold.
> Here where they died in twos and threes,
>   Leave them in their brotherhood.
> Nor regiment in well kept rows among the flowers
>   Those whose last hours
> Ran in this shell-tormented wood.
> Rather let the earth cave in upon their grave
>   And their cross decay,

Plate 9   Lieut.-Col. R. Mathieson, D.S.O., O.B.E., T.D.

Or let the cactus with its prickly fruit
    Be symbol for their Resurrection Day.
What if Death's moods are various?
We cannot find out why, to fulfil what secret laws,
His choice should pass us by and fall on either side.
But we know the stray bullet cannot make a hero,
Nor blood more sanctify our cause.
So mock not these dead with words they cannot understand.
But to commemorate their dust
Raise a plain stone pillar, if you must,
And write upon it, in a soldier's hand.
" What man can suffer, These have suffered,
What man can do, They did."
Let all other praise be silent
And, like our grief, be hid.

We were now without a commanding officer, but Lt.-Col. A. Dunlop, who was G.S.O.1 at Division, came to our rescue. He was given command of the battalion at a very critical period, as needless to say the morale of a battalion suffers after a battle where the losses have been as heavy as they were at Gerbini. Lt.-Col. Dunlop was an officer of great ability, and quickly reorganized the battalion into a first-class fighting unit once more. We were kept occupied for the remainder of July in carrying out energetic training. We were now on a three-company basis and reinforcements continued to pour in, and so we carried out a concentrated programme of training before we were required to move again. On the 31st of July, completely reorganized and re-equipped, with our morale high, we moved off to Mont Franchetta to act as a reserve battalion to the brigade. That night an attack was launched across the River Dittaino against the Sferro Hills, the 152nd Brigade attacking on the right and the two Black Watch battalions of the 154th Brigade on the left. After some stiff fighting the objective was captured. On the late afternoon of the 1st of August the 7th Argylls were directed against Pietraperciata, a high ridge overlooking the roads leading to Centuripe Muglia.

The Field Day Battle

The plan for the attack on Pietraperciata was simple. Each company was to attack the ridge by bounding forward, each making good an intermediate objective before the next company moved on. This action has been called the Field Day Battle, as each step went according to plan, the late arrival of the anti-tank guns on the objective being the only mistake. During the battle all supporting arms other than the anti-tank guns were used in a close support role. There was little opposition, and what German rearguard spandau posts and snipers remained were driven off the ridge just before last light. In this action we lost only one soldier who was wounded. On reaching the ridge our snipers and Bren gunners were pushed forward to the crest to give warning of an enemy counter-attack, while the remainder of the battalion dug in, but there was little need for this as the enemy had cleared out completely.

In the distance on the skyline could be seen the town of Centuripe, perched precariously on a mountain top. Between the battalion's position and the town a line of parallel ridges, culminating in Mount Spezia, ran from east to west. On to these ridges it was planned to put in an attack with the 153rd Brigade on the night of the 2nd of August. Our commanding officer was convinced, however, that Mount Spezia was not held by the Germans, and he consequently sent a small patrol of one carrier up the hill to investigate. This patrol was covered by a platoon of machine-guns from the 1/7th Middlesex Regiment, whose guns were sited in the battalion area. On the top of Mount Spezia, the patrol leader found nine Germans all of whom were very tired, hungry, and thirsty. They had no fight left in them and were immediately marched back to Battalion Headquarters. A brigade night attack was therefore avoided.

CHAPTER VIII

VICTORY IN THIRTY-NINE DAYS

AT 4 o'clock in the afternoon of the 4th of August the battalion moved forward to a concentration area on Mount Poira, a hill overlooking the valley of the Simeto, opposite Adrano and Biancavilla. Paterno was no longer the divisional objective, and our brigade was directed upon the two towns which it was now overlooking.

Shortly after dawn on the 5th of August the 154th Brigade attacked across the River Simeto with the 7th Argylls on the right and the 1st Black Watch on the left. The plan was to capture Biancavilla and St. Maria Di Licodia, making good three intermediate bounds, named Richman, Poorman, Beggarman. B company, under command of Major A. F. Hendry, M.C., was ordered to filter down the steep slope of Mt. Poira, cross the river, and infiltrate through the orange groves on the north side to make good Richman, and if no opposition was met to seize Poorman. This bound was the main lateral road running below the two towns. Obviously it was much used by the enemy, and B company was therefore ordered to cut it by a road block and inflict what casualties they could upon the enemy. B company crossed the river unseen by the enemy and deployed two platoons on Poorman, leaving one on Richman. Meanwhile the company of the 1st Black Watch had met some opposition on crossing the river, and orders were received that no further advance was to be made. Our B company captured one German officer and fourteen other ranks, one motorcycle combination, one self-propelled 75-mm. gun, and destroyed one Mercedes 10-seater car, all with no loss to themselves. This was probably the largest and most varied bag of Germans and equipment to fall to one platoon during the campaign.

Meanwhile our transport had found considerable difficulty in finding a satisfactory crossing of the river. One was eventually found, however, and the battalion moved up into the area round B company. C company went forward to guard the left flank, while D company covered the right flank, and A company came into reserve.

On the following day carrier and foot patrols were pushed forward and Biancavilla was occupied. This was the last action of the battalion in Sicily, and for the next fortnight it stayed in the area just south of St. Maria Di Licodia, training and resting and preparing for further battles should they come. Reinforcements continued to arrive, many of them old members of the unit who were rejoining after having been in hospital.

One day the battalion was ordered to prepare for battle on a pack-mule basis, and we fully expected to follow the 153rd Brigade round the east of Mount Etna to the final divisional objective of Castiglione Di Sicilia, but the enemy withdrew and Linguaglossa was occupied without fighting, so that the 154th Brigade was not required. The news of the fall of Messina came through on the 16th of August, and our brigade, which had been lying back for a few days, moved up into the Messina area to guard the beaches.

The campaign in Sicily was at an end. After a lightning campaign of only thirty-nine days all Axis forces had been decisively defeated, and none now remained on the island. From the start the invasion of Sicily went well. The first nine days was a race with small actions which became stiffer, culminating in the Battle of Gerbini. At Gerbini took place the most savage fighting probably of any unit in the army during the campaign, and undoubtedly the Argylls were in a large measure responsible for the crack which eventually came in the German forces in Sicily. To commemorate the Division's part in the lightning campaign, and in memory of those of the Division who fell fighting, a stone monument was raised near the Gerbini battlefield.

Shortly afterwards the following honours and awards were made known :

D.S.O.	The late Lieut.-Colonel R. Mathieson, T.D.
	Captain A. F. C. Buchanan
Military Cross	Captain N. C. Faid
Military Medal	Sergeant Duncanson
	Corporal Williamson
	Corporal Godden
	Corporal Ginty
	Private Stewart
D.C.M.	Sergeant Alexander
	Sergeant Thornton
	C.S.M. Louden

During the period after the Battle of Gerbini, until the end of the Sicilian campaign, several of us were in hospital and found many difficulties and obstacles in our way on attempting to return to our units. After being evacuated by ambulance to Syracuse from Gerbini, we were conveyed in an air ambulance to Malta. On the evening of the 23rd of July, we were flown again to El Aouina Aerodrome at Tunis where we were admitted to an R.A.F. hospital in Carthage. There we stayed for one day and were flown to Phillipville on the 24th of July, where we were admitted to the 67th General Hospital. After receiving the necessary attention at this hospital we were discharged on the 23rd of August and posted to a Reinforcement and Holding Unit. On reporting to the adjutant there, an amusing incident occurred when a private of the Argylls who had been downgraded, and was on the permanent staff of the camp, walked in and saluted. The adjutant looked up at him in amazement, and knowing that he was not in the habit of saluting, remarked, " Ah, Jock, you saluted." The soldier's reply was, " Yes, I recognized one of my own officers here."

On the 5th of September several officers and men from the Highland Division were posted to English units of an English Division. A protest was lodged, and the posting was cancelled after some considerable difficulty. On the 25th of September, we were at last attached to a draft for Bizerta which was supposed to be bound for Sicily. Instead of arriving in Sicily, however, we were landed at Taranto in the heel of Italy. Here we stayed only long enough to arrange for a lift back to Malta, from where we hoped to reach Sicily. After staying two days in Valetta, Malta, we were at long last conveyed by plane to Catania, Sicily. Strangely enough, we landed on the airfield at Gerbini which was the scene of our bloody battle on the night of the 20th of July. Not until the 9th of October did we arrive back with the battalion, but on arrival we were greeted with the joyful news that the Highland Division was going home to England along with the 50th Division.

Before coming home our brigade's last operation was to take over the Canadian bridgehead in the Calabrian peninsula of Italy on the 1st of September, which operation they completed on the 7th of September, when they returned to Messina.

Homeward Bound

Preparations were now in full swing for our return to the United Kingdom, and an advance party was sent off. On the 9th of November we embarked at Augusta, Sicily, and set off on the 11th of November for home, after an absence of approximately eighteen months. It was no longer necessary to make the long voyage round the Cape of Good Hope, as the danger of enemy attacks in the Mediterranean had by now ceased, and we were able to steam through the Straits of Gibraltar without interference. As we looked on Sicily for the last time, we could not help thinking of our comrades whom we had to leave behind. Gerbini, although now long past, could never be forgotten. The last we saw of Sicily was the snow-capped peak of Mount Etna towering above the horizon in a clear blue sky. Our voyage home took us only fourteen days. We passed through the Straits of Gibraltar at 6 o'clock in the morning, and could just make out the great dark shape of the rock in the early morning half-light. On the African side the lights of Tangier could be seen twinkling in the distance. Our ship was an American troopship called the *Edmund B. Alexander*, and on the whole was fairly comfortable. Two colossal meals per day were served aboard, which was very satisfying at the time, but in between meals one felt very hungry. After a rather uneventful trip we disembarked at Liverpool on the 25th of November, glad once again to be home, although we knew we had been brought home for the purpose of training for the invasion of Europe.

Our first location in the United Kingdom was at Hartwell House in Buckinghamshire, where we stayed for a few weeks, after which we moved to a camp near Great Missenden in the same county. After we all had disembarkation leave, we started intensive training for the invasion of Europe, which, we felt would not be long delayed. During our stay at Great Missenden we had a change of command. Lt.-Col. A. Dunlop, D.S.O., left us to take over the command of a brigade in the 49th Division, and command of the battalion was given to Lt.-Col. Angus Rose, who had previously seen service in the Far East. From Great Missenden we moved to Lowestoft in Norfolk, and started training in country which in many respects was similar to the country over which we later fought on the continent of Europe. During all this time we carried out intensive training until we moved to our final concentration area, where we were sealed in for some days before the invasion of Europe began. The training consisted of river-crossing exercises and co-operation with tanks. This type of training was different from the training we carried out in the desert before El Alamein, but the general principles were the same.

At the beginning of June 1944, we began to feel that the great invasion could not now be far off if it was to take place that year, but when or where it would take place we had not the least idea. At this stage Lt.-Col. Rose left the battalion, and Lt.-Col. J. C. Meiklejohn, D.S.O., then took over command. Lt.-Col. Meiklejohn who had previously been our adjutant in Scotland before we went to Africa, was an old Fettes boy and originally hailed from St. Andrews. In the desert he commanded a rifle company with distinction and won the D.S.O. at El Alamein. He was a born soldier, and served for many years with the London Scottish. As the days wore on rumours about the invasion began to get around, but we received no indication of the date until we moved to a sealed camp at Purfleet on the 4th of June. We were then told that the operation of landing on the Continent was called "Overlord." The battalion had been previously organized to land in three flights, containing approximately 60 per cent. for the first flight, 25 per cent. for the second, and 15 per cent. for the third flight of the battalion strength. The 60 per cent. flight consisted of the four rifle companies, S company, less half of the carrier platoon, and sufficient of H.Q. company to control the battalion in battle, together with transport essential for operations. The 25 per cent. flight comprised the remainder of what might be termed the "fighting elements" of the battalion, and the 15 per cent.

Plate 10   Lieut.-Col. J. C. Meiklejohn, D.S.O.

flight consisted of the administrative elements. The 60 per cent. flight was subdivided into a transport echelon under the command of the C.O. and a walking echelon under the command of Major J. R. Sloan. In the walking echelon the men were loaded with their full equipment, respirators, tools, ammunition, 24-hour ration packs, a greatcoat, and a blanket, and indeed it was a heavy load, but there was no other way of getting the stuff across.

After four unpleasant days in the sealed camp where we were marshalled into shiploads, the transport echelon embarked on the 8th of June. On the following day W echelon embarked for Newhaven, crossing the Thames ferry to Gravesend. Bad weather and lack of space made it impossible for W echelon to embark at Newhaven, and so we were diverted via Portsmouth to Southampton where we embarked on the *Maid of Orleans* at 11 o'clock that night.

PART III

THE INVASION OF NORTH-WEST EUROPE

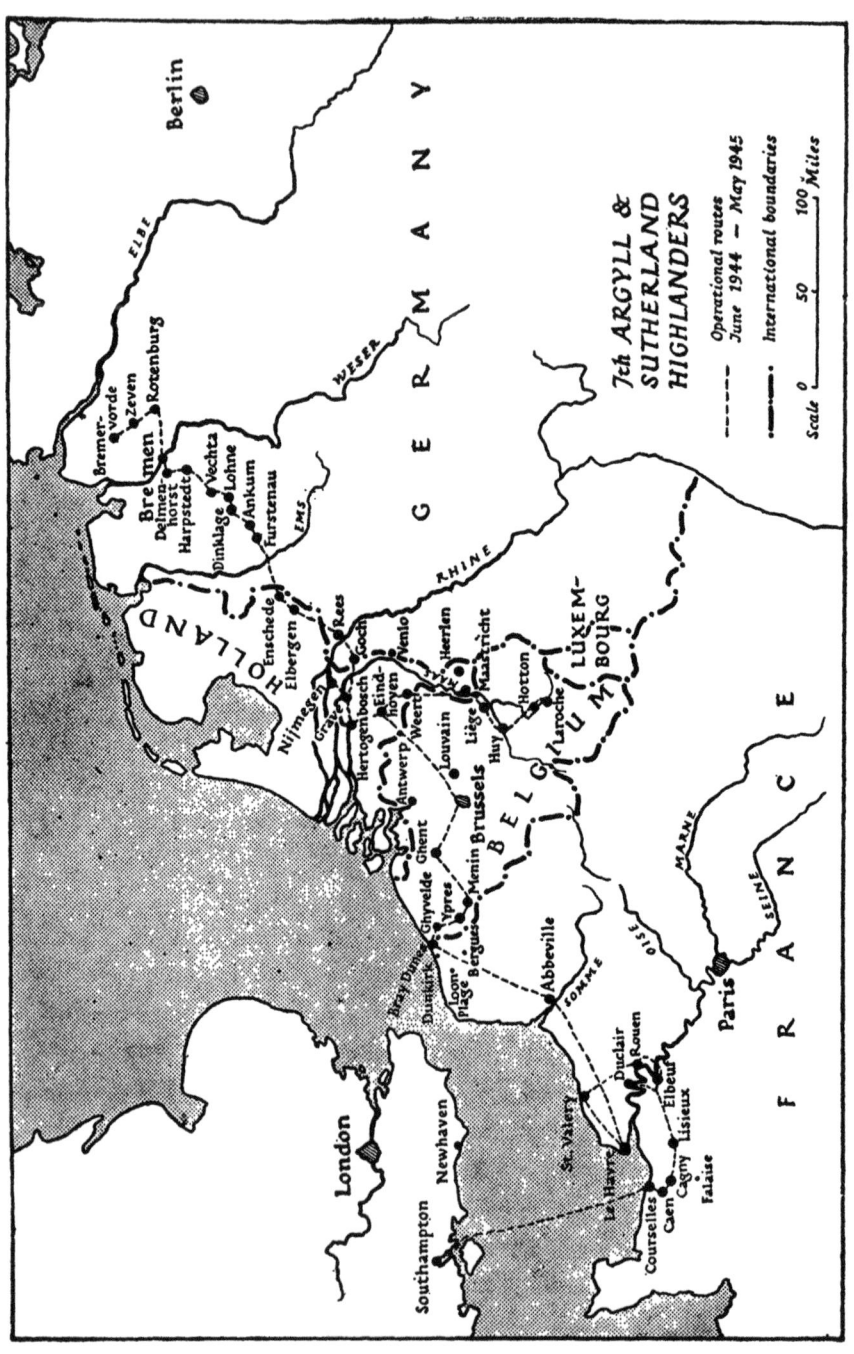

CHAPTER IX

THE NORMANDY LANDINGS

AT one o'clock in the morning of the 10th of June 1944 we set off on the most hazardous operation in the history of modern warfare. The invasion had already been in full swing four days previously, and the 51st Highland Division was being held for the heavy fighting which we all knew would face us as we pushed inland through the outer defences of Rommel's forces in Normandy. After having been at sea all night our ship was unable to pick up her escort, and we consequently returned to the area of Cowes in the Isle of Wight, where we remained until two o'clock on the morning of the 11th of June. Off we then went and landed on the Normandy beaches near Courseulles sur Mer at 11 o'clock the same morning. The weather was very hot, but having been accustomed to the terrific heat of the desert, we thought nothing of it. Immediately on landing we marched inland for a distance of approximately six miles and camped for the night at Reviers, where we had no operational role. The following day was spent mostly in carrying out reconnaissances, and on the 13th of June we occupied positions behind the 3rd Canadian Division, acting as a long-stop firm base to deal with enemy counter-attacks in the area of Colomby sur Thaon. This position was occupied in conjunction with the 4th Armoured Brigade. On the 14th of June, the battalion was placed under the command of the 6th Airborne Division, who had been fighting very severe battles ever since their successful capture of the bridges over the River Orne. The role of the battalion was the close defence of these bridges, and to carry this out it took up a defensive position on the high ground on the east side of the River Orne.

East of the Orne

The ground in front of the battalion position was littered with the gliders which the 6th Airborne Division had used in landing. Although our position was strong, these gliders hampered our fields of fire, and indeed, in previous actions had afforded cover for German snipers. Consequently we towed some of these gliders out of the way.

On the 16th of June the enemy launched attacks at Breville to the east of us and at Escoville to the south, but these attacks were smashed on the start-line by our own artillery, and the enemy were unable to infiltrate at any point. Intermittent shelling of the bridges took place day and night in this area, and very often the enemy made desperate attempts to bomb the bridges after darkness had fallen, but all these attempts failed. On the 18th of June we carried out a reconnaissance of the area of the Bois de Bavent. This area was very thickly wooded, and at the most we had only a field of fire of about 50 yards. Owing to the close nature of the country the area was a snipers' paradise. On the following day the battalion again came under the command of the 154th Infantry Brigade, and the whole brigade was placed under the command of the 6th Airborne Division. The task of the brigade was to hold the extreme southern position of the bridgehead to the east of the River Orne. This position consisted of a wooded ridge in the Bois de Bavent. The position commanded all the low ground of the bridgehead. The country was appallingly close with dense forest, scrub, small orchards, and thick hedges.

At the time the 155th Brigade were holding the position. The Boche had been very active and often infiltrated into their positions. Consequently, the 155th Brigade had sometimes to employ a whole company and a troop of tanks to winkle the enemy out of a copse or an orchard. When our brigade took over the positions they therefore adopted a more compact layout, with much closer contact between battalions. On the 19th of June, then, we moved to a concentration area at Herouvillette, where we had a foretaste of the heavy shelling and mortaring which was to be our lot for many days to come. The following day we took over the positions of the 5th Black Watch as reserve battalion to the brigade. The reserve position was below and to the west of the ridge. Longer fields of fire allowed us to adopt a more normal layout than the position on the ridge would have afforded. We had under our command considerable support in the form of anti-tank guns and tanks, and we felt that our position was fairly strong. Not a day passed without the battalion area being subjected to heavy shelling and mortaring, and although our casualties were not heavy, there was a continual drain on personnel. In addition, in former campaigns the 51st Division had always been used aggressively, and wherever there was an attack the Division always took part in it. This was the first time that the battalion had to sit for lengthy periods in a defensive position without launching an attack, and this became very monotonous. In addition, the Division was not used as a Division, but had battalions attached to other divisions here, there, and everywhere. Naturally we all longed for the day when the Division would be used as such, and in a more aggressive role.

The Germans used their six-barrelled mortar quite a lot in this area. This weapon was nicknamed " Moaning Minnie " from the wailing noise it made in flight. Whenever the wail was heard all troops usually dived for their trenches, and as the flight of the bomb took about 5 seconds one usually had time to get down. The fragmentation of the " Moaning Minnie " bombs was very poor, and the effect on morale was greater than the material damage they caused.

On the night of the 24th of June, around midnight, an

unusually heavy enemy artillery and mortar concentration was put down over the whole brigade area. Prior to this we had been warned that sounds of heavy tracked vehicles could be heard approaching the positions occupied by the 7th Black Watch, who were left forward battalion. Our battalion was ordered to " stand to," and soon the enemy launched an attack against the 7th Black Watch. Tremendous small-arms fire continued to chatter away in the woods in the 7th Black Watch area, and a good proportion of the " overs " reached us. The noise was deafening, and the whole area was battered so continuously that it was difficult to tell what was happening. The 7th Black Watch had been expending a lot of ammunition, particularly 3-inch mortar bombs, and they soon began to run short. At this stage Capt. Bob Porteous was sent up with six carrier loads. He had a difficult job, as the night was black and the tracks steep and twisting among the trees. Shells and mortar bombs continuously crashed down, and the track through the woods to the 7th Black Watch positions received more than its share of these. When Capt. Porteous had nearly got up to the 7th Black Watch, his leading carrier received a direct hit from a " Moaning Minnie." The carrier was, consequently, put out of action and blocked the track. Although the bomb burst underneath the driver of the carrier, he escaped with only the loss of a foot. Bob Porteous then managed to get the remaining carriers unloaded, and man-handled the ammunition past the knocked-out carrier. Later the 7th Black Watch asked for more ammunition, and this time the carriers were sent round another way, during which Pte. Harrow gave a display of clever driving and coolness by driving his carrier while under intense fire.

The battalion had a counter-attack role on the 7th Black Watch positions, and at one time it appeared likely that we would be required for this role. By 3.30 in the morning the firing began to die down, and we were not called upon for our counter-attack role. In any case it is doubtful whether we would have carried out this role if required in darkness, and it is more probable that we would have waited until first light. Although the enemy did not use many troops in his attack, it appears that his intention was to endeavour to shell us off the position, when he would then occupy it with his infantry. The total number of casualties caused in our battalion by the shelling were 3 killed and 6 wounded, which was fairly light considering the number of craters we found the following morning.

The following day we relieved the 7th Black Watch in their positions on the ridge, which relief was safely accomplished, although it took place during some particularly heavy stonks which caught several of the companies in the open whilst they were on the move. We remained in this position until the 8th of July, during which time we were continually shelled and mortared and sniped at. It was a period of very considerable strain, and we had to keep a very high degree of alertness all the time. Sometimes the battalion would have to " stand to " for two or three hours at night in anticipation of an attack. It was difficult to tell whether the considerable amount of mortar and spandau fire was the beginning of an attack, or whether it was merely due to windiness on the part of the Boche. Actually we were not attacked and things quietened down considerably after a bit. One platoon of the battalion was detached to a position about 400 yards in the woods in front of the foremost defended localities, where they had command of the junction of several important tracks, and this platoon, which was relieved each day, had the unpleasant task of " standing to " all day and all night.

Our snipers' section had many a good bag, and in one afternoon killed 5 Germans. During the day considerable patrolling was done, but at night it was much too thick. Deserters came in to our lines and gave themselves up in small groups. They were mostly Russians and Poles, and by the 30th of June we had nine. Our own casualties had not been heavy, but they were continuous, and we lost an officer, Lieut. David Reekie, who was slightly wounded in the knee. It was discovered that the enemy were using powerful radio transmitters and were posing as one of our local receiving stations. Their practice was to ask for the password and to countermand fire orders previously issued by us. In addition some of them were discovered to be wearing British battledress.

Periodically we changed the company positions in order to relieve the strain on the forward companies. A small defensive minefield consisting of anti-personnel and anti-tank mines was laid by our assault pioneer platoon across the road running from Breville. On the 5th of July some more Polish deserters gave themselves up, and one of the " Jocks " who had always something to say passed the remark, " There are more Poles here than there are in Falkirk." On the 6th of July propaganda messages in German and Russian were broadcast from a loudspeaker van, the object being to encourage deserters to come across to our lines. At last on the 8th of July we were relieved by the 2nd battalion of the Seaforth Highlanders, after which we moved to a rest area near Ranville. While in the Ranville area the troops had a much-needed bath and rest, but our rest was soon cut short, for on the following day reconnaissance parties went off to have a look at positions south of the Bas de Ranville with a view to taking over from the 5th Black Watch of the 153rd Brigade who were to launch an attack in the Colombelles area. C company under Captain Boyle was sent to St. Honorine, where they were under the command of the 5/7th Battalion of the Gordon Highlanders. The remainder of the battalion moved at 2 o'clock on the 10th of July to take over the positions of the 5th Black Watch. The layout of the battalion in this area was A company as right flank protection company, D company on the ridge overlooking the canal, with the carrier platoon dismounted in the area of Battalion Headquarters. C company of the 12th Devons took over positions on the right and came under our command. In addition one platoon of the 1/7th Middlesex Machine Gun Battalion and one troop from the 241st Anti-tank Battery, with 17-pounder guns, were under our command.

On the 11th of July the 5th Black Watch and the 1st Gordons were ordered to attack the Colombelles area, the object being to hold the factory there long enough for the sappers to blow the chimney up, as the chimney was being used as an enemy observation post. The 5th Black Watch captured their objective, but owing to particularly heavy shelling, they had to withdraw again. The Germans counter-attacked with Tiger tanks and knocked out ten of our Shermans. The attack by the 1st Gordons also failed, and they were ordered to withdraw to the area of Longueval.

At 4 o'clock in the afternoon of the 12th of July we carried out a reconnaissance in the St. Honorine area, where our brigade were ordered to take over the positions of the 153rd Brigade. Our battalion was to hold the area with five companies, and to be able to do this B company of the 7th Black Watch was placed under our command. We took over from the 5/7th Gordon Highlanders, and the relief was carried out so silently that we attracted no enemy shelling whatever. The position was a very important one, and as it was very open and continual shelling kept us mostly confined to our trenches day and night, it was inclined to become a bit irksome. It had been decided to leave all our transport with the exception of our carriers behind, and also we carried one complete day's rations in reserve.

CHAPTER X

THE CAEN BREAK-THROUGH

On the 15th of July it was revealed that the High Command planned an attack through our position, and consequently certain minefields which had been laid by our predecessors would have to be lifted, and gaps would have to be made in the wiring. The offensive, which was to be preceded by colossal bombing of enemy strong-points, was to take place on the 18th of July. As we were fairly near to some of the bombing targets, it was decided to draw back out of St. Honorine to the area of the stone quarries just behind Longueval on the river bank. B company under Major J. D. Milne was the only company to remain in the St. Honorine area, but even they were to be brought back to the wooded area just behind the village of St. Honorine. It was estimated that at least 2,000 bombers were to take part in this colossal air assault. Following the air bombardment six hundred guns were to fire a terrific barrage on the enemy positions, and at 8.30 in the morning a brigade of the 3rd British Division along with a brigade of the 3rd Canadian Division were to move forward to attack the enemy in their positions.

The move back from St. Honorine to the area of the stone quarries commenced at 2.30 on the morning of the 18th of July. It was a very tricky business moving out of the positions without making much noise, and during the process some of the companies, which were moving out at fifteen-minute intervals, came under some enemy shelling. The night was dark, which was perhaps fortunate, as two enemy raiders flew low over our convoy strafing the ground below them, but caused no damage to us. By 5.30 a.m. we were safely established in the area of the stone quarries, away from St. Honorine, and waiting with great excitement for the start of the air offensive. We did not take the trouble to dig in, but instead we endeavoured to find the best vantage point from which we could watch the bombing. It was now getting light, and we could see the troops of the leading brigades of the 3rd British and 3rd Canadian Divisions waiting for the order to move forward. While we were waiting for the bombers breakfast was cooked, but in the middle of breakfast we suddenly heard the distant roar of hundreds of heavy bombers. It was 5.45 a.m. when the first of the bombers arrived escorted by numerous fighters, which, flying at great height and speed, chased all enemy planes out of the sky. As the bombers drew near the noise became deafening, and in our excitement, we forgot all about our breakfasts, but who worried about breakfasts at a time like this! In a few seconds the sky was black with planes which were blasting away at the enemy positions. Smoke and flames rose to a height of about 5,000 feet, and the spectacle was the most amazing and grimmest we had ever had the opportunity of witnessing. After the bombing had ceased, the battalion moved back to the defensive positions previously occupied in St. Honorine, each company keeping about 300 yards apart while on the move. Unfortunately heavy shelling was encountered on the way, and several casualties were sustained. Not for long did we stay in St. Honorine, however, as we again moved forward to take over Cuverville. As it was anticipated that we might meet some opposition *en route*, the companies moved tactically and were well dispersed, the order of march being the carrier platoon, C company, D company, A company, Battalion H.Q., and B company. Again heavy shelling was encountered, and C company alone sustained 28 casualties, 7 of which were fatal. Lieut. Menzies of A company and Lieut. A. Rankin of B company were both killed, and Capt. Mitchell of A company was wounded.

In the afternoon a fighting patrol from B company with one section of carriers under command went out to the area of a wood on the right flank, but before reaching the wood ran into a considerable number of Germans in the cornfields. This patrol did extremely well and captured no fewer than 35 prisoners, along with much valuable booty. Altogether about 60 Germans prisoners were sent back through the battalion during the day. The dispositions of the companies in the Cuverville area were, right forward company, D company, whose responsibilities were the roads to Gibberville and Demouville. A company were left forward company, and were responsible for the area between the Demouville and Sannerville roads, and B company, being right flank company, were responsible for the Colombelles and Gibberville roads, while C company on the left were responsible for the Sannerville road. A considerable amount of shelling took place during the day, but by the 19th of July all was quiet.

On the 20th of July a reconnaissance party set off for the Cagny area, as we had been ordered to take over from a battalion of the Guards Brigade who were located in the area. Particularly heavy rainfall at this time made it impossible for wheeled transport to move as all the roads were several inches thick in mud, and the move was postponed meantime. Not until the 22nd of July did we move to the Cagny area to take over from the 1st Battalion of the Grenadier Guards. Of the remainder of the brigade, the 1st Black Watch were located in Frenouville and the 7th Black Watch in Le Poirier. Under our command were one troop of the 241st Anti-tank Battery and one platoon of the 1/7th Middlesex Machine Gun Battalion. At 1.45 p.m. we set off, and by 6 o'clock that evening the move was completed without incident except for some spasmodic shelling. The dispositions of the companies in the area were, starting from the right : A company were responsible for the road running south-east to Frenouville, and B company, who were left flank protection company, were responsible for the road to Emieville. The carrier platoon had the role of a rifle company, and were in position between B and C companies, and the mortar platoon was batterized.

Heavy shelling and mortaring of our positions continued each day, and as our positions were dug in a cornfield the mosquitoes were particularly troublesome. At night heavy bombing of the areas surrounding our positions caused a number of casualties in our A echelon. A large number of flares were dropped by enemy aircraft, making night into day, and anti-personnel bombs were dropped over a wide area. Fortunately little damage was done to us. We remained in this position until relieved by the 7th Duke of Wellington's Regiment on the 25th of July. Our next location was a rest area at Le Landel, approximately two miles south of Cazelle. Our move to Le Landel was carried out without much enemy interference, although as Battalion Headquarters were leaving the Cagny area uncomfortably heavy shelling of our positions caused an anxious minute or two. We marched to Le Landel via St. Honorine, the scene of our previous unpleasant experiences from enemy shelling. There we embussed in troop-carrying vehicles which took us to our destination. At Le Landel we all had a bath and a change of clothing, which had tremendous morale-lifting effect. Ten per cent. of the battalion were allowed to Bayeux daily, and ceremonial guards, concerts, and Retreat programmes by the Divisional massed pipes and drums helped to relieve the monotony. The Château Le Landel, a beautiful French country mansion, had been used, like many others, as a German fortress, and it was, indeed, a pitiable sight to see so many châteaux ruined

Advance of Battalion through France and Belgium

by shelling and bombing. Le Landel, however, although damaged, was in comparatively good condition.

Our rest came to an end on the 29th of July, when our brigade once more took over the positions of the 152nd Brigade in the triangle area in the Bois de Bavent. The layout of the brigade, which included the 9th Para Battalion of the 6th Airborne Division, who were on our left, was: the 7th Black Watch on our right and the 1st Black Watch in reserve. Our two forward companies were D company on the right, who were responsible for the drive to the château in the area, and A company, who were responsible for the area of the apex of the triangle. A troop of tanks was located in D company area, and our own anti-tank guns were responsible for covering the apex of the triangle and shooting up the drive to the château and the Troarn road. A echelon was established in Ranville, and B echelon in Hermanville. We had a fairly easy time in the area, as there was little enemy artillery or mortar activity, probably owing to the fact that the enemy were in poor heart after having received previously quite a battering from our artillery. A certain amount of enemy air activity took place each morning and evening, however, and although some bombs were dropped and our positions were machine gunned, few casualties were sustained. On the 31st of July we once more moved back to the Cazelle area, this time to prepare for a large-scale offensive which we hoped would be the final break-through in the Caen area before the great chase across the Continent began.

Although Cazelle was supposed to be a semi-rest area we were subjected to some heavy shelling by 88-mm. and 170-mm. guns, one of which had a delayed-action fuse. In one instance a shell landed a few feet away from where a number of us were sleeping, penetrated deep into the ground and exploded underneath without coming to the surface, causing a mound of earth about one foot high and two feet in diameter. The following day, the 2nd of August, I said good-bye to the battalion and took up a post as a general staff officer at brigade headquarters. Although I looked forward with enthusiasm to my new post, it was with a certain feeling of regret that I left the battalion with which I had been since August 1940. Many of my friends who had been in the battalion in 1940 were long since dead, but the spirit of the battalion was the same, and a number of the original members still remained. Staff work at brigade gave me a better idea of what was happening within the brigade as a whole.

On the 3rd of August the course of future operations was outlined to us. A completely new form of advance was to be made by the Division as a whole and by our brigade in particular. Each battalion was to receive a certain number of what were called " Priests," which were armoured vehicles with self-propelled guns, armoured half-track vehicles, and carriers which were to convey the fighting personnel from the start-line of the attack to a debussing area near the objective. The object of this novel form of advance from start-line to objective was three-fold. Casualties were kept down to a minimum during the initial advance, as the personnel riding in armoured vehicles were protected from small-arms fire and splinters and also from anti-personnel mines. On previous occasions when our infantry had to advance on foot, a great many casualties by enemy mortaring, shelling, and machine-gun fire were sustained long before we ever reached the objective. In addition the unpleasant task of wading through enemy minefields on foot where anti-personnel mines caused such havoc was done away with. Secondly, another advantage gained by infantry being conveyed in armoured vehicles was that the infantry arrived fresh on the objective instead of exhausted through a long and harassing advance from the start-line on foot. Lastly, by the speed of the advance it was hoped that the enemy would be taken by surprise. Special training had therefore to be carried out, and training areas were selected in the areas of Anisy, Couvre Chef, Epron, and Lebisey. During the months of June and July the battalion had suffered in casualties 2 officers killed and 5 wounded, and 32 other ranks killed and 105 wounded.

At this stage it might be of interest to give a list of the officers who landed with the battalion in Normandy. This list shows how many of these officers were at present with the battalion, and also shows what happened to the remainder.

			Remarks
105771	Lt.-Col. J. C. Meiklejohn, D.S.O.	With Unit	C.O.
86494	Major A. McKinnon, M.C.	,,	2 i/c
88687	Major I. A. Campbell	,,	O.C. S Coy.
137054	Major J. D. Milne	,,	O.C. B Coy.
124589	Major J. R. Sloan	,,	O.C. A Coy.
137939	Major J. L. Robertson	,,	O.C. D Coy.
95536	Capt. A. D. Boyle	,,	O.C. C Coy.
200416	Capt. J. F. Robertson	,,	O.C. H.Q. Coy.
164922	Capt. W. D. Williamson	,,	Adjt.
92198	Capt. W. T. Thomson	,,	M.T.O.
88298	Capt. J. Richardson	,,	Q.M.
189569	Capt. A. McElwee	,,	2 i/c A Coy.
117830	Capt. M. J. G. Bate	,,	2 i/c B Coy.
200306	Capt. R. M. Morton	,,	2 i/c S Coy.
101393	Capt. D. A. Goodall	,,	O.C. 5 Pl.
256426	Capt. R. D. Porteous	,,	4 Pl.
255825	Capt. J. I. Balleny	,,	3 Pl.
139347	Capt. W. Blair (R.A.M.C.)	,,	M.O.
133255	Capt. H. Campbell (R.A.Ch.D.)	,,	C.F.
249367	Lieut. J. R. Cutland	,,	I.O.
256456	Lieut. E. J. Harris	,,	S.O.
308588	Lieut. H. D. Archibald	,,	
287839	Lieut. J. C. M. Austin	,,	
258354	Lieut. I. Buchanan	,,	
CDN80	Lieut. J. R. Harrison (Calgary Hse.)	,,	
307402	Lieut. J. Chapman	,,	

299011	Lieut. J. Cowling	With Unit
226924	Lieut. A. M. Leslie	,,
261705	Lieut. D. McGee	,,
243554	Lieut. J. C. S. Wylie	,,
177750	Lieut. D Menzies	Killed in action, 18/7/44
256409	Lieut. A. Rankine	Died of wounds, 18/7/44
237974	Lieut. R. Williams	Wounded 8/7/44
172421	Capt. J. I. Mitchell	Wounded, 18/7/44
180726	Lieut. D. Scobbie	Wounded (accident) 23/6/44
CDN125	Lieut. A. Bartholomew (Cdn. Inf. Corps)	Wounded (accident) 19/7/44
145671	Lieut. D. G. S. Reekie	Wounded, 3/7/44
134631	Major A. F. C. Buchanan, D.S.O.	Staff College
143438	Capt. I. C. Cameron	G.III 154 Inf. Bde.
181369	Lieut. D. L. Colquhoun	L.O. 154 Inf. Bde.
78479	Capt. F. M. W. Edie	Evacuated U.K., malaria
157295	Lieut. W. Lamont	,, sick
269690	Lieut. G. P. Wood	,, sick
	Lieut. E. C. Wilkie	,, sick

The Armoured Advance

On the 5th of August the rough plan for the big advance was disclosed. The operation was called " Totalise," and the 154th Brigade were to play a prominent part in it. The plan was that the 51st Highland Division under the command of the 2nd Canadian Corps, and in conjunction with the 3rd Canadian Division on their right, were to break into the enemy positions due south of Caen, and on gaining their objectives strong armoured formations were to pass through and make for Falaise and the south-east. The operation was to be at night, and was to be supported by very heavy bombing of the flanks and a medium barrage which was to move forward at the rate of 100 yards in one minute. Various aids to keeping direction were to be used, such as Bofors firing along the flanks, and the artillery were to fire green smoke on to the objectives. The 154th Brigade were to lead, and each battalion in the brigade was to have

Plate 11 Major-General T. G. Rennie, Commander of the Highland Division in Europe

one armoured regiment in support, along with various other supporting arms. The order of march for the advance was to be : 1st Black Watch on the left, 7th Argylls on the right, and the 7th Black Watch following up the Argylls. The 1st Black Watch were to capture St. Aignon de Crasmesnil, the Argylls had as their objective Crasmesnil itself, and the 7th Black Watch were to attack and capture Garcelles Sequeville. This entailed an advance into the enemy lines to a depth of approximately 5,000 metres. On the right the Canadians were given objectives parallel to us. The advance was to be divided into two columns, each column being four vehicles abreast with vehicles approximately twenty yards apart laterally. All vehicles were to have dimmed tail-lights at night. The armoured brigade were entirely responsible for conveying the infantry from the start-line to the debussing area, where the infantry were to debuss and make straight for the objective. The brigade attack was to take place in two stages, the first being the advance from the start-line to the debussing areas in armoured vehicles. The second stage consisted of the attack and clearing of the objectives by our infantry to allow our tanks to take up battle positions by first light. The routes from the forming-up place to the start-line were to be lit with lamps on five-foot pickets, the right column being green and the left column being amber.

It is obvious that an operation of this nature required a great deal of staff work and training, and as the attack was scheduled to take place on the night of the 8th of August, time was indeed limited. On the 6th of August it was considered that the battalions were well enough trained for their new role, and we moved to our concentration area in a powder factory at Cormelles that afternoon. At 9 o'clock the same evening, brigade moved their Tac. H.Q. to a previously reconnaissanced area at Hubert Folie. At this stage we were told that the operation was put forward 24 hours to fit in with the bigger picture. During the night the battalion was shelled by a heavy gun, probably a 210-mm., and as a result B company sustained 2 killed and 10 wounded.

The morning of the 7th August was spent mostly in checking up the final details, briefing the men, and so on, and at 9 o'clock that night the column started to form up just south of Cormelles. The column consisted of two troops of tanks of A squadron of the Armoured Brigade, four abreast with a navigator in each troop, five troops of Flails in line ahead, the R.E. party, A.V.R.E.s, two armoured bulldozers, Squadron H.Q. of the tanks. After this followed another squadron of tanks, the infantry block, and finally the reserve squadron of tanks. Nose to tail the column stretched for approximately 600 yards. The forming-up was carried out successfully at last light, and off the column went at 10.50 p.m. and crossed the start-line at 11.30 p.m.

The barrage started at 11.30 p.m. and the bombing on the flanks about the same time. It was a terrific din. The guns kept up their thunderous roar and the bombs came crashing down with deadly accuracy, fairly obliterating enemy positions with a sickening thud. While the battalion was on the move, however, the full effect of the noise was lost, as the vehicles effectively drowned it.

For about the first mile all went well with the column, but after this it began to get rather spread out, and the vehicles were no longer in station. After having gone about half-way to the objective three of the leading tanks and one of the Flails disappeared into a huge bomb crater. It was unfortunate that these tanks contained the navigators, and there was considerable delay before the column was able to continue. It was at this stage that the first enemy were encountered, and B company came under fire from a spandau machine-gun post. In addition several hand grenades were thrown at one of the troop carriers, one of which landed inside, but was promptly picked up by Pte. Jarvis of B company and thrown out again before it had time to explode. Capt. M. J. G. Bate, when dismounting to deal with this post, was seriously wounded, and had to be left behind in charge of a stretcher bearer. The post was soon dealt with, however, 2 Germans being killed and 3 taken prisoner. Shortly after this a railway had to be crossed, and this further disrupted the column. Things now became a bit confused, with a few tanks running here and there and spandau fire on all sides. The debussing point was reached at about 4 o'clock in the morning. Here B company collected itself by degrees and moved off to its objective, which was the rear of the village of Crasmesnil. The objective was captured without much trouble, 5 Germans having been killed and 7 taken prisoner. A company, whose objective was forward of B company on the right, arrived at the debussing point in driblets. D company then dribbled in, but both companies soon collected themselves and reached their objectives successfully despite a heavy ground mist. D company's objective was forward and to the left of B company. A company had the stiffest opposition, and it was while they were attacking a spandau post that Capt. Andrew McElwee and one other rank was killed. However, by 5 o'clock that morning the battalion had completed its job, with 8 Germans killed and about 35 taken prisoner. All companies then consolidated their positions and prepared for the expected counter-attack. Battalion H.Q. was established in B company area, and the tanks and supporting arms were forward with the rifle companies. Although some nasty fighting had taken place the casualties in the battalion were slight, and consisted of 1 officer and 2 other ranks killed, and 1 officer and 18 other ranks wounded. Tank casualties were a bit heavier, as eight tanks had been knocked out and Major

Lovibond, the second-in-command of the regiment, and their signals officer were killed, their tank having been set on fire by a German " bazooka " on entering Crasmesnil.

A company quickly made contact with the Canadians on the right, and D company got in touch with the 1st Black Watch on the left, and the situation now looked pretty heartening. At 9 o'clock the expected counter-attack developed on the 1st Black Watch front. A number of Tiger tanks and approximately 200 infantry appeared, but our medium guns put down terrific defensive fire and the tanks with infantry on board were soon making off south. The Northamptonshire Yeomanry, who were supporting the 1st Black Watch, had a good morning, knocking out sixteen Tiger tanks to a loss of eighteen of their own. This they rightly considered a fair exchange. There was ample evidence that our 17-pounder anti-tank guns would make mince-meat of the Tiger tanks if hit on the side plates.

At mid-day 600 American heavy bombers came over to support the forward movement of the armour which was to start at 2 o'clock. One stick of bombs landed just in front of D company, but fortunately caused no casualties. We later heard that two flights had mistaken their target to such a degree as to heavily bomb the Canadians near Cormelles, causing very heavy casualties. Heavy shelling of the battalion area was carried out during the remainder of the day, but no more counter-attacks developed. By now the Canadian armour was reported to have pushed on rather well, but the Polish Armoured Division was not so successful. Some hard remarks about the Poles were passed at the time, but on going over the ground later there was little doubt from the number of Shermans burnt out that they had had a pretty sticky time.

The new experiment called artificial moonlight which was used during the attack, and which consisted of a number of searchlights shining into the clouds, was a complete success. This artificial moonlight had the double benefit to us of blinding the enemy and lighting the way for us. There is no doubt that the battalion would have suffered much heavier casualties if the advance had been on foot and not in armoured vehicles. This new technique of penetrating deeply into the enemy positions and by-passing certain strong-points on the way met with great success. These strong-points were dealt with by the follow-up battalions. For instance, Tilly La Campagne, which had been by-passed by the Argylls *en route*, was captured by the 2nd Battalion Seaforth Highlanders, while at the same time the 5th Camerons, advancing on foot behind the column, captured Lorguichon.

The Polish Armoured Division, who were to send forward armoured patrols that afternoon, did not do so until the following day at midday. Their task was to exploit to the south-west of the battalion's positions. Later in the day the Poles reported that the village of St. Sylvain was in their hands, and two battalions of the 153rd Infantry Brigade were immediately ordered to take over from the Poles. As a result of this the 7th Black Watch were sent forward to take over from the 5th Black Watch of the 153rd Brigade in order to release them for their new role of the occupation of St. Sylvain with the 1st Gordon Highlanders.

The Attack on the Woods of St. Sylvain

On the 10th of August our brigade were ordered to attack with two battalions the wooded area to the south-east of St. Sylvain. This attack, which was carried out by the 7th Argylls and 1st Black Watch, was divided into two phases. In phase 1 the 7th Argylls by silent attack were to secure lodgement areas in the woods to the south-east of the village of St. Sylvain, after which they were to push outwards and clear by patrols. In phase 2 the woods were to be cleared still further after daylight. The start-time for the attack was 15 minutes after midnight. As the ground from the 7th Black Watch positions in the area of Robertmesnil sloped towards the enemy and was under observation, no forward movement took place past the 7th Black Watch positions before 10.15 that night. One squadron of the 144th R.A.C. in support of each battalion was to be in position by first light in order to be ready for the support of our infantry should an enemy counter-attack develop. The 1st Black Watch were to move behind the 7th Argylls by the same route and form up behind them to attack the woods. Although the attack by the Argylls was a silent one, certain pre-arranged artillery targets were laid down by corps, and considerable artillery concentrations were brought down on the enemy positions farther inland after the Argylls captured their objectives.

The battalion got on to the start-line without much difficulty, and passed through St. Sylvain at the appointed time. A company were right forward company, and D company on the left, with B company in reserve. Very shortly after crossing the start-line, intense machine-gun fire was encountered from both flanks and also from directly in front. Casualties soon began to mount up, particularly with D company. The advance was not a pleasant one for the forward companies, and they showed great determination and courage in a very difficult and unpleasant operation, where the resistance was heavier than anticipated. At first light, prisoners started to come in, and about 40 in all were captured. A bunch of 16 were fired on by a spandau, which killed 1 and wounded 3 — a typical German trick. B company commander, with the help of two tanks, soon dealt with this post. At this juncture an unfortunate accident occurred when one of the 75-mm. guns from one of the tanks opened up, the shell striking a tree about one foot from the muzzle, causing it to explode beside Cpl. Laird of B company, who was killed along with another man.

At about midday on the 11th of August A company reported that a counter-attack was developing on their front. This counter-attack was accompanied by very heavy shelling and mortaring. The counter-attack was eventually broken up at about 12.20 p.m. only to be followed shortly afterwards by two other counter-attacks. Each attack was launched with about 200 infantry, but all of them were successfully beaten off with heavy loss to the enemy. One complete platoon led by a German officer surrendered to the 1st Black Watch. The Argylls, who had had a very exhausting day, having had no sleep the previous night and having beaten off three strong counter-attacks, were considerably weakened, and consequently A company of the 5th Black Watch was placed temporarily under their command.

About this time we were informed that the Polish Armoured Division and the 4th Canadian Armoured Division were coming into the area behind our brigade with the intention of sending forward armoured patrols. Elements of the Polish Armoured Division were to pass through the brigade positions at 8 o'clock in the morning of the 12th of August. The Polish patrols reached the village of Bu-sur-Rouvres, and there they found one company of German infantry ready to surrender. However, as the Poles were about to return, the Germans launched a counter-attack with infantry and about 16 tanks. This attack, which came from the south-west, caused the loss of four tanks to the Poles and compelled the remainder to withdraw. As a result of the Polish withdrawal, the 7th Argylls and the 1st Black Watch were subjected to a considerable amount of shelling and mortaring, which caused quite an increase in the number of casualties which had so far been sustained.

Active patrolling was now carried out, and a patrol from the Argylls reported that the ridge just to the north of their position was definitely occupied by the enemy. On the afternoon of the 12th of August the Poles were withdrawn from the area, and the 10th Canadian Armoured Car Regiment took over their role and became very aggressive. The 2nd Derby Yeomanry then arrived to thicken up the defence, and to capture the high ground previously reported by the Argylls to be occupied by the enemy. Although the 2nd Derby Yeomanry made a gallant effort, they failed to capture the ridge. As Canadian troops were patrolling in all directions the Derby Yeomanry could not be safely supported with artillery.

During the night of the 12th of August the 7th Argylls were relieved by the 7th Black Watch, and the battalion went back to Crasmesnil to take in reinforcements and to refit. Casualties had been fairly heavy. 8 officers were wounded, 18 other ranks were killed and 71 wounded. The wounded officers were Capt. Bob Porteous, Lieuts. Wylie, Chapman, Archibald, Cowling, Austin, White, and Twinbarrow, the last two having only joined the battalion the day before.

On the night of the 14th of August the brigade area was subjected to continuous and considerable shelling. The brigade were now ordered to launch an attack against the enemy in the area of Bu-sur-Rouvres, and the 5th Black Watch, who were still under the command of our brigade, were given this task. At the start they were interrupted by heavy mortaring and shelling, but by 12.50 p.m., after fifty minutes of skirmishing, they reached their first objective. After some heavy fighting the position was captured, along with 60 prisoners, by 2 o'clock that afternoon. During this period the 7th Argylls remained in Crasmesnil, where the only exciting incident occurred on the 14th of August when, during a heavy air bombardment by the R.A.F., some Lancasters dropped their loads on the forward edge of Crasmesnil by mistake. Fortunately no bombs dropped closer to the Argylls than 200 yards, but it was most unpleasant, particularly as this form of unnecessary torture went on for three and a half hours. At about 10 o'clock in the morning of the 15th of August the 1st Black Watch were ordered forward to take over the positions of the 5th Seaforth Highlanders, and consequently the Argylls were ordered forward once more to the woods of St. Sylvain to take over the 1st Black Watch positions. The battalion remained in this position until the 16th of August, when the advance to the River Dives and beyond began.

CHAPTER XI

BEYOND THE DIVES

OUR brigade was now ordered to advance on the axis Maizieres –Ernes–Donville–St. Pierre-sur-Dives, our objective being St. Julien le Faucon. For this advance the 33rd Armoured Brigade were in support of us. The order of march was the 7th Black Watch, followed by the 7th Argylls and the 1st Black Watch. St. Pierre-sur-Dives was reported clear by about 2 o'clock in the afternoon of the 16th of August, and the advance continued into what was by now thickly wooded country. At first the advance went quickly, but strong enemy opposition was met on the high ground on the other side of the River Dives. This opposition consisted mostly of mortaring and machine-gun fire, and it was no easy task for the infantry to winkle out the enemy positions in such country. Mortar bombs kept bursting in the trees during the advance, causing a number of casualties which usually proved fatal on account of head injuries. The 7th Black Watch, who were to capture the high ground at Le Godet, found themselves minus their supporting tanks by about 6 o'clock in the evening, owing to a traffic jam on the bridge over the river. Nevertheless, they continued to advance, and captured their first objective by 6.45 that evening. By this time a squadron of the tanks had got across the river and rejoined the 7th Black Watch. Considerable opposition from enemy anti-tank guns and snipers was encountered, but this opposition was successfully dealt with.

The 7th Argylls were by now moving up on the right, but so far had met with little opposition. During all this time the bridge over the River Dives at St. Pierre-sur-Dives was being subjected to extremely accurate and heavy enemy shelling, and the transport across the bridge had to be carefully regulated. The 7th Black Watch were having a hard fight, having met considerable opposition most of the way, but by midday on the 17th of August their final objective was captured. The Argylls, who had remained on the east side of the Dives on the night of the 16th of August, were now ordered to pass through the 7th Black Watch to their objective at the crossroads about one mile short of St. Julien le Faucon. The battalion was deployed as follows: vanguard consisting of B company under Major Jim Milne, one squadron of tanks, two detachments of pioneers, two detachments of the mortar platoon, two sections of the carrier platoon, and an artillery F.O.O. This vanguard was under the command of Major A. MacKinnon, the second-in-command of the battalion. After the vanguard there was a gap of 500 yards, and then came the commanding officer with his order group, the remaining rifle companies, and the support company.

The advance started at 1 o'clock in the afternoon, and very soon the battalion came under intense mortar fire. Major Jim Milne and C.S.M. Archibald were wounded by the same shell before the battalion reached the start-line. As the country was thickly wooded the mortar bombs continually burst in the trees, and the infantry advancing along the roads had a very unpleasant time. Some of the infantry who were riding on the tanks had a particularly nasty time of it. On reaching the start-line B company sent off a platoon on either side of the road with a troop of tanks working behind each. Very soon German infantry were encountered, and a number of prisoners, a good number of them wounded, began to trickle in. The advance was slow, and the road soon came under observation from high ground above St. Julien.

About four enemy guns then opened up a very accurate and sustained fire on the column of vehicles. Lt.-Col. I. C. Meiklejohn, D.S.O., was wounded in both legs, and his bodyguard, McHarg, was killed. Major J. L. Robertson, company commander of D company, and Major J. R. Sloan, A company commander, were both wounded in the arm, all within a few minutes of one another. In addition, a number of other ranks were killed and wounded. The vanguard kept going slowly and reached a small burn running at right angles to the road where the bridge was blown. This caused considerable delay as the tanks had to make a detour, and nearly an hour elapsed before the tanks got across. In the meantime the area of the bridge was shelled by two 88-mm. guns at a range of about 200 yards. A self-propelled gun kept up a regular bombardment of the bridge area, as well as numerous mortars. When the advance to the final objective, which was the crossroads one mile short of St. Julien, began, D company on the right got held up, and two of the supporting tanks were knocked out by 88-mm. guns. Capt. R. Muir Morton, who took over command of D company when Jim Robertson got wounded, now got wounded, leaving only Lieuts. Ian Buchanan and Peter Hands. On the left, B company got on fairly well, although Lieuts. Leslie and Hope, the acting company commander, were wounded. Hope later died of wounds at the casualty clearing station. After B company were reinforced by A company they soon got moving again. The Germans on the right had had a good deal of punishment, and at this stage they started to withdraw, but not before a private from D company had knocked out one of their 88-mm. guns with a direct hit from his Piat. At last light the objective was gained, and the companies immediately consolidated. The enemy fire had slackened off considerably, and although the battalion suffered heavy casualties, the Germans suffered a great deal more. It was a long and exhausting day, in which the battalion lost 2 officers killed and 7 officers wounded. In addition 18 other ranks were killed, and about 50 other ranks wounded. The officers killed were Hope, the second-in-command of B company, and Ian Balleny, the mortar platoon officer. The 7 officers wounded were the C.O., Major Milne of B company, Major Sloan of A company, Major Robertson of D company, Captain Muir Morton, second-in-command of D company, Lieut. Leslie of B company, and Lieut. Shillingham of D company.

At about 7 o'clock in the morning of the 18th of August the 1st Black Watch were on their way forward, their task being to pass through the battalion and capture St. Julien. Fortunately, the 1st Black Watch were only required to advance on to their objective without meeting any opposition, as the enemy had by this time withdrawn. After reaching their objective, however, a certain amount of mopping-up had to be carried out, and small parties of enemy began to give themselves up. On the evening of the 19th of August, much to our annoyance, we were again bombed and machine gunned by our own aircraft. Later the same night the area was heavily bombed by the Germans, and we suffered 6 other ranks killed and 6 wounded. Again on the 20th of August Typhoons shot up our positions, and we all began frantically setting a light to yellow smoke candles in an effort to show the aircraft that we were British troops. In addition all our vehicles displayed yellow celanese triangles in an effort to appease the R.A.F. Several rude remarks were passed about the air force, and indeed it was unpleasant enough to have to stand up to the German bombing, but when our own Typhoons got on to us it was not only unpleasant but also most annoying. However, the Allies were advancing at such a rate that it is understandable that pilots were probably having their orders changed every minute of the day. In addition the country was thickly wooded, and several rivers stood out prominently from the air, thus making mistakes excusable.

The Advance to Lisieux

On the 21st of August the 7th Black Watch moved forward to take over the positions of the 5th Battalion Seaforth Highlanders, who were advancing round the right flank. The object of our brigade now was to capture the high ground north-west of Lisieux. Consequently the 7th Black Watch set off on the morning of the 22nd of August to capture the crossroads area of La Corne, which they reached at 9.30 in the morning after overcoming minor opposition. After a day of small clashes with the enemy here and there, the 7th Black Watch captured their final objective at La Bosquetture at about 6 o'clock in the evening. Spandau fire and mortaring of the 7th Black Watch had made the day a very exhausting one for them, but although they had a hard fight for it, they only sustained 5 killed and 21 wounded. About 40 German prisoners were captured, and it was estimated that approximately the same number had been killed. At 10 o'clock that night it was the turn of the 1st Black Watch to advance, which they did along the Lisieux road without meeting enemy opposition. The 1st Black Watch reached their final objective at 11 o'clock in the morning of the 23rd of August without so much as firing a shot. In the meantime the 7th Black Watch sent a patrol to Le Boissiere, which they found clear of enemy. Three days' rest was then ordered, and the usual bathing and general cleaning up occupied most of our time.

On the 25th of August the brigade group moved to a concentration at Marolles, east of Lisieux. Things began to move faster now, and the brigade, which was at one hour's notice to move, crossed the River Risle on the morning of the 27th of August, the order of march being the 1st Black Watch, 7th Black Watch, and 7th Argylls. The brigade intention was to get to Touville. The 1st Black Watch captured their objective about midday, after which the 7th Black Watch passed through them and captured Flancourt at about 2 o'clock the same afternoon, and the 7th Argylls moved up to an assembly area at La Cautellerie. Reports were received that the Germans were holding the general line of the woods in this area, but an attack launched by the 7th Argylls met no opposition whatever. We had therefore covered a considerable distance in the advance across the River Risle, and although no opposition was met during this phase, the brigade contributed to a large extent in squeezing out the last pocket of German resistance west of the River Seine.

The layout of the brigade was now a little crowded with the 1st Black Watch in Le Maupas, the 7th Black Watch in Le Bau Pin, and the 7th Argylls in Bouquetot.

On the 30th of August the 7th Black Watch were placed under the command of the 153rd Brigade, and at 8 o'clock in the morning moved forward to the area of Herville-sur-Seine with the task of mopping-up in the area of the 153rd Brigade's operations. Brigade headquarters and the 7th Argylls then moved forward to Yville-sur-Seine, and the 1st Black Watch remained at Le Maupas. The 7th Black Watch then reverted to brigade command and sent patrols across the Seine at the Duclair ferry. These patrols reported Duclair clear of enemy, and brought in 14 enemy prisoners who had been handed over to them by the Maquis.

On the morning of the 31st of August the 7th Black Watch sent a skeleton battalion across the River Seine to form a small bridgehead until the 4th S.S. Brigade arrived to take over from our brigade. At midday the 4th S.S. Brigade began to arrive, and the take over from the 7th Black Watch commenced.

It is interesting to note that in the brigade area there were hundreds of enemy vehicles of all types, most of which were destroyed by our bombers and also by our guns. Many of them had been abandoned, however, probably through lack of petrol. A large number of guns and six-barrelled mortars were also littered all over the countryside. Altogether the Germans took a tremendous lot of punishment in the valley of the Seine, both from our bombers and artillery.

About this time Field-Marshal Montgomery issued the usual personal message to be read to all troops, in which he said :

" On the 11th of August I spoke to the officers and men of the Allied armies in North-west France. I said we must ' write off' the powerful German force that was causing us so much trouble ; we must finish it once and for all, and so hasten the end of the war.

" And to-day, ten days later, it has been done.

" The German armies in North-west France have suffered a decisive defeat ; the destruction of enemy personnel and equipment in and about the so-called ' Normandy Pocket' has been terrific, and it is still going on ; any enemy units that manage to get away will not be in a fit condition to fight again for months ; there are still many surprises in store for the fleeing remnants.

" The victory has been definite, complete, and decisive.

" As soldiers, we all want to pay our tribute to the Allied Air Forces. I doubt if ever in the history of war air forces have had such opportunities, or have taken such good advantage of them. The brave and brilliant work of the pilots has aroused our greatest admiration ; without their support we soldiers could have achieved no success. Where all have done so well, it is difficult to single out any for special praise.

" As a British general I can speak for all the soldiers of the Empire, and can express our high admiration for the

Plate 12 (*Above*) Troops of the Highland Division crossing the Seine at Elbeuf. (*Below*) Greetings from the citizens of Rouen as the Highland Division pass through the town *en route* for St. Valery

brave fighting qualities of the American armies in the opening stages of the ' break in ' battle on the 25th July and following days ; and we followed with tremendous enthusiasm their great achievements during the wheel of the right flanks almost to the gates of Paris. We never want to fight alongside better soldiers.

"As an Allied commander, and the overall commander of all the land forces under General Eisenhower, I can praise the fighting qualities and tenacity in battle of the British, Canadian, and Polish troops on the eastern flank ; they fought the enemy relentlessly, and took heavy toll of him during the whole of this great battle.

"But surely it matters little who did this or that. All that matters is that it was well and truly done by the whole Allied team. The proper motto for Allies should be :

' One for all, and all for one.'

And that is our motto.

"I want to thank you all for the way you responded to the call. The victory in North-west France, south of the Seine, marks the beginning of the end of German military domination of France.

" Much still remains to be done, but it will now be done the more easily.

" And what next ?

" Having brought disaster to the German forces in Northwest France, we must now complete the destruction of such of his forces as are still available to be destroyed. After knowing what has happened to their armies in North-west France, it is unlikely that these forces will now come to us ; so we will go to them.

" The Lord, mighty in battle, has given us the victory. The news is very good from the war fronts all over the world. Let us finish off the business in record time."

Again the 7th Argylls were without a commanding officer, as Lt.-Col. John Meiklejohn, D.S.O., was wounded and evacuated. Command of the battalion was now given to Lt.-Col. Donald Nicoll, The Black Watch, who came from the 49th Division. It was unfortunate at this stage that the C.O. and company commanders were knocked out, but other reinforcements arrived to make up the numbers.

CHAPTER XII

ACROSS THE SEINE

WE had now cleared up to the River Seine and had a small bridgehead across it at Duclair, held by the 4th S.S. Brigade. We still had to cross the Seine in force, and on the afternoon of the 1st of September we were ordered to a brigade concentration area on the east side of the Seine south of Barentin. Our route was through Elbeuf, across the Seine, and along the east bank of the Seine through Rouen. The welcome we received from the French people was simply tremendous. The streets were lined from end to end with happy and enthusiastic people. In fact it was difficult to motor one's way through the crowds. Flowers were strewn in our path and our vehicles were eventually decorated with flags and flowers by French people, young and old, who left no doubt in our minds as to our welcome in Rouen. The usual cries of " Cigarette pour Papa " and " Chocolat " greeted us wherever we went. Rouen itself was badly damaged in the industrial area of the city from bombing, but it was the first large town we had seen since D-day, and to us everything seemed at a glance to be quite normal. The journey was a most interesting one and looking down into the valley of the Seine was really a beautiful sight. The surrounding country was generally flat, and dotted here and there with woods. If the Germans had decided to fight in the wooded areas of the Risle and Seine valleys it would have caused us a lot of trouble, but fortunately he beat a hasty retreat, leaving garrisons at all the main ports such as Le Havre, Boulogne, Calais, and Dunkirk.

The 51st re-enters St. Valery

The concentration area south of Barentin was never used as our brigade was directed on Cany Barville, a few miles south-west of St. Valery, so on the morning of the 2nd of September we set off. As our axis through Yvetot had not been previously checked for mines, it was decided to send the 1st Black Watch ahead as advance guard. Here again every village through which the column passed was lined with cheering crowds. On arrival in the Cany Barville area, brigade headquarters was set up in Sasseville Château, and the layout of the battalions consisted of the 1st Black Watch and 7th Argylls across the River Durdent and the 7th Black Watch east of Cany Barville. Owing to the amount of traffic on the roads, the 7th Black Watch and 7th Argylls harboured for the night north of Rouen, and came on again on the morning of the 3rd of September. It is interesting to note that the Divisional Commander laid out the Division in exactly the same locations as were occupied in 1940 before the surrender. Divisional Headquarters was established in the Château Cailleville, where the Divisional Commander of 1940 and his staff were compelled to surrender to a large German force. The " Jocks " had come back, however, after over four years, and St. Valery was ours again without a fight. On the 12th of December, St. Valery celebrated its freedom with a day of ceremonies. The massed pipes and drums and personnel of the Division were present. Later a service was held at the cemetery, and wreaths were laid on the graves of the men of the Division who fell in 1940.

The Attack on Le Havre

After a short stay in St. Valery orders were received for the Division to be directed on Le Havre, and our brigade

Plate 13 Sounding the Last Post at the service in the cemetery at St. Valery in memory of the men of the Highland Division who fell in 1940

was ordered to concentrate in the area of Criquetot, a few miles east of the town. On the 4th of September, therefore, we set off for our concentration area, and on arrival the battalions were located on either side of the road leading from Criquetot to St. Martin du Bec. The following day the 1st Black Watch were moved to St. Barthelemy, and the 7th Argylls to Marfauville, as until now our area had been overcrowded. On the 5th and 6th of September the R.A.F. pounded away at Le Havre with heavy bombers, but the weather was most unfavourable, and on several occasions the bombers had to return to England without dropping their loads. On the 7th of September the weather broke down completely, and the bombing programme had to be cancelled. On the evening of the 7th of September the plan for the attack on Le Havre was announced. The 51st Highland Division were to break through the enemy defences north of Le Havre and capture the port. The 49th Division were to attack on the left. The 51st Divisional plan was divided into three phases. The first phase, which was to commence at midnight on the 10th of September, gave the 152nd Brigade the task of securing lodgement areas and clearing three routes through the minefields and across an anti-tank ditch. In the second phase the 153rd Brigade were to neutralize the enemy gun areas, clear the divisional axis as far forward as possible, and exploit south-westwards towards the enemy command area on the high ground in the north-east part of the town. Our brigade had the third and last phase, which was to be prepared to exploit and support the other two brigades as required. For this phase the following plan was to be carried out. The 7th Black Watch, along with C Squadron of the 1st Northamptonshire Yeomanry, were organized into a mobile exploitation force, and A Squadron, 1st Northamptonshire Yeomanry, and two composite squadrons of the 2nd Derby Yeomanry were made the mopping-up force and this was called "Grayforce" after its commander. Although the 1st Black Watch and the 7th Argylls had no immediate role, their task was probably to help one of the other brigades. The 1st Black Watch were made readily available for a mobile role along with B Squadron of the 1st Northamptonshire Yeomanry, and the 7th Argylls were to be kept in reserve for a more deliberate attack. The 7th Black Watch were then ordered to move forward to an assembly area at St. Martin du Bec, and the 7th Argylls moved to an area east of St. Barthelemy. The Argylls' area was fairly quiet, and although the battalion carried out a diversionary programme, there was little retaliation. A certain amount of shelling of the area took place, however, during which Lieut. Ian Buchanan was seriously wounded. In order to distract enemy attention from the main attack, the following deceptive plan was carried out. The 1st Black Watch on the day before the attack started laid a picqueted start-line. The 61st Anti-tank Regiment sited guns in the area of St. Sulpice and astride the coast road north of Ecqueville, and in addition were to open fire on Octeville, thus making the enemy think that the attack was coming in along the coast. The 7th Argylls were to provide infantry protection for these gun areas, and were also to fire mortar bombs and lay smoke concentrations on the enemy defences in this area, and the 1st Black Watch were to fire mortar smoke on Doudeville. The attack was to be preceded by a colossal air bombardment, and promptly at 4.15 in the afternoon the first of the heavy bombers arrived and dropped their loads on the enemy defences to the north of the town. The bombing lasted until 7 o'clock in the evening, and was extremely accurate, as was later seen when the attack was over. Approximately 5,000 tons of bombs were dropped in the Le Havre area, and the devastation was simply appalling.

The attack went well at first, and the only real difficulty

was that the ground was very sodden with the heavy rainfall of some days before. An elaborate system of minefields had to be crossed, which kept the sappers very busy. Considering the large number of enemy troops in the Le Havre area, approximately 10,000, the enemy resistance was very half-hearted. This low morale was probably due to the terrrific pounding which the enemy had suffered at the hands of the R.A.F. Prisoners soon began to come rolling in. The 7th Black Watch during their attack met only minor opposition from mortaring and spandau fire. On the evening of the 11th of September the 7th Black Watch reached their objective with the loss to them of only 6 killed and 14 wounded. The morning of the 12th of September was spent mostly in mopping-up the area, and large numbers of enemy surrendered at intervals after only a short fight. The total bag of prisoners captured by the 7th Black Watch was approximately 700, and " Grayforce," who were also mopping-up, captured another 200, and so Le Havre fell in less than 36 hours and a German force of 10,000 was liquidated. The total casualties for the Division was approximately 100, and the number of prisoners captured was in the region of 4,900, including 120 officers. The battalion took no part in the actual attack, apart from their diversionary programme. When we entered the town, however, we joined in the search for German equipment, of which there was plenty lying littered about all over the town.

A large amount of equipment and stores of all kinds were captured in Le Havre, and the Germans certainly did not lack food while they occupied the town. We were left in the Le Havre area for approximately ten days, each battalion garrisoning the town in turn, and brigade headquarters was established in Montivilliers, a suburb of Le Havre. The usual cleaning up took place and mobile baths were organized. Le Havre itself was in many places completely devastated by the terrific bombing it had received, and during the time we were there, the civilians could be seen digging in the ruins and debris of their homes, and it is regretted that the civilian death-rate in the town was very high.

A war memorial service was held in the town on the 21st of September at which our pipers and buglers played " The Last Post." Later in the day a Retreat programme by the massed pipes and drums of the brigade was played in the Boulevard de Strasbourg, at which many enthusiastic French people showed their appreciation of the pipes.

Containing Dunkirk

On the 25th of September we left the Le Havre area for a new location in the Dunkirk area. Our route to Dunkirk was through flat country with woods and copses interspersed with pastureland. We crossed the Somme at Abbeville and camped the first night in the area Neuilly and Drucat, north of Abbeville. The next day we moved off again for Dunkirk via St. Omer.

Our task at Dunkirk was not to attack it as we had done at Le Havre, but to contain it with one brigade group until such time as we were relieved, when we were to rejoin the Division, who were by this time on their way through Belgium. The 7th Argylls held a part of the line encircling Dunkirk at Bray Dunes Plage, the 7th Black Watch were at Ghyvelde, and the 1st Black Watch at Loon Plage. In addition to this the three carrier platoons of the three battalions were organized into one force called " Campbell " Force, and were disposed from Bergues to Spycker.

On the early morning of the 27th of September the 7th Black Watch were attacked by a strong German fighting patrol, which demolished a windmill and set fire to their village. Later an enterprising German patrol succeeded in getting into our battalion H.Q. and in the skirmish that took place the Adjutant-Capt. Douglas Williamson was wounded and two other ranks were killed. The Germans left two of their dead behind. But for this incident, the period was fairly uneventful except for spasmodic shelling. Rest periods were arranged for a limited number of men from the rifle companies, who spent 24 hours in the pleasant little town of La Panne, only three miles from the battalion's positions and just over the Belgian frontier. During this period a noteworthy incident occurred in Campbell Force when L/Cpl. Sykes of the carrier platoon and his section were attacked by a strong patrol. The L/Cpl. managed to kill the German patrol leader, who happened to be their crack patrol leader and a holder of the " Ritter Cross." A German officer during the subsequent truce asked if he could speak to the man who had done this. On being asked why, he said he only wanted to thank him for getting him promotion.

The country surrounding Dunkirk had been flooded by the Germans, and even if an attack on the town had been intended, it would probably have been necessary to launch an amphibious operation. Campbell Force had little trouble in their area, but continual observation and patrolling had a very tiring effect on the troops.

Towards the end of September a request was received from the French Red Cross in Dunkirk regarding the evacuation of the civilian population from the town. This request was passed on to army on the 1st of October, who intimated their approval. On the 2nd of October a letter was despatched through the French Red Cross to the German commander in Dunkirk. In this letter it was suggested that a truce of 36 hours would be sufficient to complete the evacuation. The German commander was asked to state a meeting-place where terms could be discussed, and also to state the route to be taken by the emissary from our brigade. The German commander's reply was received at 7 o'clock in the morning of the 3rd of October, and our emissaries were sent off. At Gd. Predembourg farm they met the German emissaries, and from there they were escorted blindfold to the German commander's office in the town. The terms of the truce were made known to the German commander, who stated that in order to clear the defences along the road where the evacuation was to take place and to put them in order again after the completion of the evacuation, he would require an extension of 12 hours at either end. This was agreed to, and the truce commenced at 6 o'clock in the evening of the 3rd of October and was to finish at 6 o'clock in the morning on the 6th of October. Our emissary had to visit the German commander a second time with a written guarantee from us and receive one from the German commander that there would be no acts of war or change of military dispositions during the period covered by the truce.

The evacuation was slow to begin with, but by the afternoon of the 4th of October things were speeded up, and about 5,500 evacuees had come through. On the 5th of October the total was increased to 18,500, all of whom came over the bridge at Grande Mille Brugge.

As a result of the bridges over the canal collapsing on the German side, the German commander asked for an extension of the truce, which was granted until 10 o'clock on the morning of the 6th of October. When the truce ended Typhoons and Spitfires shot up enemy positions, and our artillery opened up. There was very little retaliation during the day, and later prisoners reported that the Germans thought we would launch a large-scale attack as soon as the truce ended and they, consequently, wanted to conserve their ammunition. During the night of the 6th of October several German aircraft passed over Dunkirk dropping supplies to the German garrison there. We were amused to hear that some of these supplies, including an anti-tank gun, were dropped on Boulogne, which of course was by now in British hands. On the 8th of October our brigade was relieved by the Czech Brigade, and we then moved in two stages to rejoin the Division in the area of Eindhoven in Holland.

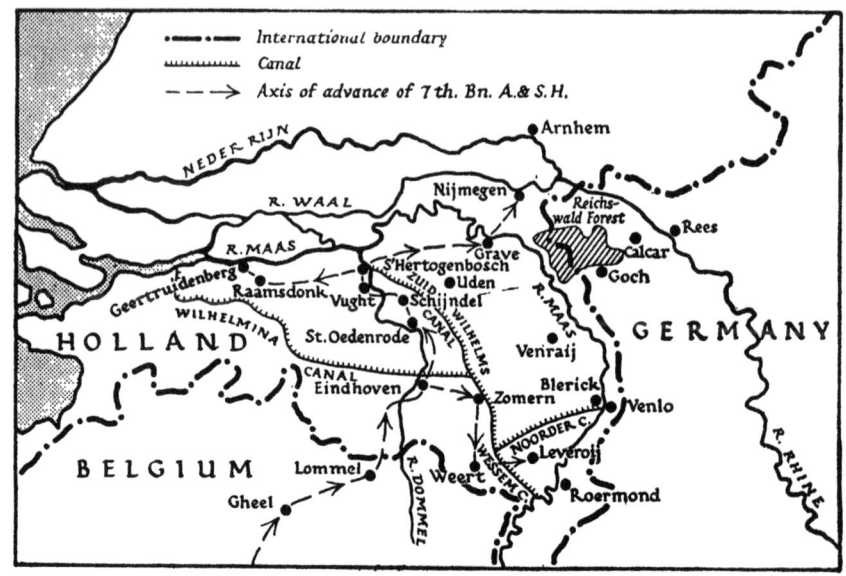

Advance of Battalion through Holland

CHAPTER XIII

THROUGH BELGIUM AND HOLLAND

AT 10 o'clock in the morning of the 9th of October we set off on our long motor move across Belgium into Holland. The journey was a most interesting one, as we passed through many places familiar to us by name from the first World War. Ypres and the Menin Gate, Messines Ridge, Armentières, Courtrai, Oudenarde and Alost near Brussels held a great fascination for us, particularly the Menin Gate. That night we camped at Alost, and some of us spent an hour or two in Brussels sight-seeing. At 8 o'clock in the morning of the 10th of October we continued our journey via Brussels–Mechlin–Heyst-op-den-Berg–Boisschot–Westerloo–Gheel–Lommel–Westerhoven–Steensel–Eindhoven–St. Oedenrode. Actually, *en route*, new orders were issued, and the original intention of going to St. Oedenrode was cancelled. Our new role was to hold the line

Plate 14 Lieut.-Col. A. MacKinnon, D.S.O., M.C.

of the Wilhelmina Canal, and to prevent enemy from crossing the canal and infiltrating south towards the airfield near Oerle. The battalions were disposed to cover the tracks and approaches most likely to be used by the enemy. As the brigade were to cease to carry out this role on the 15th of October, when the line was to be taken over by the Royals and the R.A.F. Regiment, we were ordered not to be unduly aggressive in order that there would be no noticeable change in the method of holding the front. A certain amount of shelling from both sides took place in this area, but nothing very exciting happened apart from this.

On the 17th of October the Royal Netherlands Brigade arrived to take over our positions. The Dutch Brigade consisted of three independent companies, one reconnaissance squadron, one battery of Field Artillery, and a Dutch Brigade Headquarters with a British Liaison Headquarters. After the relief was completed, our battalions moved to concentration areas prior to our move forward on the 19th of October to St. Oedenrode. The 1st Black Watch were already near Divisional Headquarters in the St. Oedenrode area, and the 7th Black Watch were concentrated at Duizel, with the 7th Argylls near them at Westerhoven and brigade headquarters at Eersel.

The intention of our brigade now was to relieve the 158th Brigade of the 53rd Division in the area of the Zuid Wilhelms Canal–Schijndel–St. Oedenrode by 2 o'clock in the afternoon of the 19th of October. We were therefore again on the move early in the morning and followed a route through Steensel–Meerveldhoven–Zeelat–Heuvel–Woensel to Keinsel. On arrival the relief of the 158th Brigade was carried out without incident. The 7th Argylls took over from the 7th R.W.F., the 7th Black Watch took over from the 1st East Lancs., and the 1st Black Watch took over from the 1/5th Welch Regiment. The 5th Seaforth Highlanders at this time came under brigade command. In support were the 1st Northamptonshire Yeomanry, two platoons of the 1/7th Middlesex, the 126th Field Regiment R.A., and the 241st Anti-tank Battery. Patrolling by both sides was very active, but only spasmodic shelling from the enemy took place. On the other hand our artillery did quite a lot of shooting.

At about 6 o'clock in the morning on the 20th of October an enemy patrol twenty strong infiltrated towards the 1st Black Watch positions. After a sharp encounter, however, the patrol withdrew, leaving behind 8 killed, including 1 officer, and 5 prisoners, 4 of which were wounded. The casualties of the 1st Black Watch were 1 killed and 9 wounded. On the night of the 21st of October a V2 landed in the battalion area, causing no damage, but gave us a fright.

The Attack on St. Michels Gestel and Vught

On the 21st of October orders for our next operation were issued. For the operation, our brigade had under command the 2nd Derby Yeomanry (initially), the 241st Anti-tank Battery, the 274th Field Company R.E., with one platoon of the 275th Field Company, B company 1/7th Middlesex, and 60 kangaroos, which were armoured vehicles for the purpose of conveying troops. As usual, in support of us were the 1st Northamptonshire Yeomanry.

The intention of the brigade was :

(1) To clear the woods south of the Zuid Wilhelms Canal.

(2) Secure bridges crossing the River Dommel at St. Michels Gestel and the Halsche Water at Halder, or crossing places and bridgeheads later in the event of the bridges being blown.

(3) The 2nd Derby Yeomanry were to relieve the 7th Argylls in their area on the 22nd of October and the 7th Argylls were then to concentrate in the area east of Eerde.

The attack was divided into three phases. In phase 1 the 7th Argylls, with in support one half squadron of the 1st Northampton Yeomanry, were to clear the woods south of the canal. The 7th Black Watch, with in support one squadron and reconnaissance troop of the Northamptonshire Yeomanry, were to pass through the 152nd and the 153rd Brigades and exploit to St. Michels Gestel to carry out the following tasks—in the second phase:

(1) If the bridge was intact, to secure all approaches both east and west of the River Dommel.

(2) If the bridge was destroyed, but little enemy opposition was encountered *en route*, to secure all approaches east and west of the River Dommel, and secure a bridgehead on the west bank to allow the 1st Black Watch to pass through.

In the third phase the 1st Black Watch, with in support one half squadron of the Northamptonshire Yeomanry, were initially to hold the firm base, and be prepared to carry out the following alternative tasks later:

(1) To relieve the 5/7th Gordon Highlanders in Weibosch.

(2) In the event of the 7th Black Watch being successful in forming the bridgehead, to secure a bridge over the Halsche Water at Halder.

(3) In the event of the 7th Black Watch being unsuccessful, to assault across the River Dommel at St. Michels Gestel and secure a bridgehead to allow bridges to be built.

The 2nd Derby Yeomanry were to hold a firm base and cover the right flank between Zuid Wilhelms Canal and the road Schijndel–St. Michels Gestel, and particularly the approaches from Dungen and Stokhoek.

The 7th Argylls were to be launched at 8 o'clock in the morning of the 23rd of October, followed by the 7th Black Watch, who were not to be launched before 9 o'clock. Lastly came the 1st Black Watch, who were not to be launched before midday. The axis of advance was via Koevering–Heertveld–

Weibosch–Schijndel–Schutsboom, and St. Michels Gestel. In all three phases of the attack considerable artillery support was available. On the afternoon of the 22nd of October Typhoons shot up enemy positions as a preliminary to the softening up by fragmentation bombing which was to come later.

On the morning of the 23rd of October the fragmentation bombing commenced and appeared to be extremely accurate. This was necessary, as the other two brigades of the Division had started their offensive at midnight on the 22nd of October, and any inaccuracy in the bombing might have seriously affected them. The 7th Argylls were launched at the arranged time, but found the going rather difficult on account of mines which held them up considerably. Not until 11.30 a.m. did the 7th Black Watch set off. To begin with they met little opposition, and by 1 o'clock had reached Brookstraat. The tanks in support of the 7th Black Watch encountered some enemy opposition at a road block, but this was soon overcome. About half an hour later the 7th Argylls had overcome the last of the mines, and reached their objective without meeting any strong resistance. The Argylls were then placed under command of the 153rd Brigade, and in their place the 5/7th Gordons came under the command of our brigade. The 7th Black Watch, although not hampered so much by mines as the Argylls were, met more opposition, and were continually running into enemy fire where small pockets of resistance were left behind by the enemy. One such pocket was encountered by the tanks at 2 o'clock in the afternoon, but by 2.45 this was overcome. By 4 p.m. the 7th Black Watch had reached the river line and found the bridge at St. Michels Gestel blown. The task was now to get across the river, and at 6 o'clock in the evening a squadron of the Northamptonshire Yeomanry were ordered to guard the north flank while the 7th Black Watch made a crossing by class 111 raft. A certain amount of enemy shelling was encountered at the river crossing, but this did not deter the Black Watch, who had the class 111 raft completed and two companies across the river by 9.30 p.m. Later class 9 and class 40 bridges were constructed over the River Dommel near the site of the old blown bridge. By 2 o'clock in the morning of the 24th of October the 7th Black Watch were all across the Dommel and meeting only minor opposition on the other side. The 1st Black Watch then began to cross, and they, along with a squadron of tanks, were successfully across by 5 o'clock in the morning.

It was decided to push two thrusts for the crossing of the Halsche Water at Halder, and during the afternoon a class 111 raft was constructed and the 1st Black Watch formed a bridgehead on the other side with two companies. This crossing was subjected to heavy enemy shelling, and on the night of the 24th October a Kapok bridge and class 9 and class 40 bridges were built, and the remainder of the 1st Black Watch crossed. An early morning patrol from the 1st Black Watch bumped into enemy infantry, and it was then estimated that the enemy in this area were fairly strong. As the country beyond the River Dommel at St. Michels Gestel was flooded, it was decided to develop the thrust made by the 1st Black Watch only, and so, at 8.30 a.m. on the morning of the 25th October, the 7th Argylls, with in support one squadron of the 2nd Derby Yeomanry, crossed the bridge and passed through the 1st Black Watch, their objective being the town of Vught. Their axis of advance was along the road running north to Vught.

The order of march was D company under Major Boyle leading. D company was supported by flamethrowers and two troops of the 1st Northampton Yeomanry. After this came the remainder of the battalion. Trouble soon started when a road block was encountered, and three of our tanks were knocked out by an 88-mm. gun. Considerable opposition was then encountered from enemy infantry, and numerous snipers who were hidden in the buildings *en route* gave a lot of trouble. In addition the enemy shelling and mortaring was very heavy. About half-way to Vught, the battalion ran into very strong opposition and a pitched battle ensued. It was later discovered on interrogating prisoners that the enemy were launching an attack at approximately the same time as the one launched by the battalion, and the unusual experience of two attacking parties clashing gave us a few anxious moments. Prisoners were taken on both sides, and the battalion destroyed a German self-propelled gun and an anti-tank gun.

A company were pushed forward to support D company on their left, but did not make much progress. Later B company were committed on the right and managed to advance a little despite heavy spandau and mortar fire. It was an exhausting day for the Argylls, and after having fought for every inch of their advance, it was decided to hold the battalion in their present positions until the morning of the 26th of October, when the 7th Black Watch would pass through. Consequently, the 7th Black Watch were concentrated at Hal in order to be ready to pass through the battalion in the morning. The next morning it was found that a number of the enemy were still in the battalion area, and prisoners came in most of the day. Capt. Billy Thomson, the M.T.O., while making a reconnaissance for a suitable place for his A echelon, about 400 yards from Battalion H.Q., had a very narrow escape when some Germans opened up on his car. His driver was killed at point-blank range, and Billy was slightly wounded in the shoulder. He had no alternative but to take to his heels, and had the mortification of seeing the Boche drive off with his jeep, which he never saw again.

On the morning of the 26th of October at 9 o'clock the 7th Black Watch passed through as arranged, and occupied the town of Vught without much opposition. Here we found a large concentration camp and ample evidence of what used to go on inside, and it appeared that little had been exaggerated by the newspapers. The position in the town was still a little confused, and the 7th Black Watch were subjected to heavy shelling and mortaring from the area of "Fort Isabella," but by 3 o'clock in the afternoon this fort was also overcome. The battle was now over and the brigade expected to have a few days' rest, and our battalion found comfortable billets in the area of a hospital south-east of Vught. On the 28th of October the battalion, along with the 7th Black Watch, were moved to a concentration area west of Helvoirt in order to make room for a brigade of the 53rd Division, whose intention was to make an assault crossing of the Aftwaterings Canal in the area of some blown bridges. At this stage the next phase of the operation was made known to us.

Raamsdonk and Geertruidenburg

Our intention now was to advance westwards through Loon op Zand and endeavour to close the enemy escape routes over the River Maas. Our route was via Udenhout, led by the 1st Black Watch followed by the Argylls and 7th Black Watch. At 9 o'clock in the morning of the 29th of October the 1st Black Watch with a squadron of tanks moved forward to Kuil, near Divisional Headquarters, and were initially camped at Schoorstraat, just to the north. It was not known how strong the enemy were in this sector, and in any case the 1st Black Watch were the only battalion to be committed initially. About midday the 1st Black Watch set off and got on quickly to begin with, until at 4 o'clock in the afternoon an enemy self-propelled gun caused a bit of trouble by knocking out the leading tank, thereby blocking the route. The 7th Black Watch were now ordered to move forward to their concentration area at Schoorstraat, where the Argylls were waiting in readiness for the word to advance, which they got at 5.30 p.m. The 1st Black Watch, who up till now had been meeting pockets of resistance here and there, were by now finding things a bit easier, until two enemy self-propelled guns supported by enemy infantry were observed advancing at about 9 o'clock that night. The 1st Black Watch were therefore ordered to remain in their present position for the night, and the 7th Argylls were brought up to form a firm defence line. The following morning the 1st Black Watch continued their advance, at first against little opposition. When they reached the river line, however, they found the bridge blown and a considerable amount of enemy opposition to the south of the railway which the 1st Black Watch had been ordered to clear. This resistance was overcome by 2 o'clock in the afternoon of the 30th of October, and the 7th Black Watch were then brought forward and were ordered to clear northwards to the line of the river from Niewe Vaart, which was carried out successfully without opposition.

The 7th Argylls were now directed on Geertruidenberg, and at 2 o'clock one company in kangaroos set off followed by the remainder of the battalion. At 3.30 p.m. two of their supporting tanks were knocked out by enemy Bazookas. Here a lot more opposition than was anticipated was encountered, and the Argylls sustained some losses from enemy mortaring, shelling, and spandau machine-gun fire. Our own artillery then opened up in order to soften the enemy defence, but at 7 o'clock that evening the opposition was still very stiff, and the Argylls were ordered to remain where they were for the present and resume their advance in the morning.

In the morning the Argylls continued their advance, and

it was found that the opposition was still very stiff. By a strange coincidence the Argylls were running into an enemy attack for the second time, and the two attacking parties clashed. At about 8 o'clock in the morning the forward companies were being subjected to aimed machine-gun fire from the area of the factory building in the area of Geertruidenburg, and the 3-inch mortars of the battalion were brought into action. Most of the opposition was on the left forward company, where the mortaring and spandau fire were exceedingly heavy. Meanwhile our artillery were firing concentrations to assist the Argylls in their advance, and by midday Raamsdonk was reached, where the Argylls were ordered to remain. Up till now the casualties sustained by them were 23 killed and 56 wounded.

It was now decided to pass the 7th Black Watch through the Argylls. Heavy artillery concentrations opened up at 3.30 p.m., and the 7th Black Watch in kangaroos, supported by a squadron of tanks, began their advance. At about 4.30 p.m. an enemy self-propelled gun was observed to be about to fire on one of our tanks when the leading kangaroo was ordered by Lieut. Ian Donaldson to ram it, which it did successfully. One kangaroo was, however, knocked out by the self-propelled gun before it was finally silenced. This caused a block in the road and the route was changed round the south of the railway. Progress after this was rapid, but at 6.30 p.m. the leading company encountered heavy machine-gun fire at the railway crossing. After a skirmish here the advance was continued, and the final objective was captured at 9 o'clock that evening without further opposition.

The 7th Black Watch had done extraordinarily well in this attack, and its success was in a measure due to the dash and speed with which the operation was carried out. Approximately 200 prisoners were captured, and the casualties of the 7th Black Watch were only 23. This was the end of a long and tiring operation which, starting on the 23rd October, continued without respite for nine days, during which time the brigade advanced a considerable distance against strong resistance. The Argylls had 3 officers killed and 3 wounded. The officers killed were Capt. Edie and Lieuts. Alsop and McLean. Major Boyle and Lieuts. Irwin and Lindsay were wounded.

The Defence of S'Hertogenbosch

The enemy had received a hammering, and as a result was much less aggressive and withdrew all his forces north of the River Maas. Our brigade's intention was now to take over the defence of S'Hertogenbosch from the 153rd Brigade, who were to go into a concentration area preparatory to an assault crossing of the Aftwaterings Canal from the south. Consequently our brigade moved on the 1st of November to a concentration area at Helvoirt and Vught prior to taking over the S'Hertogenbosch defences. The following day the brigade moved into the town and established headquarters in the governor's palace. The battalions were responsible for the defence of the town from the west, and were disposed along the western perimeter in order from north to south, 7th Argylls, 1st Black Watch, and 7th Black Watch. A certain amount of patrolling was carried out during the time we were in the S'Hertogenbosch area, but little enemy activity was encountered.

On the 3rd of November the Divisional plan for the next operation was divulged. The 51st Division, with the 152nd Brigade on the right and the 153rd Brigade on the left and our brigade in reserve, were to clear the area between the Aftwaterings Canal and the River Maas by making assault crossings over the canal from the south. The following armoured force under the command of the 33rd Armoured Brigade were to pass through the 7th Black Watch and move along the north bank of the canal after 8.30 p.m. on the 4th of November. This force, which consisted of one squadron of the 144th R.A.C., one assault bridge troop A.V.R.E., and one assault troop of the 2nd Derby Yeomanry, were to concentrate in our brigade area during the morning of the 4th of November.

So far as the 154th Brigade were concerned, a diversionary operation on the flanks was to be carried out along with the 7th Armoured Division. In the event of our brigade being required for operations elsewhere, the 2nd Derby Yeomanry were to take over the defence of S'Hertogenbosch. Under our brigade's command for this diversionary operation we had the 193rd Anti-tank Battery, B company 1/7th Middlesex, and in support of us we had the 126th Field Regiment R.A. and the 72nd Medium Regiment. The object of these diversionary operations was to distract the enemy's attention from the real operation and to cover the movement of our tanks. The 193rd Anti-tank Battery and the mortar platoon of the 1st Black Watch were to fire concentrations on certain bridges. One company of the 7th Black Watch were ordered to attack the area of a road junction west of the canal by 7 o'clock in the evening of the 4th of November, and thereafter clear any enemy that might be lurking along the canal bank. This raid was to be supported by B company 1/7th Middlesex and the mortars of the battalion. The mortar platoon of the 7th Argylls was to move to the area Cromvoirt and support the 153rd Brigade with smoke.

At 4.30 p.m. on the 4th of November the attack by the 152nd Brigade commenced, to be followed at 5.10 p.m. by the attack of the 153rd Brigade. Little opposition was encountered, and the two brigades got quickly across the canal and were established on their first objectives by 6.15 in the evening. At 7 o'clock in the evening the raiding company of the 7th Black Watch completed their task without meeting any opposition. About one hour later the armoured force under the command of the 33rd Armoured Brigade began to move forward through the 7th Black Watch, and things were going entirely according to plan. During the night two class 9 and two class 40 bridges were constructed, and it appeared that the enemy had little heart for fighting, as only occasional shelling of our area took place.

The 7th Argylls reported that numerous white flags were observed in the village of Engelen, and B company were promptly sent out to investigate and found only two enemy there, the remainder having withdrawn during the night. On the night of the 5th of November the Argylls were ordered to send a patrol to ascertain whether the village of Empel was still in enemy hands. Artillery concentrations were laid on to assist the patrol, the intention being that if enemy were still there they would probably be frightened away by our artillery. It was discovered, however, that the enemy was much stronger in the area than was anticipated, and after sustaining some casualties the patrol withdrew. As a result of this it was decided that the Argylls were to attack the area on the night of the 6th of November.

The usual artillery concentrations preceded this attack, and by midnight Empel was ours without much opposition. The enemy, probably anticipating our attack, withdrew altogether from the area. Approximately ten prisoners were captured, all of whom were of a very poor type.

Lieut.-Col. A. MacKinnon was now commanding the battalion, as Lieut.-Col. Nicoll had left to take up a staff appointment. Lieut.-Col. MacKinnon was previously the second in command of the battalion. He had seen service in the Middle East, where he won the M.C. Later he distinguished himself while in command of our battalion and was awarded the D.S.O.

CHAPTER XIV

THE BATTLES OF THE CANALS

The Crossing of the Noorder and Wessem Canals

ON the 9th of November we were again on the move. We had now been ordered to relieve the 152nd Brigade, who were holding the line south-east of Zomeren. For the next few nights active patrolling along the line of the Noorder Canal was carried out. A certain amount of enemy patrolling also took place, and on one occasion an enemy patrol infiltrated through the 1st Black Watch lines to where a platoon of the Middlesex machine-gunners was located. The Middlesex sentries were captured, along with three Seaforth Highlanders. As the enemy patrol were making their way back to the canal, B company of the 1st Black Watch challenged them and fired. The enemy patrol cleared off, leaving the Middlesex sentries and Seaforths free men again. Enemy spandau fire occasionally spattered away at our troops, and our old friend " the Moaning Minnie " made its unwelcome reappearance. On the 12th of November we were told about our next operation, which was to form a bridgehead over the Noorder and Wessem Canals, after which we were to thrust forward on the axis Maxelt–Heijthuizen. The detailed plan for the Division was divided into four phases. In phase 1 the 152nd Brigade were to cross the Noorder Canal and establish a bridgehead, while the 153rd Brigade crossed the Wessem Canal. In phase 2 the 154th Brigade were to establish crossings in the area of the lock gates at the junction of the canals. In phase 3 the 154th Brigade were to pass through the 153rd Brigade, who were to carry on mopping-up, and the 152nd Brigade were to exploit to the south-east. In phase 4 the probable final task of the 154th Brigade would be to capture Heijthuizen and Roggel, depending on how successful the previous operations were.

The intention, therefore, of the 154th Brigade was divided into three tasks. One was to hold the firm base north of the Noorder Canal. Secondly, an assault crossing for tanks at the lock gates was to be made. Lastly, the brigade was to exploit to Leveroij. Certain preliminary moves were to take place on the night of the 13th of November. The 7th Black Watch were to relieve A company of the 7th Argylls. One platoon of B company 1/7th Middlesex was to move from the 7th Black Watch area to the 1st Black Watch area. The 241st Anti-tank Battery was to relieve the anti-tank guns of the 1st Black Watch, and a composite squadron of the 2nd Derby Yeomanry was to relieve the forward platoons of the 1st Black Watch. The 7th Argylls were to give close support to the A.V.R.E. bridge team, and were also to clear the island in the vicinity of the lock gates. In addition they were also to clear a tow-path for the tanks, and afterwards capture and hold Hulsen and endeavour to make contact with a standing patrol of the 5/7th Gordons. For the task of clearing the island the Argylls were allotted stormboats.

The 1st Black Watch, with under command one troop of kangaroos and one detachment of the 274th Field Company Royal Engineers, were to clear the main axis from the limit reached by the 153rd Brigade and exploit south to the railway station in an attempt to link up with a battalion of the 53rd Division. If resistance was not severe, the 1st Black Watch was to exploit to Leveroij, and were put at one hour's notice to move from midnight on the 14th of November.

At 4 o'clock in the afternoon on the 14th of November the attack by the other two brigades started. By 5 o'clock one platoon of the Argylls was across the canal at the lock gates, and the platoon which was to land on the island was progressing well. Not much active opposition was encountered, but an enormous number of schumines caused a number of casualties among the Argylls. Some of these mines were so camouflaged that they appeared similar to the numerous bricks which were lying about. By 7 o'clock in the evening the operation generally was going extremely well, and both the 152nd and 153rd brigades had established bridgeheads across the canals. The bridging was done very quickly and satisfactorily, although the sapper officer and his sergeant were both casualties. Hulsen was quickly mopped up by the Argylls after only slight resistance. Major Joe Corcoran led with D company. About 12 casualties were sustained from the schumines, and it is interesting to note that this was the first time these mines were encountered. Invariably these mines have the effect of blowing off one's foot or seriously damaging the legs.

The advance of the 1st Black Watch in kangaroos was delayed, as the bridge was not ready for crossing until the morning of the 15th of November. When the 1st Black Watch advance in kangaroos got going it was quite unopposed, and they very quickly advanced to Leveroij. Here the road was blocked by fallen masonry.

The 7th Black Watch were then passed through the 1st Black Watch, supported by a squadron of tanks. By 3 o'clock in the afternoon they had advanced a considerable distance, when they met their first resistance from the enemy. A considerable volume of machine-gun fire was being directed on the 7th Black Watch and a self-propelled gun was causing the tanks some annoyance. This self-propelled gun was quickly silenced by our artillery, however. A company of the 7th Black Watch were ordered to debus from their kangaroos in order to deal with a batch of enemy who were dug-in around a road block, and from which a lot of the small-arms fire was coming. A certain delay was therefore caused, but by 5.45 p.m. the 7th Black Watch had moved on again and had reached the crossroads beyond Heijthuizen, where the area was considerably mined. One company was then ordered to get round the village and take up position on the eastern side.

On the 16th of November the plan was for the 153rd Brigade to pass through our brigade and occupy Roggel, and afterwards push outwards towards the Uitwaterings Canal and the River Maas. During the advance of the 153rd Brigade beyond Roggel, the 7th Black Watch sent one company to clear the area of the wood at Kinkhoven, thereby guarding the right flank of the 153rd Brigade, and by 2.45 p.m. the company of the 7th Black Watch had reached the line of the River Maas without opposition, and consequently the 7th Argylls were ordered up to Roggel to take over the role of protecting the right flank of the 153rd Brigade. A number of prisoners captured by the 7th Black Watch gave us some very valuable information. For instance, prisoners from the 741st Anti-tank Unit of the "Regiment Hermann," stated that they were in reserve and that their task was to delay us as much as possible before withdrawing over the Maas. This delaying action was carried out by mines rather than by actual opposition on the ground.

By this time the 152nd Brigade had established a bridgehead over the Uitwaterings Canal, and the intention of the 153rd Brigade was to do the same, but owing to bad weather and difficulties in bridging this was postponed until the 17th of November. On the afternoon of the 17th of November it was thought that the village of Neer had been reoccupied by the enemy, and the 7th Black Watch sent forward a company to recapture the place. They encountered a certain amount of small-arms fire and shelling, but nevertheless the advance continued, and Neer was captured by 7 o'clock in the evening. Meanwhile the 153rd Brigade had successfully established their bridgehead over the Uitwaterings Canal, but the approaches to the bridgehead were so bad that it was decided to push the 154th Brigade through the crossing formed by the 152nd Brigade.

The Attack across the Uitwaterings Canal

The 1st Black Watch were ordered to be ready to move at 9 o'clock in the morning of the 18th of November, but owing to the 152nd Brigade still using their axis it was found impossible to move before 1 o'clock in the afternoon. The plan was for the 1st Black Watch to pass through in kangaroos and occupy the area of Helden, followed by the 7th Argylls on foot who were to occupy Panningen.

The advance by the 1st Black Watch went well, and no opposition was encountered until just short of Helden. Here some enemy infantry were encountered, but by 5 o'clock this was overcome and some forty prisoners, all of whom were identified as from the 21st Para Regiment, were taken. The 7th Argylls, who were advancing on foot, arrived on their objective in Panningen at 6 o'clock without interference of any kind. Both battalions then consolidated their positions and dug-in for the night. During the night considerable enemy shelling and mortaring of the Argylls and 1st Black Watch caused a number of casualties, but apart from this there was no enemy activity until the night of the 19th of November, when an enemy patrol was discovered to be moving in an easterly direction from the area occupied by the 5/7th Gordons, and on being fired on cleared off, leaving two prisoners behind.

On the morning of the 19th of November the Derby Yeomanry sent strong reconnaissance patrols along two different axes, one through Ondar to Baarle and another southwards to Kessel. The party going to Kessel met no opposition, but had to debus on account of a large crater in the road. Quite a number of mines were encountered, but the patrol skirted round them and reached Kessel at about 3 o'clock without meeting any enemy. The party which moved eastwards to Baarle were not quite so fortunate, as enemy infantry and self-propelled guns were encountered about midday. Artillery concentrations were laid on to assist the Derby Yeomanry forward, but as they were outnumbered, it was decided to withdraw slightly and hold firm for the night. At 6 o'clock in the evening the Derby Yeomanry in the Ondar area were attacked by enemy infantry and self-propelled guns, but the attack lasted only thirty minutes when it was successfully beaten off.

On the 20th of November the brigade were ordered to clear the area of the woods in the Bong–Baarle area. Firstly, the 1st Black Watch were to clear the axis of the main road Ondar–Bong–Baarle and consolidate in the area of Baarle if opposition was slight. If, on the other hand, resistance was strong, they were to clear and consolidate Zoterboek and Bong. The 7th Argylls were then to move and clear and consolidate Rinkersfort. If the 1st Black Watch did not reach Baarle, the 7th Argylls were to advance through the wooded area and capture the town. As a result of this operation the 7th Black Watch were moved forward to the Ondar area, and the 7th Argylls were relieved in Kessel by the 5/7th Gordons and concentrated in Egghel.

At 9 o'clock in the morning of the 21st, therefore, the 1st Black Watch moved forward. All went well at first with them until about 11 o'clock they ran up against enemy infantry and mobile guns in the area of a wood. By 3.45 p.m. the 7th Argylls had reached Rinkersfort, and had so far met little opposition. Considerable shelling was encountered by both battalions, and the 1st Black Watch had in addition a fair amount of opposition from infantry and mobile guns. Two of these guns were knocked out by the tanks supporting the 1st Black Watch. By 5.15 in the afternoon the Argylls had reached Zoterboek and were consolidating, and shortly afterwards the 1st Black Watch reached their final objective, which was the main crossroads in Baarle. A number of prisoners were captured who were identified as from the 21st Luftjaeger Regiment, who had just come up from Venraij, and whose morale was fairly high. The main German forces had, however, mostly withdrawn beyond the Maas.

On the 22nd of November the 7th Argylls sent a patrol through the woods, their intention being to get to Blerick. This patrol ran into thick enemy minefields, and as darkness was coming down the patrol was temporarily withdrawn. On the following morning the patrol set off again, and after having met intense mortar and machine-gun fire from the woods to the south-east in addition to the heavy going due to mud and extensive minefields, the patrol was called off. Large parts of the area were flooded, and what was not flooded was inches deep in mud as a result of the very heavy rainfall of the last few days.

Our brigade now came under the 53rd Division, who were eventually to take over the whole sector from the 51st Division. On the 26th the Argylls were relieved by a battalion of the 53rd Division, and moved to a concentration area at Roggel preparatory to moving up with the brigade to rejoin the Division in the Nijmegen area. During the afternoon of the 27th of November, Brigade Headquarters moved to a concentration area at Heijthuizen, and the 1st Black Watch moved to Leveroij at last light. The 7th Black Watch, who were in the Ondar area, were to rejoin the brigade at Heijthuizen on the morning of the 29th of November as the column was on the move.

The brigade had now completed an operation which had compelled all German forces to withdraw to the east side of the River Maas. During these operations the brigade as part of the Division fought across a network of canals which in themselves were formidable obstacles. The weather had been appalling, and the ground over which the troops had to fight was a sea of sodden mud, inches deep. Although it had been a most unpleasant advance, the casualties in the battalion were slight, and we now looked forward to a period of rest when we could carry out some much needed administration and maintenance.

CHAPTER XV

THE NIJMEGEN FLOODS

THE move to Nijmegen was most interesting, and after having been attacking and holding the line in country which was nothing but a sea of mud and mines, it was a relief to get a change. What kind of a change we had yet to find out, but we felt that it could not be much more uncomfortable than that which we had just gone through. We did not know then that within a short time we were to be completely flooded out of our positions. We had by now got to know Holland fairly well, and we found no difficulty in moving from one location to another without even consulting a map. We found the Dutch people in many respects like the Scots, but we could make nothing of their language except that some of their words and phrases were exactly similar to " broad Scots." Their houses were very clean and tidy, but we felt that a fireplace now and again would have been much more homely than the inevitable stove which we always found.

We moved to Nijmegen early on the morning of the 29th of November. It was a dull, dreary morning to begin with, but by midday it began to brighten up, and incidentally so did we. It happened to be my responsibility to lead the convoy, which I did in a Citroen car which I had picked up in Le Havre during our attack on the town, and which had been previously used by the German Admiralty. Our route took us back over the route we had previously used on several occasions through Eindhoven, via Weert–Leende–Valkensvaard. From Eindhoven onwards we passed through St. Oedenrode, scene of our previous operations, to

Veghel–Uden–Grave and finally Nijmegen. As we travelled along the broad stretch of road approaching Grave, we noticed that the Canadians had many amusing signs posted at intervals along the roadside. One such sign had the following remarks painted on it in bold lettering: " Good Boche hunting in the woods. Tours to Berlin arranged by the direct route. We have come from Caen and Falaise, and are Second to None. What do we do now ? " This signpost caused a great deal of amusement among us, and one officer who was a bit of a wag decided to get a trumpet, and to nail it under the sign where it said, " What do we do now ? " Below the trumpet the remark, " Blow this " was painted.

The minimum of transport only was allowed across the Nijmegen bridge owing to the danger of the area between the Waal and the Neder Rijn being flooded. On arrival at our new location the brigade was laid out with the 7th Black Watch in the area of Lienden, the 1st Black Watch at Valburg, and the 7th Argylls near Herveld. As the 7th Black Watch were very exposed in their positions they were moved the following day to Andelst. Very little enemy activity took place except for shelling in the Lienden and Elst areas. In fact the area in which we were now located was much quieter than anything we had experienced for some considerable time, and was a change from the heavy and continuous fighting in which we had taken part for so long, and on which the corps commander congratulated our brigade on several occasions. The greatest threat in the area, which was generally known as the " Island " because of the fact that the area between Arnhem and Nijmegen is bounded on the north and east by the Rhine, and on the south by the Waal, was that the Germans would blow the dykes in an attempt to flood the island, and thereby force us to withdraw south across the River Waal. This actually happened on the 2nd of December, and as a result the 152nd Brigade had to pull back most of its transport. Several large explosions were heard during the night, and the following day showed that the island was gradually flooding. This flooding continued to increase, and on the afternoon of the 3rd of December it was found necessary to withdraw two battalions of the 152nd Brigade, and these crossed the River Waal *en route* for a concentration area near S'Hertogenbosch. The 5th Camerons of the 152nd Brigade remained on the island, but were pulled back a bit. So far the flooding had not seriously affected our brigade. The floods generally moved in a south-westerly direction to the lateral railway running between Resteren and Nijmegen. This railway to a great extent acted as a dyké for the area to the south, but nevertheless a certain amount of flooding south of the railway was inevitable.

The 4th of December saw the floods still rising, and the remainder of the 152nd Brigade were withdrawn, and in the afternoon the 153rd Brigade, with the exception of the 5/7th Gordons, were also withdrawn. The 5/7th Gordons came under the command of our brigade, which in turn came under the command of the 49th Division. Enemy activity was mostly in the form of spasmodic shelling which did no damage whatever. As time went on both the enemy and ourselves became much more aggressive, and amphibious patrols were periodically sent out. On the 5th of December the Argylls had to be withdrawn on account of their area becoming hopelessly flooded, and they moved to a concentration area at St. Michels Gestel. That evening further explosions were heard in the north-eastern sector of the island, and the floods began to rise steadily in all sectors at the rate of approximately one inch in four hours. On the 7th of December the 5/7th Gordons left us to rejoin the 153rd Brigade, and the Division now had only two battalions on the island. The flooding appeared to have become stabilized in brigade's sector, as no considerable change in the level had become apparent during the previous twenty-four hours.

At this stage information was received that the enemy intended to attack Nijmegen bridge in the next 48 hours, and our brigade's intention was to hold the line Lienden–Valburg–Andelst along the south edge of the flooding to De Tempel, thence along the north bank of the River Waal. The task of the 1st Black Watch was to prevent enemy infiltration across the flooded area and to hold one company at thirty minutes' notice to move to the area of Slijkewijk in the event of the enemy landing from the River Waal. The 7th Black Watch were to prevent infiltration across the flooded area, and to be responsible for the north bank of the Waal with one company. Another company was to hold Andelst and was to be ready to reinforce any point on the Bund in the 7th Black Watch sector. A squadron of the 49th Division Reconnaissance, who were under command of brigade, were to hold the Bund from De Tempel and prevent enemy infiltration south of the flooded area.

The enemy attack never materialized, probably because the operation, which would have had to be water-borne, was too difficult to control. The civilians whose homes were on the island had by this time to be evacuated, and it was a pitiful sight to see them trudging along in the rain with their few possessions, leaving behind them nothing but desolation. Their homes and farms were flooded out and ruined, and one wondered how long it would be before the country would be back to normal again.

Patrolling by both sides continued to be carried out, and exchanges in artillery fire were fairly frequent. Enemy spandau fire was occasionally encountered, but apart from this things were fairly quiet. On the 15th a patrol from the 7th Black Watch met an enemy patrol, and after a short skirmish captured 5 Boche prisoners from the 13th Para

Regiment. They had evidently crossed the Neder Rijn with instructions to find out whether or not we occupied the village of Hemmen. During this period a large number of flying bombs passed overhead, travelling in a south-westerly direction, presumably making for Antwerp. Occasionally we saw V2 rockets being launched in the area just north of Arnhem. Fortunately none of these V-weapons fell on us, although one or two flying bombs were uncomfortably close.

At last, on the 19th of December, brigade was relieved by the 152nd Brigade and moved to a concentration area at Mille. The Argylls, who were in St. Michels Gestel, moved independently. We had no operational role to begin with, but were to concentrate in the new area in order to be ready for use in an operational role if and when required. On the following day we again moved via Heesch–Uden–Veghel–St. Oedenrode–Eindhoven–Valkensvaard–Hechtel–Helchteren to a concentration area at Hasselt. *En route* the destination was changed and we eventually concentrated at Moll.

Again, on the 21st of December, we set off on an early move through Gheel–Aerschot to Louvain, where we established headquarters at Blanden, the 7th Black Watch at Vaelbeek, and the 1st Black Watch at Heverle. We were now back in Belgium, and our first words were that we hoped we had seen the last of Holland with its rain and floods. One night only we spent in Louvain, and on the morning of the 22nd of December we set off on another early move via Louvain by-pass–Diest–Hasselt–Genck–Sutendael–Lanaeken to an area east of Maastricht in Holland.

Before we moved from our comfortable billets at St. Michels Gestel, Field-Marshal Montgomery held an investiture for the Division, and the battalion was called upon to produce the guard of honour. This guard was specially selected, and Lieut. G. Wood was in command of it, and he was congratulated by the commander-in-chief for the turn-out and smartness of the guard. The following were awarded decorations at the investiture :

Lieut. P. A. Hands	M.C.
L/Sgt. Milne	M.M.
L/Cpl. Sykes	M.M.
Pte. Manning	M.M.
Pte. Patterson	M.M.

CHAPTER XVI

VON RUNDSTEDT'S ARDENNES OFFENSIVE

WE were now under the Ninth American Army, and for the present were in army reserve. Since leaving Nijmegen we had moved four times, once in Holland, twice in Belgium, and back into Holland again. At this time the Germans had been very active, and had attacked away to the south in the area of the Ardennes. Also the Germans had copied the British idea of long-range patrols in imitation of the " Long-Range Desert Group," which had done such good work for us in the desert campaign. These German patrols usually worked on the American front. The German soldiers, dressing up in American battledress, driving about in jeeps, and speaking English with an American accent, were at first very difficult to trace, but the Americans were very alert, and soon had the situation under control. I remember well the journey to Maastricht. As usual I was leading the brigade convoy, which consisted of a long line of vehicles, and as we approached Maastricht bridge two American sentries pointed their rifles at us and ordered us to halt, which we did with alacrity. We were then asked to produce our identity, give the number of vehicles in the column, and state who we were. I proudly answered that we were the 51st Highland Division who were now in the Ninth American Army, and the reply I got was, " Never heard of them." I was next ordered to draw in to the side and check all the vehicles past, but as I explained that I was leading the convoy and could not do this they agreed to let me go. Next I was asked how many sixpennies were in a half-crown, and fortunately, as I knew the answer, I was allowed to proceed. A friend of mine had not been so fortunate on another occasion, however, for when he was asked by an American sentry where the Kyle of Lochalsh was, he was so taken by surprise that he answered, " I haven't the faintest idea." Thereupon he was detained until he produced other evidence which was satisfactory. So one can see that the Americans were certainly not asleep, which was a good thing.

Accommodation in the area of Maastricht was difficult to find on account of the large number of Allied troops there. Reconnaissances were at once carried out in connection with our operational role, and as it was now Christmas Day we hoped to be left in peace to eat our Christmas dinner. Such good fortune was our lot. However, on the following day we moved off again to Ougree on the Meuse. The route took us across Maastricht Bridge and through Canne–Oupeye–Herstal and Liége. Flying bombs were our only source of worry in this area, and approximately 50 per day fell in and around Liége and Seraing. On the 28th of December the brigade plan in connection with its operational role was made known. Briefly, the brigade was to be prepared to move to and occupy a defensive position in the following areas. These areas were primarily selected as forward concentration areas, and the intention was to operate offensively from them, and thereby check any further advances made by Von Rundstedt in his Ardennes offensive. There were three plans called A, C, and D, any one of which the brigade might be called upon to carry out. In Plan A the brigade was to prevent any penetration from the east or south through the Limbourg Gap, and the brigade were therefore to be ready at a moment's notice to move via Henne–Prayen–Nessonvaux, and along the main Limbourg road through Verviers. The Argylls were to go to Limbourg, the 1st Black Watch to Tombeux, and the 7th Black Watch to Basse Mont. The brigade task in Plan C was to be prepared

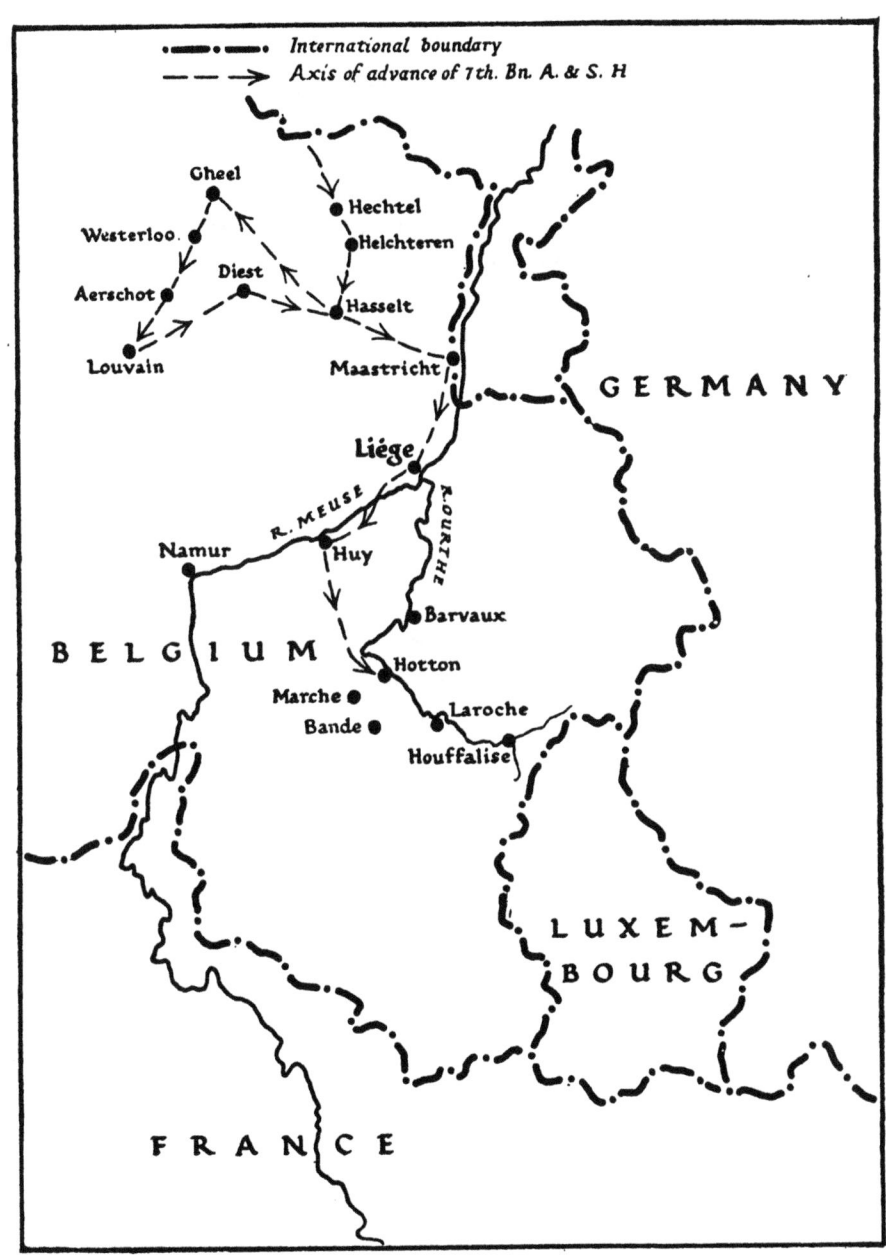

Movement of Battalion south through Belgium

to form a firm base on the general line Petit Han–Barvaux, and prevent the enemy from crossing the River Ourthe in that area. The 7th Black Watch were to be responsible for Petit Han–Durbuy, the 7th Argylls for Barvaux, and the 1st Black Watch, Tohogne. In Plan D a firm base was to be formed at Miecret–Havelange–Honze, with the 1st Black Watch in Ossogne and Honze, the 7th Black Watch in Havelange, and the Argylls in Miecret.

On the 29th of December information was received that an enemy attack was expected on the front of the 75th American Division, and consequently our Division were to take over the responsibility of guarding the bridges over the Meuse in the Liége sector. Our brigade were given the responsibility of guarding the Huy and Amay bridges, which was done with one battalion, the 7th Argylls. On the 30th of December it was decided to move the brigade out of the Seraing area, as the number of flying bombs was increasing and they had no wish to risk losing their transport. Brigade therefore moved down the river and established Brigade Headquarters in the Château Harmelle sous Huy, where the Baroness de Potesta de Waleffe lived. Here we spent the New Year's Day, where we attended an excellent party given by brigade.

Battling in the Snow

On the evening of the 6th of January we received orders to move the following day to a concentration area north-east of Ciney, with the object of concentrating the Division as part of 30th Corps who were for the present in the First American Army. Our route this time was through Terwagne and Maffe, and regardless of a blinding snowstorm and icy roads we carried out the move without any accidents, and on arrival in our new area the dispositions of the brigade were as follows : Brigade Headquarters were established in Monin, with the 1st Black Watch in Scoville, the 7th Black Watch in Hamois, and the 7th Argylls in Miecret. Our immediate intention was to relieve the 160th Brigade of the 53rd Division, who were holding a sector of the line east of Hotton on the north-western tip of the spearhead of the German break-through in the Ardennes. Accordingly, on the morning of the 8th of January we moved from our concentrations areas to carry out this relief. Two different routes were used, the 1st Black Watch moving via Menieux–Noiseux to Hotton, and the remainder of the brigade via Marche. The treacherous state of the roads, due to the hard frost and the heavy snowfall, prolonged the completion of the relief and indeed it was a wonder how the relief was carried out at all. Tanks and Bren carriers had a particularly bad time on the roads as their tracks could not obtain a grip on the slippery surface.

On arrival, however, the 7th Argylls relieved the East Lancashire Regiment in the area of Grimbiemont, the 7th Black Watch took over the positions of the 4th Welch Regiment in the wooded area south-west of Warharday, and the 1st Black Watch relieved the 2nd Monmouthshire Regiment in the Menil area. The Reconnaissance Regiment of the 53rd Division remained in the meantime under the brigade command and carried out vigorous patrolling. On the morning of the 9th of January they sent a patrol to Rendeux Bas, Ronzon, and Cheoux. The 1st Black Watch also sent a patrol to Cheoux, and at approximately 11.30 in the morning of the 9th the patrol returned and reported that the area was held by about a platoon of enemy infantry. Later in the morning the patrol from 53rd Divisional Reconnaissance Regiment reported that Rendeux was clear of enemy. About this time the 1st Black Watch were ordered to occupy Cheoux along with one squadron of tanks, which they did without opposition, as the enemy had cleared off whenever they got wind of the intention of the 1st Black Watch. On the morning of the 10th of January the 7th Argylls were relieved by the 3rd Para Brigade and moved to Bourdon. The 7th Black Watch also moved into billets in Hotton, the object being to have at least one night under cover before launching the attack on the enemy positions.

Some valuable information was obtained from an enemy deserter from the 116th Panzer Divisional Artillery who was captured by the Argylls at Grimbiemont. He stated that Lignières was clear of enemy and that the enemy had withdrawn to Bande. It was in this village of Bande that the Germans murdered thirty-four young men of the village in cold blood as suspects of collaboration with the Maquis. After the Ardennes offensive by Von Rundstedt had been written off, and we were on our way to another location, the coffins of these thirty-four victims were observed by the roadside with the Tricolor draped over them prior to the burial service. The brigade's intention was to capture and hold Laroche, Thimont, Roupage, Lavaux, and Hives. This operation was to be done in three phases. Firstly, the 1st Black Watch were to capture Laroche, and afterwards the 7th Black Watch were to pass through and capture the area Hives–Lavaux. Later the Argylls were to capture the area Thimont–Roupage. The 1st Black Watch advance was to be done on foot via Hodister and Warizy, followed by the 7th Black Watch embussed in vehicles whose route was via Laroche to Hives. The Argylls were at 30 minutes' notice to move from 9 o'clock in the morning of the 11th of January, and were also to move embussed via Hotton–Laroche–Ferme du Vivier–Thimont to Roupage, and Brigade Headquarters were to open up at Jupille at 9 o'clock in the morning.

The 2nd Derby Yeomanry in their advance met no opposition at first, but were delayed in their progress by blown bridges and mines, and two of their armoured cars were blown up on the latter. About 11 o'clock the 1st Black Watch reached Laroche without much opposition except from enemy shelling, which was particularly heavy in Laroche at the time. While the Black Watch were clearing the road beyond Laroche they encountered a certain amount of spandau and mortar fire. The advance was going well, however, and as the Americans who were attacking from the south were making good progress, we were ordered not to let any unit beyond the line Cens–Ortho–Nissramont, where patrols from the 87th American Division would eventually make contact with us. By 7.30 in the evening the 7th Black Watch reached their final objective in Hives and captured 35 prisoners from the 3rd P.G.R. Division. During their advance the 7th Black Watch had encountered quite heavy opposition from mortaring, machine gunning, and self-propelled guns. This shelling and mortaring became very heavy in Hives itself.

During the night of the 12th of January a patrol from the 1st Black Watch brought back the information that the bridges over the River Ourthe to the American sector were all blown with the exception of one, which was too badly buckled in the centre to be used with safety. On the morning of the 12th of January the 5th Black Watch, who were under the command of our brigade, moved forward with C Squadron of the 2nd Derby Yeomanry on the axis Laroche–Ferme du Vivier, their task being to capture and hold Roupage. Consequently the task of the Argylls was changed, and they were ordered to capture and hold the area of Beaulieu. During the advance of the Argylls the leading tank of the squadron of the Northamptonshire Yeomanry, which were in support, was knocked out, and a considerable amount of spandau and mortar fire was coming from the high ground on both sides of the road, and from the wooded area west of Lavaux. At this stage the opposition became rather sticky, and A company of the Argylls was temporarily held up by some Panther tanks in the wooded area. Here several casualties were sustained, including A company commander, Major Peter Samwell, M.C., who was killed. By now the 5th Black Watch having completed their task, reverted to the command of the 153rd Brigade. B company of the Argylls was then ordered forward, and by 5 o'clock in the evening the enemy resistance slackened and the Panther tanks withdrew. At 7 o'clock Lavaux was in our hands, and A company was left in Hives. Slowly the Argylls continued their advance, being harassed most of the time by lurking German tanks and self-propelled guns, but by 2 o'clock on the morning of the 13th of January Beaulieu was reached, where an attack by two Panther tanks was beaten off, one tank being knocked out. The task of the Argylls was now done, and although they had had a stiff fight they only suffered 38 casualties, including Lieut. Cutland who was wounded.

Later on the morning of the 13th the 1st Black Watch sent one company to occupy Erneuville, and the remainder of the battalion followed later. The Argylls at the same time sent patrols to Cens, which they reported clear of enemy. As a result of wireless interception, it was revealed that the Germans were withdrawing along the road Nissramont–Filly–Nadrin, and immediately heavy artillery concentrations were brought down on the enemy's lines of withdrawal. During the night of the 13th no enemy activity of any kind took place as by this time the enemy were well away to the east. A considerable amount of enemy equipment and weapons had been captured during the brigade advance, and the enemy's Ardennes salient had been liquidated with heavy losses to him.

On the morning of the 14th of January C squadron of the 2nd Derby Yeomanry were ordered to send armoured car patrols to the River Ourthe to make contact with the Americans. This they did without incident, and the operation, which from start to finish was a complete success, sent Von Rundstedt's forces reeling back towards the German frontier. More than half the German salient in Belgium was thus recaptured, and our brigade, after having advanced a distance of 12 to 15 miles in three days against stiff opposition, and in weather which was colder than anything we had yet experienced, once again added yet another page of glory to the history of the Highland Brigade. It is interesting to note that several captured prisoners stated that they were taken completely by surprise, as they did not think it possible for the Allies to launch an offensive in such weather. The brigade's casualties were fairly light and were estimated at under 150 for the whole operation.

The remainder of the period in this area was spent in cleaning up and resting, until on the 16th of January we received a warning order to move on the 17th to a concentration area at Heyst-op-den-Berg. This time we moved via Marche–Andenne–Hannut–Tirlemont–Diest–Veerle. *En route* we were informed that the Andenne bridge had been damaged, and that we would have to move via Ohey–Huy Bridge–Hannut–Tirlemont–Diest–Aerschot. It was inevitable that progress during this move would be slow on account of the very icy conditions of the roads, and also the crossing of the Huy Bridge would delay our progress to a certain extent. We did not arrive at our destination until 11.30 at night, after having taken about twelve hours to travel a distance of 105 miles.

The intention was that the Division was now to have two weeks' rest in this new area, but, as had generally been the case when a rest was ordered, we remained until the 22nd when we moved to another area near Uden. This concentration area eventually turned out to be Boxmeer and

Mil, and our route to it was via Gheel–Casterle–Turnhout–Arendonck–Bladel–Duizel–Steensel–Veldhoven–Eindhoven–Son–St. Oedenrode–Veghel–Uden to a dispersal point one mile west of Zeeland. On arrival in our new locations at 5 o'clock that evening, the layout of the brigade was as follows : Brigade Headquarters were established in Escheren, with the 1st Black Watch in Beers, the 7th Black Watch in Mil, and the 7th Argylls in St. Hubert. After a period of rest the brigade began preparations for the attack across the River Maas, and the subsequent fighting in the Reichswald Forest. Before any reconnaissances were carried out, however, all H.D. signs were removed from our uniforms and vehicles, and no unauthorized person was allowed across the Grave bridge. The object of all this secrecy was to prevent the enemy from finding out where our Division was, and to lead them to believe that we were still in the Ardennes sector.

Plate 15 While British and German officers discuss the occupation arrangements in Bremerhaven, the Argyll pipers go swinging by

CHAPTER XVII

THE REICHSWALD FOREST

THE last few days of January and the beginning of February 1945 were spent by the battalion in very comfortable billets in St. Hubert. Early in February, however, the plans for the next operation started to come in. The name given to the operation was "Veritable," and the plan was for the Canadian First Army to break the pivot of the Siegfried Line in the Reichswald Forest. The 51st Highland Division, who were at this time in the Canadian First Army, were to enter the forest at the west end and eventually emerge at the southeast end opposite Kessel.

The operation was due to start on the 8th of February, and so on the 6th of February the battalion concentrated at Cuijk on the west bank of the River Maas. The concentration in this area was made very difficult by a rapid thaw, and soon the whole area was a horrible sea of mud. Vehicles became bogged, and the weather conditions were as unpleasant as any the battalion had yet experienced. The plan for the battle of the Reichswald Forest was that the Division should attack with the 154th Infantry Brigade forward on the right. Of the 154th Brigade, the 1st and 7th Black Watch battalions were leading and the 7th Argylls were in reserve. On the morning of the 8th of February, as the leading battalions attacked the edge of the forest, supported by a terrific artillery barrage, the 7th Argylls moved up across the River Maas by the Mook Bridge and occupied a reserve position in a wood which was separated from the main part of the Reichswald Forest by a gap of approximately one mile. Many gliders left over by the Airborne Division's attack the previous summer on the

Nijmegen Bridge were scattered about in the gap. The leading battalions successfully reached and consolidated on the edge of the forest, and at 11 a.m. we moved up to attack through the 1st Black Watch. The battalion entered the forest at approximately 11 p.m., and found the going very difficult both up to and in the forest itself, as all the tracks rapidly became a muddy quagmire. At this stage all the transport had to be abandoned, and the troops had to carry extra loads in the form of wireless sets, etc. By 8 o'clock in the morning of the 9th of February, however, the necessary transport, together with one troop of Churchill tanks from the 107 R.A.C., managed to reach the battalion on the objective. It was no easy task to find one's way through this extensive, featureless forest, and indeed at times the location of the battalion was in doubt. Up to this time no enemy had been encountered or observed, which perhaps in a way was a good thing, as conditions were unpleasant enough without enemy interference, but when the battalion started to advance again at 10 o'clock to a further objective several spandau posts were immediately encountered. The Churchill tanks went into action at once, and very quickly cleared up these posts without difficulty before the battalion reached their objective.

At 6 o'clock in the evening of the 9th of February the 5th Battalion Seaforth Highlanders passed through and took over the lead. On the 11th of February the Argylls were once again in the lead, and after a very tiresome advance arrived at the edge of the forest overlooking the River Niers on the 12th of February. During our advance the battalion met little opposition, and in fact it was a much easier passage than had been expected. Casualties were fairly light so far as compared with previous operations. Lieut. Mathieson and 1 other rank were killed, and Lieuts. McGee, Binns, Nicholson, and 8 other ranks were wounded.

The battalion stayed in this area watching the Boche

in and around Kessel from two good observation posts until the 14th of February, on which date we moved off for the attack on Kessel. The 1st and 7th Black Watch battalions had secured a bridgehead the night before, and the task of the Argylls was to pass through and capture Kessel. The attack started at 10.15 p.m., led by A and D companies under Majors Johnny Sloan and Joe Corcoran respectively. Little trouble was encountered *en route*, and the battalion quickly entered the village. Some skirmishing took place in the village, but by the morning of the 15th February the village was clear and 70 prisoners had been captured. Next day was mostly spent in consolidating the positions already gained, during which time the battalion was heavily mortared, and in the afternoon the enemy launched a counter-attack which was eventually driven off. All was fairly quiet on the following day, the 16th of February, and the Churchill tanks, together with a platoon of A company, captured another 70 prisoners from dugouts only about 300 yards from the foremost defended localties. These prisoners had no fight left in them, and marched in to the battalion's lines in column of threes. Before breakfast the same day Major Hamilton, affectionately known as " Ham," our gunner from the 126th Highland Field Regiment R.A., was out for a stroll with D company commander Joe Corcoran. They climbed a local tower to view the countryside, and on reaching the top they found a German observation post complete with three Boche who were immediately made prisoners. This was possibly the reason for the very accurate mortar fire which the battalion had been enduring up to that time.

The battalion stayed in Kessel more or less peacefully reorganizing until the 21st, when they moved up to Goch, which had been partly occupied by the 15th Scottish Division and the 153rd Brigade of the Highland Division. The battalion advanced through the southern edge of the town and cleared the west edge, where they settled down on the outskirts. An unfortunate incident occurred while the battalion were passing through the town. Our own bombers were active, and they accidentally dropped several of their loads on the battalion. B company suffered more than the rest of the battalion. Four other ranks were killed and Captain M. R. Kenneth, Lieut. Knight, and 17 other ranks were wounded. During the battalion's stay in Goch they experienced heavy shelling and mortar fire, but this quietened down after the 53rd Division passed through, and it was then hoped that the battalion would be given a well-earned rest. This was not to be yet, however, as on the night of the 25th of February they were ordered to pass through the Monmouthshire Regiment of the 53rd Division and capture the village of Hulm. The opposition was stiff, but Hulm was successfully captured nevertheless. The enemy shelling and mortaring of the whole area on the 26th of February was even heavier than usual. The battalion had not yet finished, for on the night of the 27th of February D company had to make a further attack in order to secure a crossing of the anti-tank ditch. It was anticipated that this would be a stiff battle, as indeed it was, but the position was finally cleared by 2 o'clock on the morning of the 28th of February, and another day of heavy shelling was endured.

On the night of the 28th of February the battalion was relieved by the 4th battalion Royal Scots Fusiliers of the 52nd Lowland Division. Owing to the fact that the enemy were beginning to withdraw, the relief was carried out without interference. On completion of the relief the battalion returned once more to their old area in Goch, where a much-needed rest was anticipated after the tough fighting of the past week. The battalion had as usual suffered fairly heavily in casualties since the attack on the Reichswald Forest began. Altogether there were 121 casualties, consisting of 1 officer killed and 20 other ranks killed, 6 officers and 91 other ranks wounded, and 3 other ranks missing. The officers casualties were : Killed—Lieut. Mathieson ; Wounded—Capt. Kenneth, and Lieuts. Knight, McGee, Binns, Nicholson, and 2nd Lieut. Alexander.

So ended the battle of the Reichswald Forest. The 7th Argylls added more honour to the regiment. Once again they had lost heavily in manpower, but soon more reinforcements were arriving as they had done so often before. B echelon at this stage was stationed in Holland, where the people were all very friendly, while the battalion itself was in Germany. All German towns, villages, and farms in the battle area could only be described as totally destroyed. The Air Force, followed up by our terrific artillery barrages with their large proportion of medium guns, turned the countryside into an appalling desert of ruins. It was great fun, however, as there were plenty opportunities of shooting German pigs which had been left behind on the German farms. Occasionally one was able to catch some geese and chickens, and it was rather amusing to see the Jocks walking about with chickens under their arms. Major Church, M.C., joined the battalion at this stage and was appointed second-in-command. " Ginger " Richardson, the Q.M., also returned to the battalion after having had his appendix removed in hospital. He was in fine form until he found out that during his absence his rum stock had been considerably depleted. At this stage it might be of interest to give the order of battle of the battalion, as so many changes had recently taken place.

ORDER OF BATTLE

Battalion Headquarters
Lieut.-Col. A. MacKinnon, D.S.O., M.C.	Commanding officer
Major J. C. Church, M.C.	Second-in-command
Capt. A. J. A. Stewart	Adjutant
Lieut. R. Williams	I.O.
R.S.M. S. J. Morrison, M.M.	R.S.M.
C/Sgt. C. McGowan	O.R.C.

H.Q. Company
Capt. J. F. Robertson — Company Commander
Lieut. E. J. Harris — Signals Officer
Capt. W. T. Thomson — M.T.O.
Capt. (Q.M.) J. Richardson — Q.M.
R.Q.M.S. A. Mathieson — R.Q.M.S.
C.Q.M.S. W. Hutchison — C.Q.M.S.
C.S.M. J. Lloyd — C.S.M.

A Company
Major J. R. Sloan, M.C. — Company Commander
Capt. M. Macalister-Hall, M.C. — Second-in-command
Lieut. P. A. Hands, M.C. — 7 Pl.
Lieut. D. G. Aitchison — 8 Pl.
Lieut. R. D. Lindsay — 9 Pl.
C.S.M. G. Gauld, D.C.M. — C.S.M.
C.Q.M.S. W. Hardie — C.Q.M.S.

B Company
Major J. H. F. Morton, M.C. — Company Commander
Lieut. J. R. Lale — 10 Pl.
Lieut. H. A. B. Maxwell — 11 Pl.
Lieut. J. K. MacFarlane — 12 Pl.
C.S.M. E. Wildman, D.C.M. — C.S.M.
C.Q.M.S. J. Collins — C.Q.M.S.

C Company
Capt. N. G. Wykes — Company Commander
2nd Lieut. R. S. Laurie

D Company
Major J. S. Corcoran, D.S.O., M.C. — Company Commander
Capt. A. S. Bowden — Second-in-command
2nd Lieut. M. F. Green — 16 Pl.
Lieut. W. Lamont — 17 Pl.
Lieut. J. G. Burbridge — 18 Pl.
C.S.M. R. T. Boyde — C.S.M.
C.Q.M.S. W. D. Johnstone — C.Q.M.S.

S Company
Major I. A. Campbell — Company Commander
Capt. D. A. Goodall — A/Tk. Pl.
Capt. J. R. Harrison — Mortar Officer
Capt. T. Armstrong — Carrier Officer
Lieut. G. P. Wood — Pioneer Officer
C.S.M. C. Sutherland — C.S.M.
C.Q.M.S. G. Stewart — C.Q.M.S.

Attached
Capt. W. Blair, R.A.M.C. — R.M.O.
Capt. N. Campbell, R.A.Ch.D. — Padre

CHAPTER XVIII

THE RHINE CROSSING

THE first six days of March were spent in the Goch area, where the battalion rested and reorganized. During this period the Prime Minister, Mr. Churchill, accompanied by Field-Marshal Montgomery and General Sir Alan Brooke, Chief of the Imperial General Staff, visited the Division at Grafenthal. After the massed pipes and drums had played a Retreat programme, Mr. Churchill made a short speech which was greeted with enthusiastic applause, but the afternoon was unfortunately spoilt by the weather, which was cold, windy, and wet.

The 6th of March saw the end of the battalion's rest period in Goch, and an advance party was sent off that morning to make a recce of the new area at Hearlen in the south of Holland, where the battalion was to be re-equipped and where a programme of training in preparation for the next operation was to be carried out. The main body of the battalion moved to Hearlen on the 7th of March. It was an all-night move, and took from 6.15 p.m. on the 7th of March until 4 o'clock in the morning of the 8th of March. The billets were most comfortable, and the people of Hearlen were very friendly, and did all in their power to make the troops feel at home. A squadron of the Northampton Yeomanry complete with "Buffaloes" joined the battalion on arrival, and as the village was conveniently near the River Maas, the battalion soon learned how large rivers ought to be crossed. Two full-scale river crossing exercises were carried out on the River Maas just above Roermond. One was by day and the other by night. The first of these exercises was attended by Field-Marshal Montgomery, who actually crossed with one of A company's platoons. The banks of the Maas were most unsuitable for Buffaloes, and they had great difficulty in getting up the steep banks of the river on the far side.

It soon became obvious that the battalion was to be one of the assault battalions for crossing the Rhine, and although all ranks were told at this period that this was the intention, they were left in ignorance of date and place. The weather during this period was perfect, and our troops were in excellent spirits and thoroughly enjoyed themselves with the hospitable villagers. It was consequently with a feeling of regret that the battalion said farewell to Hearlen on the 21st of March and moved to a concentration area at Hansaleur, near Calcar. The Buffaloes were already concentrated there, and great care had to be taken to camouflage all vehicles as the battalion's location was only a matter of two or three miles from the Rhine. Smoke was laid continuously along the whole west bank of the Rhine to obscure our movements from the enemy, but although visibility was poor, it was sufficient to enable one to see with a feeling of relief the gently sloping, sandy banks of the Rhine on the far side which were ideal for the Buffaloes, and so unlike the steep banks of the River Maas.

Here the troops lay in the brilliant sunshine resting before the assault across the Rhine. Most civilians had left the area, but a large quantity of the livestock remained. Instructions had been received, however, that on no account was the livestock to be touched, and many a "Jock" who gazed longingly at a fine fat pullet or a plump pig, had to practice strict self-denial. However, on one occasion, the commanding officer had suddenly to reach for the telephone in the battalion office and ask to be put through to D company. When he got through to the company commander, Major Joe Coccoran, he said, " If you look out of your window you will see a pig being led towards your company area on a lead. Please see that it is released when it reaches you." Poor Joe Corcoran had been looking forward to that pig all morning !

The task of the Division was to establish a bridgehead across the Rhine at Rees. The plan was divided into phases with the 153rd Brigade on the right and the 154th Brigade on the left. In the 154th Brigade the 7th Black Watch were on the left and the 7th Argylls on the right. The plan for the 7th Argylls was to attack with A company forward on the right and B company on their left, with D company following up behind A company. A company were to make for Ratshoff, which was a small village, and B company were to make for a farm a bit to the left of this. D company were then to go through A company and make for a crossroads beyond Ratshoff. Then the 1st battalion the Black Watch were to pass through to Kl. Esserden and Speldorp, after which the 7th Argylls were to pass through them to Bienen.

D day was 23rd March 1945, and H hour was 9 p.m. By 8 p.m. all the transport and troops were loaded into the Buffaloes, and the two leading companies, A and B, entered the water on time without a hitch. The crossing was unbelievably quiet, and was really more like an exercise than an assault crossing of Germany's last great river barrier. No-one knew in advance what to expect. It was thought that the river and the banks might be mined, and one expected the enemy to have countless anti-tank guns well sited along the opposite bank in readiness to sink the Buffaloes as they swam across. It was a thrilling moment when these great clumsy vehicles lumbered into the water and started swimming across to the far bank. The noise created by our artillery was deafening, but not a shot came from the enemy side, and the 300 yards of river was crossed without interference. On reaching the far bank, the cordite and smoke

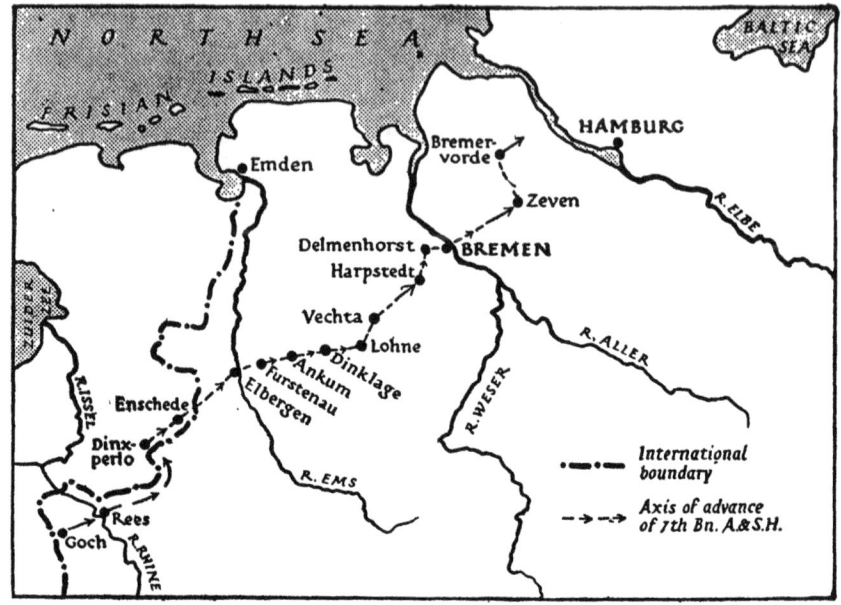

Advance of Battalion into Germany

from the creeping barrage was hanging low over the area and the general atmosphere resembled a London fog. Fortunately, however, the Buffaloes had landed the battalion at the exact spot, and it was only a matter of minutes before the companies found their bearings and set off towards their objectives. The first phase went according to plan, and all companies captured their objectives quickly against light opposition, along with about 100 prisoners.

At 11.30 p.m. the 1st Black Watch landed behind the Argylls and passed through to Kl. Esserden and Speldorp. The next move for the Argylls was to pass through the 1st Black Watch up the line of the Bund to Rosau and Bienen, but the 1st Black Watch experienced great difficulty in holding their objectives and consequently B company was sent to reinforce them at Kl. Esserden. They were later joined by a troop of DD tanks from the Staffordshire

Yeomanry. B company was later withdrawn to assist elsewhere, and A company was then passed through B company and moved up the line of the Bund to Rosau, which they captured with little difficulty. It was clear, however, that resistance was stiffening, and as the 1st Black Watch had difficulty in holding on to what they had already gained, it was decided that the Argylls would not pass through to their final objectives until the 24th of March. When the Argylls did launch their attack on Bienen, in spite of determined efforts it failed, and B company suffered heavy casualties. The battalion tried again that night and again failed to get into the village, and so it was decided that Bienen was not a one or two company attack, and the leading Canadian battalion following up was given the task while the Argylls formed a firm base. If the crossing of the Rhine had been peaceful, the tale was different now, and some of the enemy's best Panzer Grenadiers were fighting back desperately. Before the village of Bienen was finally captured, two Canadian battalions had to be used. The Argylls had suffered heavy casualties during their gallant and desperate attempts to capture Bienen. Self-propelled guns were in evidence in large numbers, and enemy spandau posts were chattering away all along the Bund. A platoon under Lieut. Maxwell tried to rush a farm and were never seen again. It was discovered later that the farm was held by at least 50 Boche. B company commander, Major J. H. F. Morton, M.C., along with all the platoon officers was wounded, and the company sergeant-major was killed. After a grim battle B company had eventually to be withdrawn to A company's position at Rosau. It was that night at 8 o'clock that D company moved up through A company to make another attempt to get the farm. D company had also a very sticky time, and most of the spandau posts had to be taken at the point of the bayonet. By about midnight the position at the farm had been taken, along with 60 Boche prisoners, mostly from the 115th Panzer Grenadiers of the 15th Panzer Division. The C.O. then decided to pass A company through D company to the southern half of Bienen, and if this was successful D company were then to go through to the northern half of Bienen. At 2.30 in the morning of the 25th of March A company moved off, supported by one troop of DD tanks from the Staffordshire Yeomanry. Meanwhile Bienen was subjected to heavy artillery concentrations. After passing through D company, A company immediately ran into very heavy opposition from spandaus and self-propelled guns mostly sited along the southern edge of Bienen. The tank troop commander was killed, and Lieut. Laurie, one of our platoon commanders, was wounded. Everything possible was tried to get into Bienen, but without success. Finally A company tried an outflanking movement to the right with one platoon. They had, however, only gone a short distance when they again ran into withering machine-gun fire. It was then decided by the brigadier that it was not possible to capture Bienen with one or two companies, and it was at this stage that the Nova Scotia Highlanders of Canada passed through to attack Bienen. Not only to the Argylls, but also to the Canadians, it was a lengthy process and cost them heavy casualties. Before Bienen was captured the enemy launched a counter-attack against the Argylls at approximately 5 o'clock in the morning of the 25th of March after the battalion had been fighting for 48 hours without sleep. Heavy defensive fire was brought down continuously, however, and the counter-attack was broken up. The Canadian H.L.I. had eventually to be passed through the Nova Scotia Highlanders before the village was finally captured.

On the 25th of March all the troops were stunned to hear the news that Major-General T. G. Rennie, Commander of the Highland Division, had been killed by enemy shelling on the road shortly after leaving the headquarters of the 7th Argylls. General Rennie had been with the Division in France in 1940 and was taken prisoner, but escaped. Later he commanded the 5th Black Watch in Africa, and afterwards became brigade commander of the 154th Brigade from El Agheila onwards, until he was given command of the 3rd British Division in Normandy. Shortly afterwards he was given command of the 51st Highland Division. He was a good commander and inspired confidence wherever he went.

Command of the 51st Highland Division was now given to Major-General G. H. A. MacMillan, C.B., C.B.E., D.S.O., M.C. General MacMillan had command of a brigade of the Highland Division in Sicily, and before taking over command of the Highland Division, he had commanded the 15th Scottish Division and the 49th Division. Furthermore, he was an Argyll, which, of course, we were all very pleased about. Shortly after the war in Europe was over, General MacMillan was appointed Colonel of the regiment.

Casualties suffered by the Argylls so far were fairly heavy. They were: 1 officer killed—Lieut. Peter Hands, M.C., 1 officer missing—Lieut. Maxwell, and 5 officers wounded, viz. Major J. H. F. Morton, M.C., Lieuts. Wilson, Laurie, and MacFarlane, and 2nd Lieut. Green. There were 18 others killed, 8 missing, and 70 wounded.

On the 26th of March the battalion moved again. This time the move was over on to the right flank of the brigade axis—the Rees–Isselberg road—and launched an attack that night. It was a two-battalion attack with the 1st Black Watch attacking across the lake in Buffaloes, just to the south of a road and railway crossing. At 10 o'clock at night the Argylls attacked across the lake, also in Buffaloes, with the usual artillery barrage. A company made for a crossroads and surrounding houses, while D company made for the northern edge of a wood and the houses on the main road to the left of the wood. Both objectives were captured easily, after which D company captured a group of farmhouses without difficulty. At this period the 1st Black Watch were having great difficulty with four self-propelled guns which were still in the houses behind them. Eventually, when the enemy withdrew his self-propelled guns up the main road towards Isselberg, A and D companies of the Argylls made good use of their Piats, knocking out at least one self-propelled gun and damaging several others. Artillery fire was also brought down on the retreating enemy guns, and it was later discovered that three guns had been knocked out. The casualties of the battalion had been very light, as they consisted of 1 officer killed—Lieut. Brammer, who commanded Battalion Headquarters' defence platoon, which had reinforced B company after Bienen. In addition only 1 other rank was killed and 4 other ranks were wounded. Altogether approximately 100 prisoners were captured.

The following morning the 27th Brigade of the 43rd Division passed through us, and the battalion settled down to a well-earned rest in whatever shelter it could find in the ruins of the area. Reinforcements soon began to roll in, and on the 27th of March two drafts totalling 135 other ranks and 1 officer, Lieut. A. Haig, arrived. Our rest was very short-lived, as on the 28th of March the brigade were ordered to attack that night with the purpose of deepening the bridgehead and securing an important gap to allow the Guards Armoured Division to pass through the following morning. The Corps Commander said that this would be the last attack the battalion would have to carry out before getting a real rest. Consequently, during the afternoon of the 28th of March the battalion moved up to an assembly area for the attack. The plan was that the 1st Black Watch were to attack the southern half of Dinxperlo, after which the Argylls were to pass through to the area of Beggelder.

The 7th Black Watch were then to pass through to the northern half of Dinxperlo. At 9 p.m. the 1st Black Watch attacked, and an hour later the Argylls launched their attack, with D company leading and making for a crossroads and a cluster of houses. A company followed ten minutes later, their objective also being a crossroads and a group of houses. Lastly came B company, who had as their objective a group of houses. The objectives were captured, and the only enemy interference was from airbursts which kept bursting over the area, but no casualties were sustained. On the morning of the 29th of March all was quiet. In the afternoon the battalion sent off a company to rescue a bogged tank belonging to the Sherwood Rangers as the Boche were hampering the L.A.D. operation party. D company were given this task, and after the tank was rescued the company withdrew. It was found, however, that while D company were driving off the enemy that were hampering the L.A.D. squad, one section of a platoon which had moved a little farther out than the rest were pinned down by a 20-mm. self-propelled gun and some spandaus. Apparently on hearing the tank withdrawing the enemy had returned and caught this section in the act of withdrawing. The company commander, Major J. S. Corcoran, D.S.O., M.C., lost his leg while attempting to reach this section. The tanks could not get near enough to help because of the enemy S.P. guns, but eventually the area was fairly heavily stonked by our artillery and a smoke screen was laid. It was decided to wait until dark, however, when the section withdrew without difficulty. It was an unfortunate episode, as the action was probably unnecessary, and as a result of it one of the best company commanders in the battalion lost his leg, 1 other rank was killed, and 4 other ranks were wounded.

At last the Guards Armoured Division were through, and

what a relief it was to the battalion to see them go after having had such bitter fighting from the 23rd of March onwards. The passage of the armour was the beginning of the great advance across the northern plains of Germany.

Germany's slogan of " Keep the Watch on the Rhine " was of no avail against the mighty Allied forces which were launched across. We now knew it was only a matter of time until the complete collapse of Germany's armed forces. Even during the grimmest fighting the " Jocks " find time for humorous remarks. For instance, on the far side of the Rhine some wag put up a notice, " Have no fear, the Argylls are here." The battalion suffered severely in casualties, however, and if the foregoing account of the battle for the Rhine describes the fighting in too little detail, the following list of casualties will give too clear an indication of the extent and ferocity of the fighting :

Officers killed	Lieut. P. A. Hands, M.C. (Ox. and Bucks)
	Lieut. E. G. Brammer
Officers wounded	Major J. S. Corcoran, D.S.O., M.C.
	Major J. H. F. Morton, M.C.
	Lieut. J. G. Burbridge
	Lieut. J. K. McFarlane
	2nd Lieut. R. S. Laurie
	2nd Lieut. M. F. Green (Beds. and Herts)
	Lieut. P. A. G. Wilson
Officer missing	Lieut. H. A. B. Maxwell
Other ranks killed	28, including
	2987111 C.S.M. E. Wildman, D.C.M.
	14366840 Sergeant E. Spencer
	2987360 Pte. O'May (late of the 1st Bn.)
Other ranks wounded	96, including
	2978744 Sgt. J. Proffitt
	2990636 Sgt. H. Platts
	2979240 C.S.M. R. T. Boyde was wounded in the hand but remained on duty
Other ranks missing	9

Plate 16 (*Above*) Victory March Past by the Highland Division at Bremerhaven. Salute taken by Lieut.-General B. G. Horrocks (30th Corps Commander). (*Below*) Lieut.-General Horrocks takes the salute at the handover of Bremerhaven by the 51st Highland Division to the 29th U.S. Division. With him are Major-General G. H. A. MacMillan, C.B., C.B.E., D.S.O., M.C., Commander of the 51st Highland Division, and the Commander of the 29th U.S. Division

CHAPTER XIX

THE FINAL ADVANCE

THE battalion remained at Beggelder in corps reserve until the 6th of April, on which date they moved forward into Holland once again to comfortable civilian houses in the village of Enschede, where they were given a great welcome by the friendly population. As usual this rest period was cut short and at 9 o'clock on the 8th of April the battalion was on the move again. This time the move was to a concentration area at Elbergen. On the following morning the battalion moved at 1.30 a.m. over the River Ems to take over a position from the 1st battalion the K.O.S.B. of the 3rd British Division. Just over a day was spent in this new position, and on the 10th at 5 p.m. the battalion moved to a concentration area near Furstenau. On the 11th of April the battalion was given the task of clearing Ankum. A company, with one troop of tanks from the 8th Armoured Brigade, moved off at 6.30 a.m. followed by the defence platoon, Tac. Battalion Headquarters, B company and a section of R.E.s, and lastly D company. The armoured cars of the Derby Yeomanry went forward to recce the route. At 7.30 a.m. A company reported Besyen clear of enemy, and by 8.30 a.m. they had reached the outskirts of Ankum without meeting any opposition. B company were then passed through, followed by D company, after which the 1st and 7th Black Watch passed through. At 6.30 p.m. the battalion moved forward again to a concentration area at Badbergen and spent the night there. The pace of the German retreat was quickening, and in consequence the battalion was never left long in one spot. Dinklage was the next objective given to the battalion, and at 9.45 a.m. on the 12th of April the battalion moved forward with D company and Tac. H.Q. in kangaroos, followed by B, A, and S companies in troop-carrying vehicles. Dinklage was reached at 10.50 a.m., but the town was found to be empty, and so the battalion pushed on to Lohne, which was reached without opposition. A hospital was found here with 250 German wounded. The troop-carrying vehicles were now sent back to pick up the Black Watch, who were to occupy Lohne, while the Argylls pushed on to Vechta. It was a new and pleasant experience to be given an objective, prepare for battle, but find the position unoccupied on arrival. It was indeed very thrilling to be chasing the German army up the centre of the Peninsula between Bremen and Hamburg with armour clearing the way in front.

While the battalion was on the move to Vechta, the Derby Yeomanry reported that their cars had reached the village without meeting any opposition and had taken 14 prisoners. It was later found, however, that a few enemy still remained in the northern part of the village, and D company with a troop of tanks went forward to deal with them, but on seeing the tanks they surrendered. There was a certain amount of sniping, and Lieut. Sedgeley got wounded, and Lieut. McFarlane lost his leg when the tank in which he was riding got panzerjausted. The battalion remained in Vechta for the night, during which time prisoners came straggling in. Altogether 4 officers and 107 other ranks gave themselves up during the evening. A military hospital with between 2,000 and 3,000 German wounded and a small number of British wounded prisoners was also in the town.

On the 16th of April at 6 a.m. the battalion was once again on the move, this time to Harpstedt to take over a position from the 2nd R.U.R. of the 3rd British Division. The battalion was to have remained in this position for the

1st and 7th Black Watch battalions to pass through, but the plan was changed, and the battalion was given Ippener as its next objective, and the 7th Black Watch was to go to Horstadt. Consequently, at 9 a.m. A company moved off with a troop of tanks, followed by B company, Tac. Battalion Headquarters, and D company. A company's progress was slow at first because of mines, but a group of carriers from the Derby Yeomanry were met who had come by another route, and the pace was then speeded up. At one period thirty enemy were observed coming south towards Gr. Ippener, but whenever our artillery opened up they made off. About 12.30 p.m. an S.P. gun was giving some trouble, and Captain John Harrison, the mortar officer, was killed, along with 1 other rank. In addition 3 other ranks were wounded. By about 1.30 p.m. all companies were in position on their objectives, after which the 1st Black Watch passed through.

On the 18th of April an interpreter brought in a young Pole who was able to point out the houses of the local Volksturm leaders. The houses were immediately searched, and a large number of papers, two Nazi flags, and some Wehrmacht uniforms, several revolvers, rifles, and shotguns were found. Incidentally, the weapons were buried in the garden. The civilian occupants of the houses were placed under arrest immediately. On the 19th the Derby Yeomanry reported they had observed some enemy in farm buildings, and so a platoon of A company was sent forward, supported by a troop of tanks and followed by the rest of the company. The objective was captured without any trouble except from a single S.P. gun. No casualties were suffered, and on arrival on the objective it was found that the enemy had disappeared. During the evening B company moved forward through A company, and D company moved up to Annen to take over a position from the 1st Black Watch, and the 1st Black Watch, who were at this stage placed under the command of the 153rd Brigade, were to assault Delmenhorst with that brigade. However, the 153rd Brigade were able to enter Delmenhorst unopposed, and consequently plans were again changed. At 10.30 a.m. on the 21st of April the battalion moved to Varrel, as the 154th Brigade were to take over the sector from the 3rd British Division. The battalion remained in this area until the morning of the 25th of April, when the 154th Brigade moved across the River Weser to take over a sector from the 43rd Division. The enemy were either non-existent or else they were lying low, as the area was very peaceful. Patrols were sent out to make contact with the 7th Black Watch in the area of the road between Hellwege and Ahausen. In addition a carrier patrol was sent out to make contact with elements of the 53rd Division in the region of the Forst Rotenberg.

On the 27th of April the battalion was again on the move. In order to avoid an assault crossing over a deep river obstacle with bridges blown on the immediate front, the battalion was moved 17 miles to a flank to a concentration area at Waffensen, from where an attack starting on the far side of the river could be launched at dawn the next day. Waffensen and the crossing over the obstacle were held by the 53rd Division, and from there our battalion advanced from the flank against Gr. Sottrum after a detour of some 35 miles in all, thus clearing the way for the Division to continue on its northerly axis once the bridges south of Gr. Sottrum had been secured and repaired. The first to move were B company, who set off at 9.30 p.m. through Hassendorf to Gr. Sottrum. B company's advance was quite unopposed, and the next to move was A company, who followed the same route and took Kl. Sottrum without any difficulty. Finally, D company went straight along the road from Waffensen past Sottrum and over the autobahn to

Stukenborstel. The roadside was mined along the verges in certain places, and unfortunately one other rank was killed and another was wounded. The bridge in front of Stukenborstel was found to be blown, but was soon bulldozed in, and the town was reached by D company without meeting any enemy opposition. D company was later side-stepped up to just outside Otterstedt. At this stage the 1st Black Watch passed through the battalion, followed by the 5th Black Watch. At 6 p.m. our battalion were on the move again, and this time made for Ostertinke, where they remained in a reserve position.

The speed of the Allied advance across the northern plains of Germany had not slackened. Our armour was still smashing on against a broken and disillusioned German army. The once proud and conquering German army was now a pitiful rabble of disorganized men. Move after move took place at short notice until the end came. On the 1st of May the battalion moved up to Zeven, where it stayed for two nights. On the 3rd of May the battalion again moved to a harbouring area on the southern outskirts of Bremervorde and remained there until 5 o'clock the same evening, when they were once again on the move. This time the battalion embussed in kangaroos, and were ordered to go through Lintig. The order of march was D company, B company, Battalion Headquarters with the commanding officer, Lt.-Col. A. MacKinnon, and A company. At Meckelstedt the battalion debussed and went forward into Lintig without meeting any enemy opposition. D company went to Hainmuhlen, and B company, who sent a patrol to inspect the bridge near Beorkesa, were fired on from the west side of the canal, where the bridge was blown. During the afternoon of the 4th of May two German Red Cross men from Beorkesa came into our lines with a white flag and asked that we should stop shelling the village as there was a hospital full of wounded there. We promised this on the condition that any German troops in the district would surrender to us immediately. A time limit for this surrender was fixed, but nothing happened, so the war went on. For two hours that afternoon the battalion area was shelled fairly heavily, but only one casualty was sustained. This was the first shelling that the battalion had had for some time. Later in the afternoon rumours began to trickle in about negotiations for the surrender of the 15th Panzer Grenadier Division. A meeting with a German officer took place at Battalion Headquarters, where the brigadier passed on the terms of surrender. With effect from 8 a.m., 5th May, all hostilities ceased on the British Second Army front and on the 1st Canadian Army front. So far as the Argylls were concerned the war on their part of the globe was over. An international bridge was established at Ringstadt, and D company moved down there. Their position at Hainmuhlen was taken over by A company. Stragglers in hundreds continued to pour in day and night, so that it became impossible to count them. On the 8th the battalion moved to Wollingst in order to be near to the German battalions which had surrendered, and which had to be disarmed and disembodied. In Appeln were concentrated the two German battalions forming the 104 P.G. Regiment, with which we were concerned.

The End of the War in Europe

On the morning of the 7th of May an important message was received. The message contained the news that we had all been waiting for so long. The war in Europe was at an end, and after five years and eight months, during which time the British people had not only suffered the loss of their fine soldiers, but also remained stout-hearted against the blitzing of their homes by the enemy's bombers and his V weapons. The British soldier had once more proved himself superior to the German soldier in battle, and along with the rest of the Allies, saved the British Empire and the world from the brutality of the Nazi aggressor and would-be invader. The so-called " Master Race " were humble enough now.

This historic message read :

" A representative of the German High Command signed the unconditional surrender of all German land, sea, and air forces in Europe to the Allied Expeditionary Force and simultaneously to the Soviet High Command at 01.41 hours Central European time, 7th May, under which all forces will cease active operations at 00.01 hours 9th May. Effective immediately all offensive operations by Allied Expeditionary Force will cease and troops will remain in present positions. Moves involved in occupational duties will continue. Due to difficulties of communication there may be some delay in similar orders reaching enemy troops, so full defensive precautions will be taken."

Germany had been well and truly beaten, and one had only to glance at some of her cities to witness the appalling devastation. Where prosperous cities used to stand, now only a heap of rubble remained. The industrial Ruhr was now only a smoking shell, and Germany's war factories were blasted beyond all hope of recovery. It was now the task of the Army of Occupation to begin the tremendous problem of re-education so as to ensure that never again would Germany be able to use her armed might in another attempt at conquering the world.

" Eclipse " was the name given to the final occupation of Germany by the Allies, and indeed it was a complete eclipse for the once mighty and proud German nation, now beaten to her knees and completely bewildered and disillusioned by the appalling catastrophe which had overtaken her. The whole country was in a complete state of chaos. Millions upon millions of slave workers wandered aimlessly all over the countryside. Half the nationalities of Europe were on the march: French, Dutch, Belgians, Czechs, Poles, and Italians, and finally vast numbers of Russians in their bright green uniforms with " S.U."—Soviet Union—painted in white on their backs. These millions lived a vagabond existence, slowly making their way westwards towards the British and American lines in the hope of finding food and shelter. The Germans were terrified of these wandering slave workers, especially the Russians, and they had good reason to be. The war had ended, but still Europe was in a turmoil. The German people looked to the British and Americans for protection. What a change from the dark days of 1939, when the then arrogant German nation was all bent on conquering the world without regard to the right of nations to govern themselves.

APPENDIX I

Nominal Roll of Officers who went overseas with the 7th Battalion the Argyll and Sutherland Highlanders in 1940

    Lt.-Col. E. P. Buchanan, M.C.
    Major E. Rowley-Orr
    Major Younger, M.C.
    Major R. M. Young
    Capt. A. T. Roper-Caldbeck
    Capt. G. Handley
    Capt. E. P. A. Hewitt
    Capt. A. Irvine-Robertson
    Capt. J. Logan
    Capt. A. F. Hendry, M.C.
    Capt. J. Ritchie
    Lieut. A. D. Brown
    Lieut. D. M. Fisher, M.C.
    Lieut. J. B. Mathieson
    Lieut. W. D. Clark
    Lieut. R. G. Dawson
    2nd Lieut. J. C. Muirhead
    2nd Lieut. A. S. Haig
    2nd Lieut. D. A. Orr Ewing
    2nd Lieut. A. Orr Ewing
    2nd Lieut. C. G. Mackie
    2nd Lieut. W. A. Atkinson Clark
    2nd Lieut. D. H. Macalaster Hall
    2nd Lieut. R. L. Powell, M.C.
    2nd Lieut. H. S. Spens
    2nd Lieut. P. McLaren
    2nd Lieut. J. E. M. Atkinson
    2nd Lieut. J. V. Parnell
    2nd Lieut. P. S. Moore
    2nd Lieut. N. C. W. Green
    2nd Lieut. H. McIlwraith
    Lieut. and Q.M. C. H. Ditcham
    Lieut. I. A. R. Mackenzie, R.A.M.C.
    Capt. D. MacInnes, M.C., R.A.Ch.D.

Also served

    2nd Lieut. H. Ross
    Capt. J. E. McEwan

APPENDIX II

Awards to Officers and Men of the 7th Battalion during the campaign of 1940

Military Cross
> Capt. A. F. Hendry
> 2nd Lieut. Alan Orr Ewing
> Capt. D. MacInnes, C.F.
>
> *Gazette of 9th October, 1945*
> Major O. B. Younger
> Lieut. D. M. Fisher
> 2nd Lieut. R. L. Powell

Distinguished Conduct Medal
> *Gazette of 9th October, 1945*
> R.S.M. W. Lockie

Military Medal
> *Gazette of 9th October, 1945*
> C.S.M. J. Milne
> Sgt. W. Livingstone

Mentioned in Despatches
> Capt. A. Irvine-Robertson
> 2nd Lieut. C. G. Mackie
> Pte. C. McIvor
>
> *Gazette of 9th October, 1945*
> Lt.-Col. E. P. Buchanan, M.C.
> Capt. G. Handley
> 2nd Lieut. Alan Orr Ewing
> 2nd Lieut. J. V. Parnell
> C.Q.M.S. J. C. Bell
> C.Q.M.S. A. Watson
> Sgt. Gray
> Sgt. P. G. Hunter
> Cpl. A. Newton
> Pte. J. S. Rennie

N.B.—Those officers and other ranks whose awards were published in the Gazette of 9th October, 1945, had been captured during the fighting on the Somme in 1940.

APPENDIX III

Nominal Roll of Officers who served for varying periods with the 7th Battalion the Argyll and Sutherland Highlanders between 23rd October 1942 and 8th May 1945

Capt. D. E. Adamson	Killed in action at Wadi Akarit on 6/4/43
Lieut. D. G. Aitchison	
2nd Lieut. D. Alexander	Wounded, B.L.A., February 1945
Lieut. R. Alsop	Killed in action, B.L.A., 31/10/44
Lieut. H. D. Archibald	Wounded, B.L.A., 11/8/44
Capt. T. Armstrong	
Lieut. J. G. Austin	Wounded, B.L.A., 11/8/44
Lieut. I. Balleny	Killed in action, B.L.A., 17/8/44
Lieut. A. Bartholemew	Wounded (accident), B.L.A., 19/7/44
Capt. M. J. G. Bate	Wounded Wadi Akarit, 6/4/43
	Wounded, B.L.A., 8/8/44
Capt. W. D. C. Binns	Wounded, B.L.A., 9/2/45
Capt. W. Blair, M.C., R.A.M.C.	
Capt. A. S. Bowden	Wounded, Alamein, 23/10/42
	Wounded, Wadi Akarit, 6/4/43
Major A. D. F. Boyle	Wounded, B.L.A., 31/10/43
Lieut. E. G. Brammer	Killed in action, B.L.A., 26/3/45
Capt. W. A. Brechin	Killed in action, Africa, December 1942
Major A. F. C. Buchanan, D.S.O.	Left Bn. for Staff College, August 1944
Capt. D. Buchanan	Wounded, Alamein, 23/10/42
Lieut. I. Buchanan	Wounded, B.L.A., 7/9/44
Lieut. J. G. Burbridge	Wounded, B.L.A., 24/3/45
Capt. R. L. Callan	
Major K. P. Calderwood, M.C.	
Capt. I. C. Cameron	Wounded, Wadi Akarit, 6/4/43
	Wounded, Gerbini, Sicily, 20/7/43
	Wounded (accident), B.L.A. 8/5/45
Major I. A. Campbell	
Brig. L. M. Campbell, V.C., D.S.O. and Bar, T.D.	Left Bn. to command Bde. in 5th Div., May 1943
Capt. N. Campbell, R.A.Ch.D.	

APPENDIX III

Lieut. J. Chapman	Wounded, B.L.A., 11/8/44
Lt.-Col. J. C. Church, M.C.	
Lieut. D. L. Colquhoun	Killed in action, B.L.A., February 1945
Major J. S. Corcoran, D.S.O., M.C.	Wounded, Gerbini, Sicily, 20/7/43
	Wounded, B.L.A., 29/3/45
Lieut. W. F. Cormack	P.O.W., Gerbini, 20/7/43
Lieut. J. Cowling	Wounded, B.L.A., 11/8/44
Capt. M. A. Currie	
Lieut. J. Cutland	Wounded, B.L.A., 13/1/45
Major K. B. L. Davidson	
Lt.-Col. A. Dunlop, D.S.O.	Left Bn. to command Bde. in 49th Div., April 1944
Lieut. W. A. Dunsmuir	
Lieut. F. M. W. Edie	Killed in action, B.L.A. 31/10/44
Capt. N. E. Faid, M.C.	Wounded, Wadi Akarit, 6/4/43
Lieut. G. Fortune	
Lieut. R. Gibb	P.O.W., Gerbini, 20/7/43
Lieut. J. Gilmour	Killed in action, Alamein, 23/10/42
Capt. D. A. Goodall	
Lieut. J. A. Gray	
2nd Lieut. M. F. Green	Wounded, B.L.A., 24/3/45
Lieut. J. Groves	
Lieut. P. A. Hands, M.C.	Killed in action, B.L.A., 24/3/45
Lieut. A. S. Haig	Posted to 51st Division as Staff Captain
Lieut. E. J. Harris	
Capt. J. R. Harrison	Killed in action, B.L.A., 16/4/45
Major A. F. Hendry, M.C.	Left Bn. in Sicily to become Town Major of Augusta
Capt. J. A. Hope	Died of wounds, B.L.A., 17/8/44
Capt. G. B. Horsburgh	Wounded, Alamein, 23/10/42
	P.O.W., Gerbini, 20/7/43
Lieut. W. Howat	Left Bn. in Africa and appointed Camp Comdt., 154th Bde.
Lieut. N. Irwin	Wounded, B.L.A., 31/10/44
Capt. A. D. Jackson	
Lieut. R. B. Jones	Killed in action, Gerbini, 20/7/43
Capt. M. R. Kenneth	Wounded, B.L.A., 21/2/45
Lieut. R. F. Kinghorn	Wounded, Alamein, 23/10/42
	Wounded, Wadi Akarit, 6/4/43
	Wounded, Gerbini, 20/7/43
Lieut. J. R. Knight	Wounded, B.L.A., 21/2/45
Lieut. J. R. Lale	
Capt. W. Lamont	

APPENDIX III

2nd Lieut. R. S. Lawrie	Wounded, B.L.A., 25/3/45
Lieut. W. C. Lees	P.O.W., Africa, 4/4/43
Lieut. A. M. Leslie	Wounded, Mareth Line, 16/3/43
	Wounded, B.L.A., 17/8/44
Lieut. J. Lindsay	
Lieut. R. D. Lindsay	Wounded, B.L.A., 31/10/44
Lieut. R. Marshall	Wounded, Alamein, 23/10/42
	Wounded, Wadi Akarit, 6/4/43
Lieut. Mathers	Killed in action, Gerbini, 20/7/43
Lt.-Col. R. Mathieson, O.B.E., D.S.O., T.D.	Killed in action, Gerbini, 20/7/43
Lieut. R. Mathieson	Wounded, Alamein, 23/10/42
Lieut. R. H. Mathieson	Killed in action, B.L.A., 9/2/45
Lieut. H. A. B. Maxwell	P.O.W., B.L.A., 24/3/45
2nd Lieut. M. D. Maxwell	Died of wounds, B.L.A., 5/11/44
Lt.-Col. J. C. Meiklejohn, D.S.O.	Wounded, B.L.A., 17/8/44
Lieut. D. Menzies	Killed in action, B.L.A., 18/7/44
Major J. D. Milne, M.C.	Wounded, B.L.A., 17/8/44
Capt. J. I. Mitchell	Wounded, B.L.A., 18/7/44
Major J. H. F. Morton, M.C. and Bar	Wounded, B.L.A., 24/3/45
Capt. R. Muir Morton	Wounded, Wadi Akarit, 6/4/43
	Wounded, B.L.A., 17/8/44
Major K. Muir	Left Bn. in the U.K.
Capt. J. Muirhead	Left Bn. in Africa for O.E.T.A. staff
Capt. C. G. Mackie	Left Bn. in Africa and appointed I.O., 154th Brigade
Major M. McAlister-Hall, M.C.	
Major J. S. Lindsay Macdougall, D.S.O., M.C.	Wounded, Alamein, 23/10/42
	Wounded, Wadi Akarit, 6/4/43
	Wounded, Gerbini, 20/7/43
	Died of wounds as P.O.W.
Capt. A. McElwee	Killed in action, B.L.A., 8/8/44
Lieut. J. K. MacFarlane, M.C.	Wounded, B.L.A., 24/3/45
Lieut. D. McGee	Wounded, B.L.A., 9/2/45
Lieut. T. McGill	Killed in action, Wadi Akarit, 6/4/43
Lt.-Col. A. MacKinnon, D.S.O., M.C.	
Lieut. A. McLean	Killed in action, B.L.A., 31/10/44
Lieut. T. McNaught	P.O.W., Gerbini, 20/7/43
Lieut. A. McVicar	Wounded, Alamein, 23/10/42
	Died of wounds, Gerbini, 20/7/43
Lieut. J. K. Nicholson	Wounded, B.L.A., 9/2/45
Lt.-Col. D. N. Nicoll	Left Bn. in Holland
Major G. E. Paton	
Capt. R. D. Porteous	Wounded, B.L.A., 11/8/44
Capt. H. R. Patullo	Left Bn. in Africa and appointed to O.E.T.A. staff

APPENDIX III

Lieut. A. Rankin	Killed in action, B.L.A., 18/7/44
Lieut. E. J. Reed	
Capt. D. G. B. Reekie	Wounded, B.L.A., 3/7/44
Capt. (Q.M.) J. Richardson, M.B.E.	
Capt. J. Roberts	
Lieut. J. Robertson	P.O.W., Africa, 4/4/43
Major J. F. Robertson	
Major J. L. Robertson	Wounded, Alamein, 23/10/42
	Wounded, B.L.A., 17/8/44
Lt.-Col. A. J. C. Rose	Left Bn. in the U.K.
Lieut. A. Roxburgh	
Major H. P. Samwell, M.C.	Wounded, Alamein, 23/10/42
	Wounded, Medenine, 4/3/43
	Killed in action, B.L.A., 12/1/45
Lieut. D. Scobbie	Wounded (accident), B.L.A. 23/6/44
Lieut. Sedgeley	Wounded, B.L.A., 13/4/45
Lieut. Shilling	Wounded, B.L.A., 17/8/44
Lieut. Sills	Killed in action, Alamein, 23/10/42
Major J. R. Sloan, M.C. and Bar	Wounded, B.L.A., 17/8/44
Capt. A. J. A. Stewart	
Lieut. P. J. Stewart-Bam	Killed in action, Wadi Akarit, 6/4/43
Capt. T. C. J. Sinton, R.A.Ch.D.	Died of malaria, Sicily
Capt. W. T. Thomson	Wounded, Alamein, 23/10/42
	Wounded, B.L.A., 26/10/44
Major Pat. Tweedie	Wounded, Gerbini, 20/7/43
Lieut. J. Twinbarrow	Wounded, B.L.A., 11/8/44
Lieut. R. Williams	Wounded, B.L.A., 8/7/44
Capt. W. D. Williamson	Wounded, Sicily, 18/7/43
	Wounded, B.L.A., 27/9/44
Lieut. White	Wounded, B.L.A., 17/8/44
Major W. L. N. White	Left Bn. in Africa for staff appointment
Lieut. E. C. Wilkie	
Major A. R. Wilson, M.C., R.A.M.C.	
Lieut. P. A. G. Wilson	Wounded, B.L.A., 24/3/45
Capt. G. P. Wood, M.C.	
Capt. N. G. Wykes	
Lieut. J. Wyllie	Wounded, B.L.A., 11/8/44
Capt. D. E. Young	Wounded, Alamein, 23/10/42
	Killed in action, Gerbini, 20/7/43

APPENDIX IV

Honours and Awards to the Officers and Men of the 7th Battalion the Argyll and Sutherland Highlanders between 23rd October 1942 and 8th May 1945

Name	Award	Place
Brig. Lorne M. Campbell	D.S.O.	France, 1940
	Bar to D.S.O.	Medenine
	V.C.	Wadi Akarit
* Lieut.-Col. R. Mathieson	O.B.E.	El Alamein
	D.S.O.	Wadi Akarit
Lieut.-Col. J. C. Meiklejohn	D.S.O.	El Alamein
Lieut.-Col. A. Dunlop	D.S.O.	Sicily
Lieut.-Col. A. MacKinnon	D.S.O.	B.L.A.
	M.C.	M.E.F.
* Major J. S. Lindsay Macdougall	D.S.O.	Wadi Akarit
	M.C.	El Alamein
Major J. S. Corcoran	D.S.O.	Gerbini, Sicily
	M.C.	Medenine
	Bar to M.C.	B.L.A.
Major A. F. C. Buchanan	D.S.O.	Gerbini, Sicily
Major J. H. F. Morton	M.C.	Sicily
	Bar to M.C.	B.L.A.
Major J. R. Sloan, K.O.S.B.	M.C.	B.L.A.
	Bar to M.C.	B.L.A.
Major J. D. Milne	M.C.	B.L.A.
* Major H. P. Samwell	M.C.	Medenine
Major A. R. Wilson, R.A.M.C.	M.C.	El Alamein
Capt. N. E. Faid, Cameronians	M.C.	Wadi Akarit
Capt. (Q.M.) J. Richardson	M.B.E.	B.L.A.
Capt. W. Blair, R.A.M.C.	M.C.	B.L.A.
Capt. G. P. Wood	M.C.	B.L.A.
* Lieut. P. A. Hands	M.C.	B.L.A.
Lieut. J. K. MacFarlane	M.C.	B.L.A.
C.S.M. M. J. Archibald	D.C.M.	Wadi Akarit
	M.M.	Medenine
C.S.M. G. Gauld	D.C.M.	El Alamein
C.S.M. W. Louden	D.C.M.	Gerbini, Sicily
* C.S.M. E. Wildman	D.C.M.	B.L.A.
C.S.M. R. T. Boyde	D.C.M.	B.L.A.
C.S.M. D. Duncanson	M.M.	Wadi Akarit

* Deceased

APPENDIX IV

Pipe-Major J. Smith	M.M.	El Alamein
Sgt. H. Platts	M.M.	B.L.A.
Sgt. A. Plant	M.M.	B.L.A.
Sgt. R. Thornton	M.M.	Gerbini, Sicily
Sgt. A. Alexander	M.M.	Gerbini, Sicily
Sgt. W. Hemphill	M.M.	Wadi Akarit
Sgt. J. Bauld	M.M.	El Alamein
* Sgt. E. Lake	M.M.	El Alamein
L/Sgt. D. MacRae	M.M.	Mareth Line
L/Sgt. J. Milne	M.M.	B.L.A.
L/Sgt. J. Harte	M.M.	B.L.A.
L/Sgt. J. Wallace	M.M.	Medenine
C/Sgt. C. McGowan	B.E.M.	B.L.A.
Cpl. J. Ginty	M.M.	Wadi Akarit
Cpl. W. McColl	M.M.	El Alamein
L/Cpl. J. Williamson	M.M.	Wadi Akarit
* L/Cpl. J. Watson	M.M.	Wadi Akarit
L/Cpl. H. Godden, R.E.M.E.	M.M.	Sicily
Pte. S. Shields	M.M.	El Alamein
Pte. J. Snadden	M.M.	Gabes
Pte. R. Stewart	M.M.	Gerbini, Sicily
Pte. A. Paterson	M.M.	B.L.A.
Pte. A. Manning	M.M.	B.L.A.
Pte. D Sykes	M.M.	B.L.A.
Pte. J. Gracie, R.A.S.C.	M.M.	Medenine
Pte. W. Monaghan	M.M.	El Alamein
Pte. A. Greig	M.M.	B.L.A.
Pte. J. Ritchie	M.M.	B.L.A.

* Deceased

www.ingramcontent.com/pod-product-compliance
Ingram Content Group UK Ltd.
Pitfield, Milton Keynes, MK11 3LW, UK
UKHW021329180426
11947UKWH00017B/1522